REDEEMING RELIGION

VOLUME II
Living Toward the End

Caleb J. Breedlove

Copyright © 2026 by Caleb Breedlove

All rights reserved. No part of this publication may be reproduced, stored in a retrieval system, or transmitted in any form or by any means—electronic, mechanical, photocopy, recording, or any other—except for brief quotations in printed reviews, without the prior permission of the publisher.

Published by TBG Studio Press, a subsidiary of TBG Holdings Co.

Unless otherwise noted, all Scripture quotations are from the ESV® Bible (The Holy Bible, English Standard Version®), copyright © 2001 by Crossway, a publishing ministry of Good News Publishers. Used by permission. All rights reserved. The ESV text may not be quoted in any publication made available to the public by a Creative Commons license. The ESV may not be translated into any other language.
Scripture quotations marked (NKJV) are taken from the New King James Version®. Copyright © 1982 by Thomas Nelson. Used by permission. All rights reserved.
Scripture quotations marked (KJV) are from the King James Version. Public domain.
Scripture quotations marked (J.B. Phillips) are from The New Testament in Modern English by J.B. Phillips, copyright © 1960, 1972 J.B. Phillips. Administered by The Archbishops' Council of the Church of England. Used by permission.

ISBN: 979-8-9944345-0-5 (paperback)

First Edition

DEDICATION

This book was forged in a furnace I did not enter alone.

To my spiritual director—for wisdom that waited.
To my therapist—for truth that healed.
To my friends—for hands that held.
To Cassie—for love that remained.

What you gave me, I have tried to give away.

CONTENTS

TWO SOULS IN A WILDERNESS 3
THE DISCIPLINE RELIGION 66
THE GROANING AND THE GLORY 133
THE PERSEVERING RELIGION 170
THE MYSTERY OF RELIGION 222
WHEN THE HEAVENS ROLLED BACK 259
THE RELIGION OF THE GREAT HARLOT 296
THE ANTICIPATION OF RELIGION 365
BIBLIOGRAPHY 398

A RULE OF READING

Dear Reader,

You hold the second half of a single vision. In Volume One, we walked together through the diagnosis of a dying faith and laid the foundations of true religion—humility at the basin, communion at the table, the spiritual life breathed by the Spirit, doctrine that shapes the soul, community that carries us, and incarnational discipleship that gives flesh to our creed. There we asked: What is the religion that God delights in?

Now we enter the wilderness.

This volume opens with two souls separated by seventeen centuries yet united by the same ache—an ancient monk in the Egyptian desert and a modern man drowning in blue light at 2:47 AM. Their parallel stories frame the question that animates every page that follows: How do we live this religion through the long night of faith?

Here you will find the disciplines that form us, the groaning that accompanies glory, the perseverance that refuses to let go. We will speak of mystery—not as a defect in our theology but as its crowning achievement. We will stand at the edge of apocalypse and ask what faithful religion looks like when the heavens roll back. We will name the counterfeit and anticipate the consummation.

If Volume One taught us to receive, Volume Two teaches us to remain.

Read slowly. These chapters were written in prayer and are meant to be received in the same spirit. Let the narratives work on you before you work on them. Where conviction comes, do not flee it. Where hope rises, do suppress it. Where the call to endure sounds harsh, remember: the One who calls you has Himself endured to the end.

The storm is upon us. The wheat and the tares grow together toward harvest. And somewhere in the tension between the already and the not-yet, between the basin and the throne, between the cross and the crown we are invited to become the kind of people who can say with Paul, "I have finished the race. I have kept the faith."

May this volume equip you for the journey.

In hope of glory,
Caleb

I

TWO SOULS IN A WILDERNESS

A Story of Desert and City, of Ancients and Moderns, of Grace Received

Prologue: The Same Thirst

"As a deer pants for flowing streams, so pants my soul for you, O God." — Psalm 42:1

Two men. Separated by seventeen centuries. United by the same ache.

One knelt on sand still warm from the Egyptian sun, his knees calloused from ten thousand genuflections, his heart cold as the coming night.

The other sat in a glow of blue light at 2:47 AM, thumb scrolling through an infinite feed, his eyes burning, his soul emptier than the notifications he craved.

Both were dying of thirst beside the water.

And over both, unseen but not unfelt, a Presence brooded—patient as a mother hen gathering her chicks, persistent as a lover who will not let go, gentle as breath and relentless as the tide.

Return to Me, the Presence whispered. *I am hemming you in. I am closing the doors you thought were escapes. I am making the wilderness a pathway home.*

They could not hear it yet. But they would.

Part One: The Unraveling

Marcus

The Nitrian Desert, Egypt — 387 AD

The bell for Vespers had rung an hour ago. Marcus had not moved.

He sat at the mouth of his cave, watching the sun bleed out across the western dunes, and he felt nothing. No, that wasn't true. He felt the absence of feeling, which was its own particular agony—the way a man who has lost his arm still feels the phantom limb reaching for what is no longer there.

Twelve years.

Twelve years since he had walked away from the counting houses of Alexandria. Twelve years since he had traded silk for sackcloth, the weight of gold for the weight of silence. He had been thirty then, wealthy, respected, his name spoken in the marble halls where merchants became princes.

Now he was forty-two, and he could not remember why he had come.

I traded everything for nothing. The thought rose unbidden, in his own voice, with his own certainty. *I could have had a villa by the sea. Servants. A wife with soft hands and softer eyes. Children who would carry my name. Instead, I have sand in my bread and loneliness in my bed. I am a fool. I have always been a fool.*

"I came for God," Marcus said aloud, but his voice cracked on the word.

And where is He? Twelve years of prayers. Twelve years of fasting until my ribs showed like the hull of a wrecked ship. Twelve years of silence, of solitude, of sacred rhythms. And what do I have? An empty cave. An empty heart. I am no holier than when I arrived. I am worse—I have lost everything and gained nothing.

Marcus closed his eyes. The voice was not wrong. That was the horror of it. The voice was never entirely wrong.

He remembered the morning prayers—*Lauds* at dawn, when the sky turned rose and gold and the brothers lifted their voices in antiphonal psalms. He remembered how his heart had once swelled with the words: *"O Lord, open my lips, and my mouth shall declare your praise."* Now his mouth formed the syllables while his mind wandered back to Alexandria, to the smell of cinnamon in the warehouses, to the clink of coins being counted, to the respect in men's eyes when Marcus ben Ezra entered a room.

No one here even knows my name. I am just another brown robe, another sunburned face. Anonymous. Forgotten. I gave up being someone to become no one, and I didn't even get God in the bargain. What kind of man does that? What kind of fool?

Marcus pressed his palms against his eyes until colors burst behind his lids. "Spirit of the Living God," he breathed, "Spirit of the Living God—"

But the prayer died on his tongue. He could not feel the Presence. He had not felt it in months. Perhaps years. The sacred rhythms that had once been a dance had become a march, a grinding duty, a weight upon his shoulders rather than wings upon his back.

I should go home. There is still time. I am not so old. I remember the trade routes, the customs, the languages. I could rebuild. I could have everything I gave up and more. God would understand—He knows I tried. He knows I gave it my best. Surely He would not begrudge me a comfortable old age after all these years of sacrifice.

The sun sank below the horizon, and the desert went from gold to gray to the deep purple of a bruise. Marcus did not go to Vespers. He lay on his pallet of woven reeds and stared at the ceiling of his cave, and he felt the foundations of his vocation crumbling like sandstone in the rain.

He did not notice that the road to Alexandria had become strangely difficult of late. That every time he imagined leaving, something intervened—an illness, a sandstorm, a visiting pilgrim who needed guidance. He did not notice that the doors he thought were open were slowly, gently closing.

He did not hear the whisper beneath his despair:

I will hedge up your way with thorns. I will build a wall against you, so that you cannot find your paths. You will chase your lovers but not overtake them. You will seek them but not find them. Then you will say, "I will go and return to my first husband, for it was better for me then than now."

The Spirit brooded over Marcus like wind over water, like a mother over a fevered child. Patient. Persistent. Already at work in the darkness, even when Marcus could see nothing but the dark.

David

Austin, Texas — Present Day

David Chen stared at the notification on his phone: *Your daily average screen time this week: 7 hours 23 minutes.*

Seven hours. Twenty-three minutes. More than a third of his waking life, fed into the glowing rectangle in his hand. And for what? What could he remember from those hours? A blur of faces, takes, opinions, outrage, beauty, horror, all of it bleeding together into a kind of digital static that left him wired and exhausted at the same time.

He sat on the edge of his bed in his studio apartment, the blue light washing over his face, his Bible on the nightstand still open to Psalm 63 from three days ago when he'd made his last attempt at morning devotions. *"My soul thirsts for you; my flesh faints for you, as in a dry and weary land where there is no water."*

David, the man who'd led worship last Sunday. David, the small group leader who spoke so eloquently about intimacy with God. David, who'd been baptized in the Spirit at a revival seven years ago, who'd felt the fire in his bones, who'd wept with joy and spoken in a tongue he didn't know.

Where was that David now?

1 TWO SOULS IN A WILDERNESS

I'm a fraud. The thought came with the weight of absolute certainty. *I stand up there every Sunday with my hands raised, and I'm thinking about how I look. About whether Hannah is watching. About whether anyone captured a good photo for Instagram. I'm performing. I've always been performing. And everyone can see it except me.*

David's thumb hovered over the Instagram icon. Then over a different app, one buried three folders deep, one that had no name displayed, one that represented his deepest shame.

I've already ruined tonight's devotional time. I already feel like garbage. What's the difference now? At least I'll feel something. At least for a few minutes I won't feel this emptiness.

"No," David said, but his thumb didn't move away. "No, I'm not going to—"

Isn't this the fourth time this month I've said that? The seventh? I've lost count. All my worship, all my small group leadership, all my spiritual language—and I can't even control my own eyes. I can't even control my own hands. I'm pathetic. I'm disgusting. God must be so tired of me.

The shame was like acid in his throat. Because he knew what he wanted to be. He could see it so clearly: David the man of prayer, rising at 5 AM for lectio divina. David the fasting warrior, setting aside food for feasting on God's Word. David the servant, anonymously giving half his income to the homeless ministry. David the evangelist, naturally weaving gospel conversations into every relationship. David the mystic, lost for hours in contemplative silence, hearing the still small voice.

That David was beautiful. That David was holy. That David was a figment of his imagination, a religious avatar he'd constructed from podcasts and books and Instagram feeds of celebrity Christians who seemed to have it all together.

This David—the real one—was sitting in his underwear at 2:52 AM, thumb trembling over an app that would deliver a dopamine hit and a shame spiral in equal measure, having not opened his Bible in three days, having skipped small group last week because he "wasn't feeling well," having lied to his accountability partner when asked if he was staying pure.

But God's grace is sufficient, isn't it? Another voice now, smoother, more reasonable. *That's the whole point of the gospel. I'm not saved by works. I'm saved by grace. So if I fall tonight, I can confess tomorrow. God will forgive me—He always does. That's His job. And maybe getting this out of my system will help me focus better tomorrow. Maybe I need to hit bottom before I can really change.*

David recognized this voice too. It had been his companion for years—the voice of cheap grace, the voice that turned forgiveness into permission, the voice that said *sin now, repent later* as if confession were a get-out-of-jail-free card he could play indefinitely.

But that's not how it works, a third voice whispered, fainter than the others. *You know that's not how it works. Every time you plan the sin and the confession together, something dies in you. The repentance gets shallower. The cycle gets tighter. You're not fooling God. You're only fooling yourself.*

Who cares? the first voice snapped back. *I'm already a failure. I'm already a hypocrite. At least this way I get some pleasure before the inevitable guilt. The guilt is coming anyway—it always comes. Might as well earn it.*

But God's grace—

God's grace is for real Christians. Not for frauds like me. Not for people who can't go three days without falling. I'm beyond grace. I'm too broken to fix.

No, that's not true either. Grace covers everything. Even this. Even tonight. So why not—

The voices warred in his skull, each one claiming to speak truth, each one pulling him in a different direction. David sat paralyzed, his thumb still hovering, his heart racing, his mind a battlefield.

I hate myself, he thought, and that was the one voice that rang truest of all. *I hate what I've become. I hate that I can't stop. I hate that I don't even know which voice is mine anymore.*

He threw the phone across the room where it hit the wall and clattered to the floor. He sat in the sudden darkness, his breath ragged, his hands shaking.

I'll just pick it back up. I always do. I'm weak. I'm nothing. I'm—

"Stop it," David said aloud. "Stop it, stop it, stop it."

But the voices didn't stop. They never stopped. They were the constant background noise of his existence, and he had forgotten what silence sounded like.

Where are You? he asked the darkness. It was almost—almost—a prayer. *Where are You, God? I used to feel You. I used to burn for You. What happened to me? What happened to us?*

The silence that answered was the loudest thing he'd ever heard.

But beneath the silence, beneath the accusation and the excuse, beneath even David's awareness, Something stirred. Something that had been stirring for months, arranging circumstances, closing doors, making the old escapes less satisfying, the old numbing agents less effective.

The app that used to bring relief now brought only deeper emptiness. The social media that used to distract now only amplified the loneliness. The patterns that used to work were failing, one by one, and David did not understand why.

He did not hear the whisper:

I am alluring you. I am bringing you into the wilderness. And there I will speak tenderly to you. I will give you back your vineyards, and make the Valley of Trouble a door of hope.

The Spirit brooded over David's chaos like wind over the face of the deep. Creating. Calling forth. Already speaking light into the darkness, even when David could see nothing but the dark.

The Descent

Marcus — Three Months Later

The abbot had noticed.

Father Paphnutius, ancient and weathered as the desert itself, his eyes still sharp as a falcon's despite his ninety years, had summoned Marcus to his cave after the Eucharist—which Marcus had attended with the expression of a man walking to his own execution.

"You did not take the Bread," Paphnutius said. It was not an accusation. It was an observation, the way one might note that the sun had risen or that sand was dry.

Marcus stood before him, his head bowed, his hands clasped behind his back like a schoolboy caught cheating. "I did not feel worthy, Abba."

"Ah." Paphnutius nodded slowly. "And do you think any of us feel worthy? Do you think I, who have served Christ for seventy years, who have seen visions and worked healings and raised men from spiritual death—do you think I feel worthy when I approach the Table?"

"I am sure you do not, Abba. But my unworthiness is... different."

"How so?"

The silence stretched. A scorpion scuttled across the floor of the cave, its tail curved like a question mark. Marcus watched it disappear into a crack in the rock before he spoke.

"I want to leave."

There. He had said it. The words hung in the air between them, almost visible, like smoke from the oil lamp that flickered in the corner.

Paphnutius did not react. His weathered face remained as still as the stone walls around them. "Tell me more."

"I think..." Marcus's voice broke. He had not cried in years—tears were a luxury he had denied himself along with all the others—but now he felt the pressure building behind his eyes like water behind a dam. "I think I made a mistake. Coming here. I thought I was called. I felt certain. But now, after twelve years, I feel nothing. The prayers are ashes in my mouth. The fasting is mere hunger. The psalms are just words. I go through the sacred rhythms like a donkey turning a millstone, round and round, and nothing—*nothing*—changes inside me."

I'm wasting my life, the inner voice added. *Even the abbot can see it. He's looking at me with pity. Twelve years, and I'm still the same broken man who arrived. Worse—at least that man had hope.*

"And what do you think would change if you left?" Paphnutius asked.

"I don't know." Marcus ran his hands over his face. "Maybe nothing. Maybe I would just be miserable in a different way. But at least in Alexandria, my misery would have silk sheets. At least my emptiness would be surrounded by beauty and comfort. At least—" He stopped, hearing how pathetic he sounded.

"At least you would have the distractions to numb the pain," Paphnutius finished for him.

Marcus nodded, ashamed.

He understands, the voice whispered. *He knows I'm not cut out for this. He's probably relieved I'm leaving. One less failure to worry about.*

The old abbot rose from his stool with a grace that belied his years and crossed the small cave to stand before Marcus. He placed his hands on the younger man's shoulders, and Marcus felt the weight of them—light as bird bones, heavy as mountains.

"My son," Paphnutius said, "you are in the Desert of the Soul. It is different from this desert of sand. More barren. More terrible. More holy."

"Holy?" The word tasted bitter. "There is nothing holy about what I feel. Only emptiness. Only death."

Only failure. Only the proof that I was never meant for this. That God never really called me. That I heard what I wanted to hear and threw away my life for an illusion.

"Yes. Death." Paphnutius's eyes held a distant light. "The death of the false self. The death of all your striving. The death of the Marcus who came here twelve years ago, who thought he could *earn* God's love through discipline, who thought he could *achieve* holiness through effort, who thought the sacred rhythms were a ladder he could climb to reach heaven."

Marcus flinched. It was as if the old man had read his soul.

"That Marcus must die," Paphnutius continued. "And it is a terrible death. A crucifixion. But on the other side of that death, my son, is resurrection. On the other side is a life you cannot yet imagine—a life in which you do not *strive* for God but *receive* Him, in which the disciplines are not a ladder to climb but a table set before you, a feast prepared by Love itself."

He's wrong, the voice insisted. *He has to be wrong. If there were something on the other side, I would have found it by now. Twelve years is enough time. I've done everything right. The problem isn't my approach—the problem is me. I'm unfixable.*

"How?" Marcus whispered. "How do I get to the other side?"

Paphnutius smiled, and for a moment, his face was luminous. "You cannot get there. You can only be carried. But first, you must let go of everything you are clinging to—including your idea of who you should be. Including your despair. Including your plans to leave."

He reached into the folds of his robe and withdrew a small scrap of parchment, creased and worn as if it had been handled many times.

"I am sending you to the mountain cave three days' journey south. There you will find two visitors from Hispania—a woman named Teresa and a man named Juan. They have come seeking the wisdom of the Desert Fathers, but I suspect they have more to give than to receive. Stay with them. Listen to them. They know the dark night better than anyone I have ever met."

Marcus took the parchment. On it was a crude map and a single sentence in Latin: *"Where I am weak, there I am strong."*

As he turned to leave, Paphnutius spoke once more: "Marcus. The Spirit has been working in you all along. Even in the darkness. Especially in the darkness. He is like a mother bird brooding over her nest—you cannot see

Him, but He is there, warming what has grown cold, incubating what is not yet born. Do not mistake His patience for absence. Do not mistake His silence for abandonment. He is hemming you in, closing the doors that lead to death, opening the one door that leads to life. Trust the hemming. It is love."

Marcus walked out into the desert night, and for the first time in months, he felt something other than despair. Not hope, exactly. Not yet. But something like the memory of hope, or the anticipation of it—a distant warmth, like a fire glimpsed across a dark valley.

Come, something whispered beneath his thoughts. *Come to Me. I am making a way in the wilderness. I am making rivers in the desert.*

He did not know if the whisper was real or imagined. But he turned south, toward the mountain cave, and he began to walk.

David — Three Weeks Later

He was sitting in his car in the church parking lot, crying.

The worship service had been beautiful. The presence of God had been tangible—he could see it in the faces of the people around him, hands raised, tears streaming, some of them on their knees. The pastor had preached on the prodigal son, and at the invitation, six people had gone forward for salvation, three for rededication.

David had stood in his row, mouthing the words to the closing hymn, feeling like a ghost.

I don't belong here. The thought had been relentless throughout the service. *Look at them. Look at how they feel God. Why can't I feel Him? What's wrong with me? They're real Christians. I'm just pretending. They must know. They must see right through me.*

He had slipped out the side door before anyone could ask him to stay for fellowship, before Hannah could invite him to lunch with her friends, before his small group co-leader could suggest they grab coffee to plan next week's lesson.

Now he sat in his car, engine running, air conditioning blasting against the Texas heat, and he wept.

Not the cathartic weeping of someone meeting God. The bleak, hopeless weeping of someone who had been crying out in the dark for months and heard only silence in return.

His phone buzzed. Then again. Then again. The group chat was going off—probably planning where to go for lunch, probably discussing the sermon, probably being *community* in all the ways David was failing to be.

I can't face it. I can't face any of them. If they knew who I really was—what I did last night, what I do most nights—they would never look at me the same way. They think I'm a leader. They think I have something to offer. If they knew the truth, they'd be disgusted.

But maybe, the other voice suggested, *maybe you should just accept it. You've proven you can't live up to your own standards. You've proven you can't be the David you want to be. So stop fighting. Find a faith that asks less of you—or no faith at all. At least you'd stop feeling like a hypocrite.*

Or, the smoother voice added, *just lean into grace. Really lean into it. God knows you're going to keep failing, so why torture yourself? Just accept that you're a sinner saved by grace, do what you're going to do, and trust that the blood covers it. That's freedom, isn't it? That's what grace is for.*

No. The third voice, quieter but persistent. *That's not grace. That's license. Grace transforms. Grace heals. If I'm not being transformed, something is wrong—but the answer isn't to give up or to cheapen grace even further. The answer is—*

What? More effort? More discipline? You've tried that. You've tried everything. You're still the same mess you were seven years ago when you thought the revival had changed you. Face it: some people are beyond help. Some people are just broken.

I TWO SOULS IN A WILDERNESS

David stared at the steering wheel through blurred eyes. The voices circled like vultures, each one tearing off another piece of his hope.

But even as the thoughts beckoned, something deeper resisted. A memory—or was it a hope?—of what he had once tasted. The revival where fire had fallen. The moment in worship when he'd lost himself and found something infinitely greater. The still small voice that had once whispered *"Beloved"* to his restless heart.

"I can't give up," he whispered. "But I can't keep going like this either. Something has to change. *I* have to change. But I don't know how. I've read the books. I've tried the programs. I've made the commitments. And I keep failing."

Because I'm a failure. That's who I am. That's all I'll ever be.

He sat in silence for a long time, watching families stream out of the church, watching couples hold hands, watching children run and laugh in the parking lot. All of them seemed to have something he lacked. All of them seemed to know a secret he had never been told.

And then—so quietly he almost missed it—something else. Not the accusing voice. Not the excusing voice. Something underneath both, like a current beneath the waves.

David.

He startled, looking around the car as if expecting to see someone.

David. I have loved you with an everlasting love. Therefore I have drawn you with lovingkindness.

It was not audible. It was barely even a thought. It was more like a pressure in his chest, a warmth behind his eyes, a knowing that bypassed his mind entirely and spoke directly to something deeper.

I am not finished with you. I have been working even when you could not see Me. I have been hemming you in—closing the doors that lead to death, making the old escapes bitter in your mouth. Not to punish you. To save you. To bring you home.

David's tears changed. He did not know how or why, but suddenly they were different—still painful, still raw, but no longer hopeless. Something was breaking open in him that had been sealed shut for years.

"I don't know how to find You," he whispered to the empty car, to the Presence he could almost feel. "I've tried. I keep trying. I keep failing."

Stop trying to find Me. Let Me find you. I am already here. I have always been here. Brooding over your chaos like wind over water. Waiting for you to stop running.

His phone buzzed again. This time, it was a text from an unknown number:

"David—this is Roger Morrison. Pastor James gave me your number. Said you might be looking for someone to talk to. I'm retired, but I've got nothing but time. Coffee tomorrow? My treat. Just say when and where."

David stared at the message. Roger Morrison. He knew that name. The pastor who had served twenty-three years at Redeemer before retiring last spring. The one everyone called a "father in the faith." The one with the quiet eyes and the gentle laugh.

This is Me, the whisper came again. *I am sending help. I am making a way. Will you walk through the door I am opening?*

His thumb hovered over the keyboard. Part of him wanted to delete the message, to avoid one more person who would discover how broken he really was.

He'll see through me, the accusing voice warned. *He'll realize I'm not worth his time. Better to spare us both the embarrassment.*

But maybe, the quieter voice—the new voice, the one that was not his own—whispered, *maybe he has seen this before. Maybe I have sent him because he knows the way. Trust Me, David. Trust the hemming.*

His thumb typed:

"Tomorrow works. Black Swan Coffee. 9 AM. Thank you."

Part Two: The Mentors

I TWO SOULS IN A WILDERNESS

Teresa and Juan

The Mountain Cave — 387 AD

Marcus found them at sunset on the third day, just as Paphnutius had said he would.

The cave was larger than his own, its mouth facing west so that the dying light poured in like liquid gold. Inside, two figures sat on simple mats woven from palm fronds—a woman perhaps fifty years old with dark eyes that seemed to hold both laughter and sorrow in equal measure, and a man younger than her, gaunt and intense, his hands scarred as if by fire or torture.

"You are Marcus," the woman said. It was not a question. Her accent was strange—the Latin of Hispania, softer than the Egyptian pronunciation. "Paphnutius sent word you were coming. I am Teresa. This is Juan."

Marcus hesitated at the entrance, suddenly shy. He had heard rumors in the desert about these two—that they were reformers of some great order in their own land, that they had suffered persecution for their love of prayer, that they had seen visions that made even the Desert Fathers pause.

I shouldn't be here, the inner voice hissed. *These are holy people—real saints. They'll see immediately that I'm a fraud. They'll wonder why Paphnutius wasted their time with someone so far from God.*

"Come," Teresa said, patting the ground beside her. "Sit. You have walked three days through the wilderness. Your feet are tired. But I think your soul is more tired still."

Marcus sat. The stone floor was warm from the day's heat, and the cave smelled of incense and something else—olive oil, perhaps, or the residue of prayers offered over many years.

"Paphnutius said you know the dark night," Marcus said. "He said you could help me."

Juan laughed softly—not mocking, but understanding. "The dark night is not something one 'knows' like a fact. It is something one survives, like a shipwreck. Teresa and I have both drowned in those waters. By God's grace, we were pulled from the depths."

"I am drowning now," Marcus admitted. "I have been a monk for twelve years. I have practiced every discipline the fathers taught—prayer at the canonical hours, fasting, silence, solitude, the gathering for Eucharist, giving what little I have to the poor who sometimes wander through the desert. I have sung the psalms until my voice cracked. I have meditated on Scripture until the words danced before my eyes. And now—" His voice caught. "Now I feel nothing. Worse than nothing. I feel the absence of God like a wound in my chest."

I sound pathetic, the voice sneered. *Twelve years and I'm complaining like a child. They must be laughing at me inside.*

Teresa nodded slowly, her dark eyes soft with compassion. "Tell me, Marcus—when you began these disciplines, what did you hope they would do?"

The question surprised him. "I hoped… I hoped they would make me holy. Transform me. Bring me closer to God."

"And did you think of them as something you *did* for God, or something you *received* from God?"

Marcus opened his mouth to answer, then closed it again. He had never considered the question.

"I thought…" he said slowly, "I thought of them as my offering. My sacrifice. The price I paid to earn His presence."

Juan leaned forward, and the fading light caught the hollows of his cheeks. "There," he said quietly. "There is the root. You have been climbing a ladder you built yourself, and you are surprised that it does not reach heaven."

"But the fathers taught—"

"The fathers taught truly," Teresa interrupted gently. "But teachings can be heard wrongly. The sacred rhythms—the prayers, the fasting, the silence, the gathering, the songs of praise—these are not rungs on a ladder. They are windows. They are openings through which grace flows into us. They are not the work we do for God; they are the spaces where we allow God to work in us."

She reached out and took Marcus's hands in her own. Her fingers were rough with calluses, her grip surprisingly strong.

"Let me tell you what I have learned, my son. The soul is like an interior castle with many rooms. At the center dwells the King—Christ Himself—in light so brilliant that it would blind us if we saw it all at once. But Marcus—" She paused, her eyes searching his. "There is a third Presence you must learn to recognize. The Holy Spirit. He is the One who guides us through the castle's rooms. He is the One who has been working in you all along, even in your darkest nights."

Marcus felt something stir in his chest. "The Spirit?"

"Yes. He is not like the voices that accuse you or the voices that excuse you. He does not condemn, though He convicts. He does not offer cheap comfort, though He comforts deeply. He is like—" Teresa paused, searching for words. "He is like a mother hen brooding over her eggs, patient and warm. He is like a lover wooing His beloved back from exile. He is like the prophet Hosea, pursuing wayward Israel with a love that will not let go."

Juan spoke now, his voice low and intense. "The Spirit has been hemming you in, Marcus. Have you not noticed? Every door you thought was an escape—has it not closed? Every path back to your old life—has it not become harder to walk?"

Marcus thought of the sandstorms that had blocked the road to Alexandria. The illness that had struck when he had begun packing his few possessions. The visiting pilgrim who had needed guidance for a month, just when Marcus had been ready to announce his departure.

"I thought those were coincidences," he said slowly. "Or punishments."

"Neither," Teresa said. "They were love. *'I will hedge up her way with thorns,'* the Spirit says through Hosea. *'I will build a wall against her, so that she cannot find her paths.'* This is not cruelty, Marcus. This is the desperate love of One who will not let you destroy yourself. He is closing the doors to death so you will finally walk through the door to life."

Marcus's eyes burned. "But why doesn't He speak to me? Why can't I feel Him?"

"You have not been listening for the right voice," Juan said. "You have been listening to the accuser, who tells you that you are worthless and beyond hope. You have been listening to the excuser, who tells you that grace requires nothing and changes nothing. But there is a third voice—quieter than both, beneath both, more patient than either. That voice says: *Come. Return. I have loved you with an everlasting love. My kindness has drawn you, even when you thought you were lost.*"

Teresa squeezed his hands. "The Spirit speaks in the silence between your prayers. He speaks in the ache you feel when you long for home without knowing what home is. He speaks in the strange dissatisfaction that makes your old pleasures taste like dust. That dissatisfaction is not punishment—it is wooing. He is making you hungry for the only Bread that satisfies."

They talked through the night.

Teresa spoke of prayer as *"intimate conversation with the One who loves us,"* not a duty to be performed but a relationship to be enjoyed. She taught him to begin each morning not with petitions but with simple presence—sitting in silence before God, letting himself be seen, letting himself be loved, without trying to produce anything or prove anything.

"Morning prayer," she said, *"is like a lover waking beside their beloved. You do not immediately begin listing requests. You simply rest in the joy of being together. And as you rest, learn to listen for the Spirit's voice. He will not shout over your noise. He will wait until you are quiet enough to hear Him whisper."*

1 TWO SOULS IN A WILDERNESS

Juan spoke of meditation not as intellectual study but as *savoring*—taking a single word or phrase of Scripture and holding it in the mouth of the soul like a piece of bread, letting it slowly dissolve, letting its nourishment seep into every part of the inner life.

"Noon prayer," he said, *"is a returning. The world pulls at us, even in the desert. The thoughts scatter like birds. The noon pause gathers them again, brings the soul back to center, reminds us whose we are. And as you return, pay attention: the Spirit will often speak in that moment of turning. He will say, 'Here. This is where I am. This is where you belong.'"*

They spoke of fasting—not as self-punishment but as *hunger made holy*, the body's emptiness becoming a prayer the mind could not articulate, a longing made tangible.

"Weekly hunger," Teresa said, *"is not God's rejection of pleasure but His invitation to deeper pleasure. We fast from bread that we might feast on the Bread of Life. And the hunger itself—the ache in your belly—this is a prayer the Spirit prays through you. He groans within us with groanings too deep for words. Let your hunger join His groaning."*

They spoke of giving—the release of possessions as a loosening of the grip, a practical proclamation that the Kingdom of God was worth more than gold.

"When you give to the poor who wander through your desert," Juan said, *"you are not earning favor. You are participating in the Missio Dei—God's mission to restore all things. You become a channel through which His compassion flows. And the Spirit—He is the One who creates compassion in you. When you feel your heart moved toward the poor, that is His work. Thank Him. Follow Him. Let Him lead you into the Father's mission."*

They spoke of song—the psalms and hymns that Marcus had sung until they became mere words.

"Sing them as if for the first time," Teresa urged. *"Each psalm is a door into a room of the interior castle. The hymns are not performance; they are wings. Let them carry you. And listen—the Spirit sings with you. He takes your*

broken notes and weaves them into the eternal chorus. You are never singing alone."

They spoke of community—the gathering Marcus had begun to resent, seeing it as intrusion rather than gift.

"You cannot reach heaven alone," Juan said. *"The politeia—the common life, the citizenship in God's Kingdom—is not optional. It is the very shape of salvation. Christ came as the Head of a Body, not as a teacher of isolated monks. When you gather for Eucharist, you take your place in that Body. You are not alone. You never were. And the Spirit—He is the bond of unity. He knits you to your brothers in ways you cannot see. When you resist community, you resist Him."*

And they spoke of the Eucharist itself—the Table Marcus had fled from.

"You think you must be worthy to receive," Teresa said gently. *"But the Table is not a reward for the worthy. It is medicine for the sick. Christ offers Himself to you not because you have earned Him but because you need Him. Every time you refuse the Bread, you are saying your unworthiness is greater than His grace. That is pride, Marcus, dressed in the robes of humility. And the Spirit—He is grieved when you refuse. He has been preparing you for this meal. He wants to feed you. Let Him."*

At dawn, Marcus wept.

Not the bleak tears of despair he had shed so many times in his cave. These were different—a loosening, a release, the cracking open of something that had been sealed too long. He wept, and Teresa held him like a mother, and Juan prayed over him in a language Marcus did not recognize, and in the golden light of morning, something began—not to end, but to transform.

"I see now," Marcus managed through his tears. "I see what I was doing wrong. But the feelings—the dryness—it has not changed. How do I practice differently when my heart is still stone?"

Juan smiled. "The feelings will come. Or they will not. It does not matter. What matters is the turning—the shift from earning to receiving, from striving to resting, from climbing to falling into the arms that were waiting all along. Do the practices. But do them as one who is already loved. That is all. The transformation is the Spirit's work, not yours."

"How long will the darkness last?"

"As long as it needs to. Some nights are longer than others. But Marcus—" Juan's eyes held a light that seemed to come from somewhere beyond the cave. "The night always ends. Always. And when morning comes, you will wonder how you ever lived without it. The Spirit is faithful. He will finish what He has begun."

Teresa spoke once more: "Listen for Him, Marcus. In the days ahead, in the practices you return to, listen for the third voice. Not the one that accuses. Not the one that excuses. The one that woos. The one that says, *Beloved. Return. I have been waiting.* That is the Spirit. That is your guide. Follow Him home."

Roger and Chenè

Austin, Texas — The Next Morning

The coffee shop was already busy when David arrived—the usual mix of remote workers, students, and retired couples enjoying the morning cool before the Texas heat descended. He spotted Roger Morrison immediately: a man in his late sixties with silver hair, kind eyes behind wire-rimmed glasses, and the kind of weathered face that suggested he had lived fully and suffered genuinely.

"David." Roger stood and extended a hand. His grip was firm but gentle. "Thanks for coming."

"Thanks for reaching out." David slid into the seat across from him, clutching his coffee like a lifeline. "I have to be honest—I'm not sure why you wanted to meet. I'm not exactly in a great spiritual place right now."

This is a mistake, the inner voice warned. *He's going to see through me in about thirty seconds. Then he'll politely end the meeting and tell Pastor James not to bother him with broken toys.*

"I know." Roger smiled, and there was something in that smile—not pity, not judgment, but a recognition that disarmed David immediately. "James told me. He said you've been struggling. Said you might need someone to talk to who wasn't, well, trying to fix you or recruit you for something."

David laughed despite himself. "That obvious, huh?"

"To someone who's been there? Yes." Roger sipped his own coffee—black, David noticed, no sugar. "Can I tell you a story before you tell me yours?"

David nodded.

"Twenty-seven years ago, I was you. Different specifics—I didn't have a smartphone to wrestle with—but the same disease. I was leading a thriving church, preaching powerful sermons, seeing lives changed, and inside, I was dying. Burned out. Addicted to affirmation. Secretly envious of every pastor more successful than me. I prayed, but my prayers were performances. I read Scripture, but I was mining for sermon material, not meeting God. I served the poor, but I was building a reputation, not entering the kingdom."

He paused, turning his coffee cup between his hands.

"And then I crashed. Hard. Public sin, public shame, nearly lost my marriage and my ministry. The elders confronted me, and I remember thinking, 'This is it. This is the end of everything.'"

David's throat tightened. "What happened?"

"An old Benedictine brother happened. Father Gregory. He showed up at my lowest moment—my wife had moved out, my church had suspended me, I was sitting in an empty parsonage thinking about whether to keep living—and he didn't offer counsel or condemnation. He just sat with me. For hours. In silence. And then he said something I'll never forget."

1 TWO SOULS IN A WILDERNESS

Roger leaned forward.

"He said, 'Roger, your problem isn't that you sinned. Everyone sins. Your problem is that you've been trying to become holy through your own efforts, and you've used the spiritual disciplines as tools in that project. But holiness isn't achieved. It's received. The disciplines aren't ladders to climb or penances to perform. They're hands cupped to receive grace. You've been working when you should have been resting.'"

David felt the words land somewhere deep, in a place he hadn't known was wounded.

"That's... that's exactly what I do," he said slowly. "The morning devotions—when I do them—I'm trying to earn something. To prove something. To check a box. And when I fail, I feel like a fraud. Like God must be so disappointed in me."

Because He is disappointed, the voice insisted. *How could He not be? Look at what I do. Look at who I am.*

"And the other struggles?" Roger asked gently. "The ones you haven't mentioned yet?"

David's face flushed. "Pastor James told you about—"

"He told me you're struggling with technology and purity. He didn't give details. You don't have to either, not today. But I want you to know something: whatever it is, I've either done it, heard it in confession from someone else, or struggled with the desire for it. Nothing you tell me is going to shock me. And nothing is going to change my desire to walk with you."

The tears came without warning. David tried to stop them, but they kept falling, running down his cheeks into his coffee.

"I'm addicted to my phone," he whispered. "I can't put it down. My screen time is seven hours a day, and that's not counting when I use it for work. I scroll through social media comparing myself to everyone, feeling worse about myself with every post. I have... there are apps I shouldn't have. Sites I visit. It started as occasional temptation and now it's... it's a prison.

I've tried accountability apps. I've tried software locks. I've tried giving my phone to friends on the weekends. Nothing works."

Nothing works because I don't really want to stop, the smooth voice added. *Be honest. Part of me likes it. Part of me needs it. And grace covers that, right? God knows I'm weak. He made me this way. He can't be that surprised when I act accordingly.*

"And the worst part—" David struggled to form the words.

"Go on."

"The worst part is the cycle. I tell myself I'm going to stop. I pray about it. I feel genuinely convicted. And then... the temptation comes, and there's this voice that says, 'Just do it and confess later. God's grace is sufficient. You're not saved by works anyway. You can repent tomorrow.' And I listen to it. I give in. And then I feel awful, and I confess, and I mean it—I really mean it—but even while I'm confessing, part of me knows I'm going to do it again. So is my repentance even real? Or am I just... playing a game with God?"

Roger's eyes softened. "That's an important question. And I'm not going to give you a simple answer, because there isn't one. But let me ask you this: when you confess, are you confessing to earn forgiveness, or to receive it?"

"I... I don't understand the difference."

"Earning means you're performing a transaction. You sin, you confess, the slate is wiped clean, you go back to your life until the next sin. It's a religious formula. Receiving means you're coming to a Person—not a system, a Person—and you're saying, 'I cannot save myself. I cannot even stop sinning by myself. I need You, not just for forgiveness, but for everything. I need You to do what I cannot.' Do you see the difference?"

David was silent, turning the words over in his mind. The voice that usually whispered condemnation was quiet—perhaps because it had no category for what Roger was describing.

"I've been earning," he said finally. "My whole Christian life. I've been performing a transaction."

"Most of us do. It's the default mode of the religious heart. But there's another way." Roger pulled out his phone and scrolled through his contacts. "I want you to meet someone. Her name is Chenè. She's a licensed therapist, but more importantly, she's a spiritual director—one of the best I've ever encountered. She combines psychological insight with deep contemplative spirituality. I think she could help you in ways I can't."

Great, the voice sneered. *Now I need a therapist too. More proof of how broken I am.*

But another voice—the quieter one, the one that had spoken in the parking lot—whispered something different: *This is Me. I am sending help. I am making a way. Will you trust the hemming?*

Two Days Later

Chenè's office was nothing like David expected.

He had imagined something sterile and clinical—a leather couch, a desk, diplomas on the wall. Instead, he found himself in a warm, sunlit room with plants cascading from shelves, a small fountain gurgling in the corner, and two comfortable chairs facing each other. The walls were decorated with icons—Eastern Orthodox, he thought, though he couldn't identify the saints—and a single candle burned on a low table between the chairs.

Chenè herself was a woman in her late fifties with silver-streaked dark hair, olive skin, and eyes that seemed to look not at him but into him. She wore simple clothes—jeans, a linen blouse—but there was something about her presence that made David feel simultaneously exposed and safe.

"Roger told me about you," she said, gesturing for him to sit. Her accent was subtle—South African, perhaps. "He said you're in the dark night."

"The what?"

"The dark night of the soul. It's a term from a Spanish mystic named John of the Cross—he wrote about it in the sixteenth century. But the experience is as old as faith itself. It's what happens when God begins to strip away everything we've built our spiritual lives on—including our ideas about Him, about ourselves, about what holiness looks like."

Great, the inner voice muttered. *Another person who thinks my failure is actually some kind of spiritual experience. I'm not having a 'dark night.' I'm just a mess.*

"I'm not sure that's what's happening to me," David said. "I think I'm just... failing. Repeatedly. In the same ways. And I can't seem to stop."

Chenè nodded, unsurprised. "Tell me about the failure."

So David told her. Everything. The phone addiction, the pornography, the cycles of resolve and collapse, the shame that drove him deeper into isolation, the voices that warred in his head—the one that condemned him and the one that offered cheap grace and the quieter one he could barely hear anymore.

When he finished, Chenè was silent for a long moment. Then she said something that stopped his breath.

"David, your soul is a castle with many rooms. And you've been living in the outer courtyard your whole life, never realizing there's a throne room at the center where God Himself is waiting for you."

"I don't understand."

"You're fighting your sins on the surface. You're trying to manage your behavior through willpower and accountability and guilt. But the addiction, the phone, the pornography—these aren't the problem. They're symptoms. The real problem is that you've never learned to dwell in the interior of your own soul, where you are known and loved and held. You've been living as a stranger in your own house."

She's right, the voice admitted, surprising him. *I don't know who I am. I don't know where I live. I'm always performing, always managing, always watching myself from the outside.*

I TWO SOULS IN A WILDERNESS

"How do I... get to the throne room?" David asked.

"Not by trying harder. Not by climbing another ladder. The path inward is the path of surrender—of letting go, layer by layer, of everything that keeps you from receiving the love that's already there." Chenè leaned forward. "But David—there's something else you need to understand. There is a Guide. The Holy Spirit. He has been working in you all along, even when you couldn't feel Him. Especially when you couldn't feel Him."

David felt something stir in his chest—the same strange warmth he had felt in the parking lot. "The Spirit?"

"Yes. He is not the voice that accuses you. He convicts, but He does not condemn—there is a difference. He is not the voice that offers cheap grace, permission to sin because forgiveness is easy. He offers real grace—forgiveness that transforms, not just covers. He is like—" Chenè paused, searching for words. "He is like a mother bird brooding over her eggs, patient and warm. He is like a pursuing lover. Have you read Hosea?"

David shook his head.

"It's a book about a prophet who married a prostitute named Gomer. She kept leaving him, returning to her lovers, and God kept telling Hosea to pursue her, to bring her back. It's a picture of God's love for wayward Israel—and for you. The Spirit is like Hosea. You keep running away, and He keeps pursuing. You keep choosing lesser loves, and He keeps wooing you back to the only Love that satisfies."

"But how? How does He pursue me?"

"By hemming you in." Chenè smiled gently. "Have you noticed that your old escapes don't work anymore? That the things that used to numb you now leave you emptier than before? That the doors you thought were open keep closing?"

David's breath caught. He *had* noticed. The porn that used to bring relief now brought only deeper shame. The social media that used to distract now only amplified his loneliness. The cycles that used to be manageable were becoming unbearable.

"That's the Spirit," Chenè said. "He is building walls around the paths that lead to death. Not to punish you—to save you. He is making the wilderness the only way forward, because it's in the wilderness that He can finally speak to your heart without competition from all the other voices."

She quoted softly: *"Therefore, behold, I will allure her, and bring her into the wilderness, and speak tenderly to her. And there I will give her her vineyards and make the Valley of Achor a door of hope."*

"What do I do?" David asked. "How do I... cooperate with that?"

"You learn to recognize His voice. Not the accuser, not the excuser—the third voice. The one that is quieter than both, beneath both. The one that does not condemn but calls. The one that does not excuse but transforms. When you feel convicted but not crushed, that's Him. When you feel drawn toward home even though you're ashamed to go there, that's Him. When you feel a strange dissatisfaction with the things that used to satisfy, that's Him—making you hungry for the only Bread that fills."

She led David through a practice he had never encountered. First, silence—not the anxious silence of his failed devotional attempts, but a settled silence, anchored by breath, grounded in the awareness that he was not alone. Then, an invitation to the Spirit to show him not just his sins but their roots—the fears, the wounds, the empty places that drove him toward false comfort. Then, a simple acknowledgment: *This is who I am. This is what I've done. I cannot fix myself.*

And then—this was the part that broke him—a receiving. Not earning. Receiving. Chenè had him hold out his hands, palms up, and receive the forgiveness that was already flowing toward him, that had never stopped flowing, that did not depend on the quality of his repentance.

"Now listen," Chenè said as his tears fell. "Listen for the Spirit. He wants to speak to you."

David sat in the silence, hands open, heart raw. The accusing voice was there, circling: *This is ridiculous. Nothing is going to happen. I'm too far gone.*

I TWO SOULS IN A WILDERNESS

The excusing voice was there too: *Even if I feel something, it won't last. I'll fall again tomorrow. Why bother?*

But beneath both—so quiet he had to strain to hear it—something else. *David.*

He held his breath.

Beloved. You are not a failure. You are a son. I have been pursuing you through all your wandering. I have been closing the doors that lead to death. I have been making the wilderness a path to your true home. Come home, David. Come home. Not because you have earned it—you haven't—but because I have paid for it. Not because you are worthy—you aren't—but because My love is stronger than your unworthiness. Come home.

The tears came harder now—not tears of shame, but of recognition. Of homecoming. Of being found.

"The spiritual disciplines," Chenè said gently, "are not punishments for sin. They're not penances you perform to earn back what you've lost. They're means of grace—channels through which God's love flows into the empty places of your soul. And the Spirit—He is the One who makes them come alive. Without Him, the disciplines are dead works. With Him, they become encounters with the living God."

"When you pray in the morning, you're not checking a box; you're opening a door for the Spirit to meet you. When you fast, you're not proving your commitment; you're making space for hunger that only God can fill—and the Spirit will meet you in that hunger. When you gather with others, you're not performing community; you're receiving the Body of Christ—and the Spirit is the bond that holds the Body together. Do you see? It's all gift. It's all receiving. The moment you make it about earning, you step out of the Spirit's current and start swimming against the river."

But what about the sin? the voice demanded. *What about the patterns I can't break?*

"The sin is real," Chenè acknowledged, as if she had heard the thought. "The patterns are strong. But David—the sin loses its power when you stop trying to defeat it on your own. The Spirit is the One who transforms. Your job is not to fix yourself; your job is to keep showing up, keep receiving, keep listening for His voice. He will do the work. He is already doing the work. The hemming you've been experiencing—that's His work. The dissatisfaction with your old escapes—that's His work. The fact that you're sitting here, crying, broken open—that's His work. Trust Him. Cooperate with Him. And let Him carry you where you cannot carry yourself."

David left Chenè's office that day with a new practice: each morning, before any other prayer, he was to sit in silence and listen for the Spirit. Not the accusing voice. Not the excusing voice. The third voice—the quiet one, the patient one, the One who had been pursuing him all along.

"The imaginary David has to die," Chenè had said. "He's been standing between you and God for years. Let him go. And let the real David—broken, struggling, beloved—finally come home. The Spirit will guide you. He has been guiding you. Learn to recognize Him, and you will never walk alone again."

Part Three: The Practicing

Sacred Rhythms

Marcus — Six Months Later

The bell for Lauds rang through the desert darkness, and for the first time in over a year, Marcus rose eagerly.

He had returned from the mountain cave a changed man—not changed in the sense of becoming suddenly holy, but changed in the sense of becoming honest. He no longer approached the morning prayers as a ladder to climb but as a table set before him, a gift offered by Love itself.

This morning, as every morning now, he began in silence.

1 TWO SOULS IN A WILDERNESS

Sitting on his reed mat, he did not immediately launch into petitions or recitations. Instead, he followed Teresa's teaching: he simply sat. Breathing. Present. Acknowledging the Presence.

I am here, Lord.

This is who I am. A man who still struggles. A man who still feels the pull of Alexandria. A man whose prayers sometimes feel like dust. But I am Yours. I am here.

And then, as he had learned to do, he listened. Not for the accusing voice—*You're wasting your time. You feel nothing. God is not here.* Not for the excusing voice—*You've already put in your years. You don't have to try so hard. Grace covers your laziness.* But for the third voice. The quiet one. The patient one.

Some mornings, the Spirit spoke clearly—not in audible words, but in impressions, in warmth, in a sudden knowing that bypassed his mind and settled directly into his heart. Other mornings, like this one, there was only silence.

But Marcus had learned something in the months since the mountain cave. The silence was not absence. The Spirit was brooding over him even in the dark, like a mother bird over her eggs, like wind over the face of the deep. The lack of feeling did not mean the lack of presence.

I hear You in the silence, Marcus whispered inwardly. *I trust You in the dark. I know You are working even when I cannot see.*

And then—so faint he might have imagined it—a response:

Yes, beloved. I am here. I have never left. Rest in Me.

Marcus breathed deeply. The accusing voice was there, circling at a distance: *That was just your imagination. You're making this up. Real saints have visions and ecstasies; you have nothing but wishful thinking.* But Marcus had learned not to argue with it. He simply noted it, acknowledged it, and returned his attention to the quiet Presence beneath.

Thank You, he said to the Spirit. *Thank You for not giving up on me. Thank You for hemming me in when I wanted to run. Thank You for making the wilderness a way home.*

He rose and made his way to the chapel.

The brothers were gathering—thirty men in brown robes, their faces weathered, their eyes bright with the particular alertness of the desert. Marcus took his place among them, and when the antiphon began, he opened his mouth to sing.

"*O Lord, open my lips, and my mouth shall declare Your praise...*"

The psalm was the same one he had sung a thousand times before. But now, following Juan's teaching, he savored it. He let each word settle on the tongue of his soul like a piece of bread:

Open my lips. He could not open them himself. The opening was gift. The praise was gift. And the Spirit—the Spirit was the One who gave it. *Spirit, open my lips. Spirit, give me the words. I cannot praise on my own.*

My mouth shall declare Your praise. Not because he had achieved praise, but because the praise was already there, waiting to be released, a spring bubbling up from somewhere deeper than effort.

And Marcus realized—the Spirit was singing with him. His broken voice was being woven into something larger, something eternal. He was not singing alone.

The voices rose around him, and for the first time in many months, Marcus felt himself carried on the current of sound. Not performing. Not striving. Flowing. The Spirit was the current. All Marcus had to do was float.

At noon, when the sun hung high and the desert shimmered with heat, the bell rang again. Marcus stopped his work—he had been repairing the chapel roof, his hands rough with clay and straw—and returned to his cave.

The noon pause, Juan had said. *The turning.*

He sat again. Breathed again. Returned again.

I TWO SOULS IN A WILDERNESS

The morning's prayers had scattered under the pressure of labor, the whispering of the familiar voices—*I'm not as good as Brother Pachomius; I should have stayed in Alexandria; this is all meaningless; God doesn't hear me anyway*—and simple distraction. Marcus gathered them up now like a shepherd gathering strayed sheep. He did not beat himself for the straying. He simply called the sheep home.

Spirit, he prayed, *I have wandered again. My thoughts have scattered. My heart has grown cold. But I am returning now. Meet me here. Speak to me here.*

And the Spirit answered—not in words, this time, but in warmth. A gradual thawing of the coldness in Marcus's chest. A sense of being held, being known, being welcomed back without reproach.

This is what I do, Marcus understood suddenly. *I wander, and You call me back. I stray, and You gather me. Over and over. Not because I deserve the gathering, but because You are a Shepherd who will not lose His sheep.*

Yes, the Spirit seemed to say. *This is who I am. This is who you are to Me. Beloved. Pursued. Never abandoned.*

Marcus sat in the warmth for ten minutes, twenty. He did not try to produce anything. He simply received. And when he rose to return to his work, he carried the warmth with him, a coal burning quietly in his chest.

In the evening, as the sun set and the desert cooled, he joined the brothers for Vespers. The psalms were different now—the evening psalms, with their themes of rest and gratitude and the completion of day. Marcus sang them as a man sings lullabies, not demanding response, but offering presence.

"*In peace I will both lie down and sleep; for You alone, O Lord, make me dwell in safety...*"

And the Spirit sang with him, weaving his voice into the eternal chorus, carrying his feeble notes into the throne room of heaven.

At night, in the dark hours before Matins, when the accusing voice was loudest, Marcus practiced the discipline he had most resisted: honest confession.

Not confession to earn forgiveness—he understood now that forgiveness was already given—but confession as agreement with reality. Kneeling in his cave, he spoke aloud the sins of the day:

I resented Brother Pachomius when he criticized my work.

I felt the old longing for Alexandria, for wealth, for reputation.

I compared myself to the younger monks and felt both superior and envious.

I daydreamed during the psalms.

I entertained the accusing voices longer than I should have.

I heard the smooth voice say, "God will forgive anyway—why struggle so hard?" and part of me wanted to believe it.

He did not minimize these failures, but neither did he wallow in them. He named them, released them, and then—this was the crucial part—he listened.

Spirit, he prayed, *what do You want to say to me? What do You see that I have not yet confessed? Where are You calling me deeper?*

The silence stretched. And then, gentle as breath:

Marcus, you are still trying to earn My love. You are still counting your sins like a merchant counts debts, hoping to balance the ledger. But there is no ledger. There is only love. I do not love you because you confess; I love you because you are Mine. The confession does not pay for the sin—Christ has already paid. The confession simply opens the door so you can receive what has already been given.

Marcus wept. Not tears of shame, but tears of relief. Of homecoming.

And Marcus, the Spirit continued, *there is one more thing. The longing for Alexandria—the desire for wealth, for comfort, for significance—this is not your deepest longing. It is a shadow of something real. You were made for a home, for riches, for honor. But not the home you left. Not the riches that moth and rust destroy. Not the honor that fades with death. I am preparing a place for you. An inheritance that cannot spoil or fade. When you feel the ache for Alexandria, bring it to Me. Let Me transform it into longing for your true home.*

Marcus knelt in the darkness, the Spirit's words burning in his chest like fire. He did not feel ecstasy. He did not see visions. But he knew—with a certainty deeper than feeling—that he was not alone. That he never had been. That the Spirit had been brooding over him through all the years of darkness, patient and persistent, hemming him in, wooing him home.

Thank You, he whispered. *Thank You for not giving up. Thank You for the hemming. Thank You for the long, long pursuit.*

I will never give up, the Spirit answered. *I will pursue you all the days of your life. And when the pursuit is over, you will see: it was always love. Only ever love.*

The Long Obedience

David — Eight Months Later

The alarm went off at 5:30 AM, and David woke without groaning.

This had not been true eight months ago. Eight months ago, the alarm had been an enemy, a tyrannical demand that felt like punishment. Now it was simply an invitation—an invitation to show up, to receive, to meet the One who had been waiting through the night.

He made coffee—a small pleasure both Roger and Chenè had encouraged rather than discouraged, part of learning to enjoy the disciplines rather than endure them—and settled into the worn armchair by the window where he met God every morning.

No phone. The phone stayed in the bedroom, charging, its notifications silenced until 7 AM. This had been one of Chenè's first prescriptions: *"You* cannot hear the Spirit's voice if you're drowning in digital noise. Give Him the first hour. The algorithm can wait."

David sat. Breathed. Let the silence settle.

Good morning, Spirit, he prayed. *I'm here. I'm listening. What do You want to say to me today?*

This was the practice Chenè had taught him—beginning not with petitions or confessions or Scripture reading, but with listening. *"The Spirit has been speaking all along,"* she had said. *"You just haven't been listening. Learn to listen first. Let Him set the agenda."*

Some mornings, the Spirit spoke clearly—impressions, warmth, a sudden word or phrase that seemed to come from beyond David's own mind. Other mornings, there was only silence.

Today was a silent morning. But David had learned, over eight months of practice, that silence was not absence. The Spirit was brooding over him even in the dark. The quiet was not emptiness; it was patience. The Presence was there, whether David could feel it or not.

I trust You in the silence, he prayed. *I know You're here even when I can't feel You. I know You're working even when I can't see.*

He sat for fifteen minutes, twenty. Then he opened the Book of Common Prayer and read the appointed psalm for the day:

"Create in me a clean heart, O God, and renew a right spirit within me. Cast me not away from Your presence, and take not Your Holy Spirit from me. Restore unto me the joy of Your salvation, and uphold me with a willing spirit..."

Each phrase was a small opening, a window for grace to flow through. David let the words settle, repeated them silently, noticed which ones caught his attention. *Create. Clean. Renew.* Not things he could do for himself. Things done in him, to him, through him. By the Spirit.

Spirit, create in me a clean heart. I can't make myself clean—I've tried. You have to do it. Spirit, renew a right spirit within me. My spirit is bent,

1 TWO SOULS IN A WILDERNESS

broken, pulled in a thousand wrong directions. You have to straighten it. I'm here. I'm open. Do what only You can do.

And then, after the psalm, more silence. More listening.

David.

He held his breath. There it was—the third voice. Not the accuser (*You're still a mess; nothing has changed*). Not the excuser (*You're fine; don't be so hard on yourself; grace covers everything*). The Spirit.

David, I am pleased with you.

David's eyes stung. *But I haven't achieved anything. I'm not the imaginary David—the one who prays for hours and never struggles. I'm still a mess. I still fall sometimes. I still—*

I know who you are. I know what you've done. And I am pleased with you. Not because you have achieved holiness—you haven't. Because you are here. Because you keep showing up. Because you have stopped running and started receiving. That is all I ever wanted. Your presence. Your openness. Your willingness to let Me work.

David wept. This had happened many times over the past eight months—tears in the morning silence, tears of relief and recognition and homecoming. He no longer fought them or felt ashamed of them. The tears were part of the receiving. They were the soul's way of opening wider.

I love You, he whispered. *I don't know if I've ever said that before and really meant it. But I love You. Not because of what You've done for me—though You've done everything. Because of who You are. You pursued me when I was running. You hemmed me in when I wanted to escape. You spoke tenderly to me in the wilderness. You are—*

He searched for the word. And the Spirit supplied it:

Beloved. I am your Beloved, and you are Mine. This is who we are to each other. Everything else flows from this.

At 6:30, David's alarm chimed—the reminder for his noon pause, relocated to fit his work schedule. He had discovered that literal noon was impossible (he was deep in meetings by then), so he and Roger had adapted: a brief pause during his commute, a few minutes of conscious returning before the workday swallowed him whole.

"The rhythms are servants, not masters," Roger had said. *"The desert fathers practiced them one way. You will practice them another. What matters is the turning, not the timing. And the Spirit—He will meet you whenever you turn. He is not bound by the clock."*

In the car, driving to work, David turned off the music and sat in silence. Just a few minutes. Just enough to acknowledge:

Spirit, I got scattered. Work is pulling at me. Anxieties are circling. The voices are starting up again—the one that says I'm behind, that I'll never catch up, that everyone else is doing better than me. But I'm turning to You now. Recenter me. Remind me whose I am.

And the Spirit answered—sometimes with warmth, sometimes with a word, sometimes with simple peace. The anxieties didn't always disappear. But they became smaller, more manageable, put in their proper place. David was not alone in the car. He was never alone anymore.

At work, the temptations were constant. His phone buzzed with notifications. His computer presented infinite rabbit holes of distraction. His colleagues' casual conversations about binge-watching shows or viral videos reminded him of everything he was missing by choosing a different way of life.

I'm missing out, the accusing voice whispered. *Everyone else is enjoying themselves, and I'm stuck with these rigid practices. Is this really what God wants? Doesn't He want me to be happy?*

Besides, the excusing voice added, *a little scrolling never hurt anyone. It's not like I'm going to do anything bad. I can browse social media and still be a good Christian. God's grace covers everything, right?*

But David had learned to recognize these voices now—and to wait for the third one.

David. The Spirit's voice, quiet beneath the noise. *What are you really looking for? What does the scrolling promise that it never delivers?*

David paused. Thought. *Connection, I guess. Distraction from anxiety. The feeling of being in the loop, of not being left behind.*

And do you find those things in the feed?

No. I feel more disconnected afterward. More anxious. More behind.

Then why do you return?

Because... because I don't know what else to do with the emptiness. The loneliness. The ache.

Bring the ache to Me. That is what it's for. The ache is a homing signal—it's telling you that you were made for something the feed cannot give. Stop trying to fill the ache with pixels. Let Me fill it. I am the connection you long for. I am the peace your anxiety craves. I am the home your restlessness is seeking.

David did not pick up his phone. He sat with the ache instead, offering it to the Spirit, letting it become a prayer.

On a Wednesday evening, three months into his work with Roger and Chenè, David had fallen. The pull of the old patterns had been overwhelming—stress at work, loneliness, a fight with Hannah—and at 11 PM, alone in his apartment, he had opened the forbidden app.

See? the accusing voice had crowed. *I knew it. I'm hopeless. All those disciplines, all that 'receiving,' and I'm still the same pathetic failure I always was. I should just give up.*

Or, the excusing voice had countered, *I could acknowledge that I'm human. God made me with these desires. He can't be that surprised when I act on them. I'll confess tomorrow, and everything will be fine. That's what grace is for.*

But David had learned, over months of practice, to wait for the third voice. To not react to the first two, but to listen deeper.

And the Spirit spoke—not in condemnation, not in excuse, but in something harder and more beautiful: truth wrapped in love.

David. What happened?

I fell. Again.

I know. I saw. I was with you even then—grieved, yes, but not gone. What drove you to it?

I was lonely. Hannah and I fought, and I felt rejected, and the old patterns—they promised relief.

Did they deliver?

No. I feel worse now. Emptier.

Yes. That is how the false comforts work. They promise what they cannot give. But David— and here the Spirit's voice became very tender— *the loneliness you felt, the rejection—those are real wounds. They need real healing. The porn was a false bandage on a real wound. It didn't heal you; it infected the wound further. But I can heal you. Will you bring Me the wound, not just the sin? Will you let Me speak to the loneliness, not just forgive the acting out?*

David knelt on the floor of his apartment, tears streaming. *Yes. I'll bring You the wound. Here it is—the loneliness. The fear that Hannah will leave me. The terror of being abandoned. The part of me that believes I'm not worth loving, that everyone will eventually see through me and walk away.*

That wound is old, the Spirit said. *Older than Hannah. Older than the addiction. It goes all the way back to childhood—to the father who was never satisfied, to the peers who mocked you, to the lie you believed that said you had to perform to be loved. But David—that is a lie. You do not have to perform. You are loved because I have chosen to love you. Not because of what you do, but because of who you are to Me: My beloved. My pursued. My child.*

The healing did not happen all at once. But something shifted that night. The shame that usually followed a fall was less crushing, because David had brought it to the Light instead of hiding in the dark. And the accusing voice had less power, because the Spirit had spoken louder.

1 TWO SOULS IN A WILDERNESS

The next morning, David had texted Roger: *I failed again. Can we meet?* Roger's response had come within minutes: *Of course. Coffee at 9?*

They had met, and David had confessed—not just the act, but the wound beneath it. And Roger had listened without judgment, had prayed with him, had reminded him of the truth.

"David, the fact that you're here—that you texted me, that you came to confess—that's not failure. That's success. The failure would be hiding. The failure would be pretending nothing happened and adding shame to shame until you disappeared from community entirely. You fell. And you got back up. That's the whole story of the Christian life."

"But it keeps happening," David had said. *"I keep failing. When does it stop?"*

"Maybe never," Roger had replied. *"Maybe the struggle is lifelong. I don't know. What I do know is that the Spirit's work in you is not dependent on your perfection. He is faithful even when you are not. He will finish what He has begun. Your job is not to achieve sinlessness; your job is to keep showing up, keep confessing, keep receiving. He will do the rest."*

That had been five months ago. Since then, David had fallen twice more—not good, not the victory he longed for, but fewer times than in any comparable period of his adult life. And each time, the Spirit had met him in the fall:

David. What happened?

I fell.

I know. I was there. I am still here. Let's look at the wound together. Let Me heal what drove you to it. And then—get up. Walk. I am not finished with you.

The fasting had become a conversation with the Spirit.

Every Wednesday, David ate nothing until dinner—a practice Roger called *"teaching the body to pray."* The hunger was real, uncomfortable, sometimes distracting. But David had learned to offer the hunger:

Spirit, this is how my soul longs for You. This is the emptiness that only You can fill. The growling in my stomach is a prayer I can't put into words. Receive it. Answer it. Feed me with Yourself.

And the Spirit would answer—sometimes with supernatural peace, sometimes with a word of comfort, sometimes with simply the assurance that the hunger was being heard.

Your hunger is holy, David. It is the truest prayer you pray. The body knows what the mind forgets—that you were made for more than bread. Keep hungering. Keep aching. I will satisfy you, but not yet, not fully—the full satisfaction is coming, at the Wedding Feast, when all things are made new. For now, let the hunger keep you leaning toward home.

The giving had become a participation in the Spirit's mission.

David had begun tithing—something he had always talked about but never practiced consistently—and beyond the tithe, he had begun giving to the homeless ministry, the refugee resettlement program, the church's benevolence fund. The money left his account every month with a slight sting, a relinquishing.

Spirit, this is not my money anyway. It all comes from You. I release it. Use it for Your mission. Make me a channel of Your compassion.

And the Spirit would answer:

Yes. This is the Missio Dei—My mission to restore all things. You are participating in it now. Every dollar you give loosens the grip of Mammon on your heart. Every act of generosity makes you more like Me. Keep giving. Keep loosening. And watch—I will open doors you never expected, create connections you never planned, use your small offerings for My great purposes.

The community had become the Spirit's body.

David had stopped skipping small group. He had told them—not everything, but enough—about his struggles. He had asked for prayer. He had received it.

And to his astonishment, the Spirit had used his vulnerability to open doors. Two other men in the group had approached him privately, confessing similar struggles, asking if they could talk. The secret shame that had isolated David for years became a bridge to others who had been equally isolated.

"This is the Body of Christ," Roger had said. *"The Spirit knits you together. When you suffer, they suffer. When you heal, they heal. You are not alone. You never were."*

On Sunday mornings, David took Communion again.

He approached the Table with hands open, heart exposed, not pretending worthiness but receiving mercy.

"This is My body, broken for you."

And the Spirit spoke:

This is how I come to you—broken bread, poured-out wine. I give Myself to be consumed. Take Me in. Let Me become part of you. Let My body heal your body. Let My blood cleanse your blood. You are not worthy—no one is. But you are welcome. That is what grace means.

David ate the bread and drank the wine, and every time, something was strengthened in him. Not achievement. Not progress he could measure. Something subtler and more essential: he was being knit more tightly to the Vine. The Life was flowing from Christ through the Spirit into him. He could not see it or feel it most of the time. But he knew it was happening.

Part Four: The Transformation

The Shift

Marcus — Two Years After the Mountain Cave

The younger monks had begun coming to him.

This was unexpected and, initially, unwelcome. Marcus did not think of himself as a wise man. He was not Paphnutius, not Teresa, not Juan. He was just a former merchant who had stumbled through the darkness and somehow emerged into a light he still didn't fully understand.

But they came anyway.

They came with questions about the dryness they felt in prayer. They came with confessions of temptations—longings for the world they had left, desires that seemed incompatible with their vows, memories that returned unbidden in the night. They came with doubts about their calling, with anger at God, with the full range of struggles Marcus knew all too well.

And he listened. And he spoke. And he realized, with growing wonder, that the words he spoke were not always his own.

Spirit, he would pray before each conversation, *I have nothing to offer this brother. I am empty. Fill me. Speak through me. Give me Your wisdom, not my own.*

And the Spirit would answer—sometimes with a sudden insight, sometimes with a phrase that seemed to come from nowhere, sometimes with simply the patience to listen without needing to fix.

"What do I do when I feel nothing?" a young monk named Thaddeus asked one evening. He had been in the desert only two years, and his face still had the softness of youth, the hope not yet beaten down by the long obedience.

Marcus smiled. "You do the same thing you would do if you felt everything. You show up. You receive. You trust that the Spirit is present whether you perceive Him or not."

"But how is that possible? How can I trust in a Presence I can't feel?"

Spirit, give me the words.

"Thaddeus, the Spirit is like a mother bird brooding over her eggs. You do not feel the warmth every moment—sometimes you feel only the darkness of the shell. But the warmth is there, working invisibly, bringing life out of what seems dead. The feelings come and go—they are weather, not climate. The Spirit's presence is the climate. He does not change. We are the ones who change, who lose awareness, who fall asleep. The disciplines are not ways of summoning His presence. They are ways of waking up to the presence that was there all along."

Thaddeus's eyes widened. "You make it sound so... simple."

"It is simple. Not easy—but simple. The Spirit has been pursuing you since before you were born. He drew you to this desert. He is hemming you in even now, closing the doors that lead away from Him, opening the one door that leads to life. Your job is not to generate feelings. Your job is to trust the hemming. To keep showing up. To let yourself be loved."

Another monk, Cassius, came with a different struggle. He was older than Marcus, had been in the desert for thirty years, and was wrestling with something he called "the sin of my imagination."

"I do not commit sins with my body," Cassius said. "I have kept my vows. But in my mind, I live a thousand lives—none of them holy. I imagine returning to Rome, to wealth, to women. I imagine being celebrated, being powerful, being free of these walls. And the worst part is, the imaginings feel more real than my prayers."

Marcus was silent for a long moment. This was his struggle too, though he had never spoken of it aloud.

Spirit, what do I say?

And the Spirit answered—not with words, but with a sudden clarity, a way of seeing that Marcus knew was not his own.

"Cassius, I know that war. I was a merchant before I came here. Sometimes I still count the coins in my mind. I still close deals I will never close. I still walk through streets I will never walk again."

"What do you do?"

"I acknowledge it. I do not pretend it isn't happening. And then I ask the Spirit a question: *What is this longing really for?*"

Cassius looked puzzled. "What do you mean?"

"The longing for Rome, for wealth, for women—these are not your deepest longings. They are shadows of something real. The Spirit taught me this: we were made for a home, for riches, for love. But not the home we left. Not the riches that rust. Not the love that fades. We were made for the eternal home, the incorruptible inheritance, the love that will never let us go. When I feel the ache for Alexandria, I bring it to the Spirit. I say, 'Here is my longing. It is misdirected. Redirect it. Teach me to long for what I was really made for.' And slowly—so slowly—the old longings are being transformed into new ones."

Cassius's eyes glistened. "You offer the sin itself to the Spirit?"

"I offer the sinner. Which is what I am. And I ask the Spirit to do what I cannot do: to heal the wound beneath the symptom, to fill the emptiness that drives me toward false comforts. This is not something I achieve. It is something I receive—over and over, day after day, for the rest of my life."

These conversations changed Marcus from the inside out. He realized, as he taught, that he understood things he had not known he understood. The wisdom that flowed through him was not his own—it came from the Spirit, who had been working in him all along, even during the years of darkness.

And the darkness itself, he now saw, had been the Spirit's work.

"I will allure her and bring her into the wilderness," the Spirit had said through Hosea. *"And there I will speak tenderly to her."*

The darkness had been the wilderness. The emptiness had been the stripping away. And in the stripping, in the emptying, the Spirit had been preparing a space for Himself—a space that Marcus's own striving could never have created.

1 TWO SOULS IN A WILDERNESS

"Without the night," Juan had said, *"you would not know the value of the light."*

It was true. The merchants Marcus had known in Alexandria—the successful ones, the ones who had everything—most of them were terrified. Terrified of loss, of failure, of death. They clung to their wealth with white-knuckled desperation because they knew, deep down, that it was all they had.

Marcus had nothing. And because he had nothing, he had room for the Spirit to fill him with everything. The joy that now bubbled up in him during Lauds was not the joy of achievement but the joy of a man who had been lost and was now found. It was resurrection joy. It cost everything, and it was worth everything.

"The Spirit Himself bears witness with our spirit that we are children of God," Paul had written. And Marcus knew it now—not as doctrine, but as experience. The Spirit was within him, bearing witness, whispering *Beloved, Beloved* even when the other voices screamed condemnation.

The sacred rhythms he had once despised now carried him through the day like a river carrying a boat. He did not struggle against the current anymore. He rested in it. And the current was the Spirit.

Morning prayer: the Spirit waking him, calling him, meeting him in the silence.

Noon prayer: the Spirit gathering his scattered thoughts, calling the sheep home, recentering him in love.

Evening prayer: the Spirit receiving the day, the failures and successes alike, the whole messy offering of a human life.

Night prayer: the Spirit speaking in the confession, healing the wounds beneath the sins, whispering *Beloved* into the dark.

The Eucharist: the Spirit making Christ present in bread and wine, feeding Marcus with life not his own.

The fasting: the Spirit transforming hunger into prayer, emptiness into longing, longing into homecoming.

The giving: the Spirit flowing through Marcus like a river through a channel, compassion moving from Source to need.

The psalms and hymns: the Spirit singing in Marcus and through Marcus, weaving his broken voice into the eternal chorus.

The community: the Spirit knitting Marcus to his brothers, creating a Body, making many into one.

All of it was the Spirit's work. All of it was receiving. All of it was life in God, not striving for God.

"This is what You wanted all along," Marcus prayed one night, overwhelmed by the simplicity of it. *"Not my effort. Not my achievement. Just my presence. Just my receiving. Just my 'yes.'"*

And the Spirit answered—not in words, but in a Presence so thick and warm that Marcus wept with joy:

Yes. This is what I wanted. You. Just you. Exactly as you are. Beloved.

Life in God

David — Three Years Into the Journey

Hannah said yes.

They were married in the spring, in the church where David had once felt like a ghost, surrounded by the community that had become family. Roger officiated, his words warm and wise, his voice cracking with emotion as he pronounced them man and wife. Chenè sat in the front row, her eyes bright with tears.

"I've watched David grow," Roger said during the ceremony. "Not into the imaginary perfect version of himself—thank God that David never showed up—but into something more beautiful: a man who knows he is broken and loved, who has learned to receive grace, who has stopped performing and started resting, who has learned to recognize the Spirit's voice and follow it home. That's the David I'm giving you today, Hannah.

He will fail you sometimes. So will you fail him. But both of you know where to go when you fail. Both of you know the Spirit is faithful. He will finish what He has begun."

It was not the wedding David had imagined as a younger man. It was better. It was true.

The struggles had not disappeared. That was the honest reality of the life David now lived. Some mornings, he still wanted to throw his phone across the room—not because of temptation, but because of the sheer gravitational pull of distraction. Some nights, he still felt the old hungers stirring, the old patterns beckoning.

And the voices were still there. They would always be there, he suspected—the accuser and the excuser, each one whispering from the outer rooms of his soul.

I'm not good enough, the accuser would say. *I'll never be good enough. Hannah deserves better. God deserves better. I'm still the same failure I always was.*

Don't be so hard on yourself, the excuser would reply. *You're human. Everyone struggles. Just relax. God's grace covers everything. You don't have to try so hard.*

But David had learned, over three years of practice, to wait for the third voice. The quiet one. The patient one. The Spirit.

David. The voice came in the silence between the others, beneath the others, more patient than either. *You are loved. You are being transformed. You have not arrived, but you are on the way. I am working in you—pruning what needs pruning, healing what needs healing, growing what needs growing. Trust Me. Keep receiving. Keep showing up. I am faithful, even when you are not.*

That voice—the voice of the Spirit, the voice of the Beloved—had become David's anchor. Not his achievement. His anchor.

The morning prayers had become as natural as breathing. Not every day—there were still mornings when the alarm felt like a burden, when the silence felt empty, when the Scripture felt flat. But these mornings were exceptions now, not the rule.

Most days, David came to the morning hour with genuine anticipation, knowing that Someone waited for him there. He would sit in his worn armchair, coffee in hand, and listen.

Good morning, Spirit. I'm here. What do You want to say to me today?

And the Spirit would answer—sometimes with warmth, sometimes with a word, sometimes with silence that was itself a word. David had learned that the silence was not absence. The Spirit was brooding over him even in the quiet, patient and present, working invisibly in the depths.

The fasting had taught him something about hunger.

Every Wednesday, when his stomach growled, David would offer the discomfort:

Spirit, this is how my soul longs for You. This is the emptiness that only You can fill. I'm hungry—not just for bread, but for You. Feed me with Yourself.

And the Spirit would answer:

Yes. Your hunger is prayer. Keep hungering. Keep aching. The full satisfaction is coming—at the Wedding Feast, when all things are made new. For now, let the ache keep you leaning toward home.

The giving had liberated David from anxiety about money.

As he gave more generously, his grip on his remaining resources loosened. And the Spirit would speak:

You are participating in My mission. Every dollar you release flows into the river of My redemption. Keep releasing. Watch what I do with seeds sown in faith.

The community had become David's lifeline.

The small group that had once felt like obligation now felt like family. When David fell—and he still fell, less often but not never—they caught him. They prayed with him. They reminded him of the truth.

And the Spirit would speak through them:

This is My Body. I have knit you together. You are not alone. You never were.

On Sunday mornings, David took Communion with Hannah beside him, both of them broken, both of them beloved.

"This is My body, broken for you."

And the Spirit would speak:

Take and eat. This is how I come to you—broken, poured out, given. Let My life become your life. Let My love fill your emptiness. You are not worthy—no one is. But you are welcome. That is what grace means.

David ate the bread and drank the wine, and every time, something was strengthened in him. The Life was flowing from Christ through the Spirit into him. He could not see it most of the time. But he knew it was happening.

One evening, three years into the journey, David sat with Roger one last time—not because the mentoring was ending, but because something had shifted, and both of them knew it.

"You're different," Roger said, sipping his coffee. "Not perfect—don't get me wrong. But different. Something has changed."

David nodded slowly. "I used to strive. I used to think the disciplines were ladders I could climb to reach God. Now..." He paused, searching for words. "Now I know they're just hands cupped to receive. The Spirit does the work. I just show up."

"And the voices? The accuser and the excuser?"

"Still there. They'll probably always be there. But I know a third voice now. The Spirit. He speaks underneath the noise, and His voice is the truest.

When I listen to Him, the other voices get quieter. Not silent—but quieter."

Roger smiled. "That's it. That's the whole thing. You've learned to listen for the right voice. The Spirit is faithful. He'll keep speaking, keep pursuing, keep hemming you in. And one day—" His eyes glistened. "One day the pursuit will end, and you'll see Him face to face. And you'll realize: He was there the whole time. Every moment. Every struggle. Every fall and every rising. He never left. He never gave up."

David's eyes burned. "Neither did you. Thank you, Roger. For answering the phone that day. For being His hands and voice to me."

"That's what the Body is for. I was just a channel. The Spirit did the work." Roger reached across the table and gripped David's hand. "Keep listening, David. Keep receiving. And when you're ready—pass it on. There are others in the wilderness, waiting for someone to show them the way home."

Epilogue: The Same Spring

"Deep calls to deep at the roar of Your waterfalls; all Your waves and Your breakers have gone over me." — Psalm 42:7

Two men. Separated by seventeen centuries. United by the same Spirit.

Marcus, the former merchant, died in his cave at seventy-three, surrounded by the brothers who had become his family, his lips moving in silent prayer, his face radiant with something beyond expression. His last words, witnesses said, were: *"Spirit... I hear You... take me home..."*

David, the former ghost, lived to old age, his grandchildren gathered around him, his hands still folded each morning in the posture of receiving. He never became the imaginary David, the perfect performer. He became something better: a real man, a broken man, a man who had learned to listen for the Spirit's voice and follow it through the wilderness to home.

1 TWO SOULS IN A WILDERNESS

In some sense known only to God, they had been companions. Fellow travelers in the wilderness. Pilgrims guided by the same Spirit, drinking from the same spring.

The Spirit who had brooded over them like a mother hen over her eggs.

The Spirit who had pursued them like Hosea pursued Gomer, like God pursued wayward Israel.

The Spirit who had hemmed them in with thorns, closing the doors to death, opening the one door to life.

The Spirit who had spoken tenderly in the wilderness, making the Valley of Trouble a door of hope.

The Spirit who had never—not for one moment—given up.

The sacred rhythms that sustained them—prayer morning, noon, and night; meditation and silence and solitude; the weekly hunger; the giving that loosened grip; the hymns and psalms and spiritual songs; the gathering and the Eucharist; the life in community; the participation in God's mission—these were never ladders to climb.

They were cups to fill.

They were hands to open.

They were doors to walk through.

And on the other side, waiting in every room, was the Spirit. Brooding. Wooing. Calling.

Beloved. Come in. Come home. I have been waiting.

"Come to Me, all who labor and are heavy laden, and I will give you rest."

They came. They rested. They received.

And in the receiving, they were transformed into receivers.

That was all. That was everything.

THE END

A Prayer for the Reader

Spirit of the Living God—
We are thirsty.
We have strived until our hands bled, trying to climb to the Father. We have performed until our hearts emptied, trying to earn the Son's love. And all along, You have been brooding over us—patient, persistent, pursuing.
We have listened to the voices that accuse: "I'm a failure. I'm hopeless. I'll never change."
We have listened to the voices that excuse: "I can do this and confess later. Grace covers everything. Why struggle so hard?"
Teach us to hear Your voice—the third voice—the one that speaks beneath the noise and outlasts the storms: "Beloved. You are already loved. Stop striving and receive."
You have been hemming us in. We see it now—the closed doors, the bitter escapes, the wilderness that seemed like punishment but was really pathway. You have been making us hungry for the only Bread that satisfies. You have been wooing us home.
Teach us to trust the hemming.
Teach us to receive.
Teach us that the disciplines are not punishments but prescriptions, not ladders but doors, not the work we do for the Father but the spaces where we let You work in us.
Morning, noon, and night—meet us. In silence and solitude—speak to us. In weekly hunger—feed us with Yourself. In giving—flow through us. In song—sing with us. In community—knit us together. At the Table—nourish us with Christ.
We are not the people we wish we were. We are not the people we imagine we should be. We are only this: Yours. Broken and Yours. Failing and Yours. Pursued and Yours.
Help us believe that this is enough.

Help us rest in the Love that was here all along.
Help us find the throne room.
Spirit, lead us home.
Amen.

Endnotes

1. Psalm 42:1: "As a deer pants for flowing streams, so pants my soul for you, O God" (ESV). This psalm of the Sons of Korah expresses intense spiritual longing during a period of exile or distance from God's presence. The imagery of thirst in a dry land becomes a governing metaphor for the entire narrative.
2. The image of the Spirit "brooding" (*merachefet*) derives from Genesis 1:2, where "the Spirit of God was hovering over the face of the waters" before creation. The Hebrew verb suggests the protective, nurturing movement of a bird over its nest—an image of creative patience that the narrative develops throughout.
3. The metaphor of God as "a mother hen gathering her chicks" comes from Jesus's lament over Jerusalem in Matthew 23:37: "How often would I have gathered your children together as a hen gathers her brood under her wings, and you were not willing!"
4. The Nitrian Desert (Wadi El Natrun) in Egypt was one of the major centers of early Christian monasticism, established in the fourth century. By 387 AD, the date of this chapter, it contained numerous monasteries and hermit cells, including the famous settlements of Nitria, Kellia (the Cells), and Scetis.
5. The canonical hours (Lauds, Vespers, etc.) structured monastic life around fixed times of prayer. Lauds (Morning Prayer) was typically prayed at dawn; Vespers (Evening Prayer) at sunset. This pattern, rooted in Jewish prayer practices (Psalm 119:164: "Seven times a day I praise you"), became the framework for the Divine Office.
6. The term "Abba" (Aramaic/Hebrew for "father") was the standard form of address for a monastic elder or spiritual father in the desert tradition. The feminine equivalent, "Amma," was used for Desert Mothers.
7. Hosea 2:6-7: "Therefore I will hedge up her way with thorns, and I will build a wall against her, so that she cannot find her paths. She shall pursue her lovers but not overtake them, and she shall seek them

but not find them. Then she shall say, 'I will go and return to my first husband, for it was better for me then than now'" (ESV). This passage describes God's strategy of gracious constraint—blocking the paths that lead away from Him so that His wayward people will return.
8. Psalm 63:1: "O God, you are my God; earnestly I seek you; my soul thirsts for you; my flesh faints for you, as in a dry and weary land where there is no water" (ESV). David's psalm from the wilderness of Judah provides the biblical archetype for spiritual longing in barren circumstances.
9. The concept of "cheap grace" was famously articulated by Dietrich Bonhoeffer in *The Cost of Discipleship* (1937): "Cheap grace is the preaching of forgiveness without requiring repentance, baptism without church discipline, Communion without confession... Cheap grace is grace without discipleship, grace without the cross, grace without Jesus Christ, living and incarnate."
10. Jeremiah 31:3: "I have loved you with an everlasting love; therefore I have continued my faithfulness to you" (ESV). This declaration of God's persistent, covenant love becomes a touchstone for understanding the Spirit's pursuit throughout the narrative.
11. Hosea 2:14-15: "Therefore, behold, I will allure her, and bring her into the wilderness, and speak tenderly to her. And there I will give her her vineyards and make the Valley of Achor a door of hope" (ESV). The Valley of Achor ("Valley of Trouble"), site of Achan's judgment in Joshua 7, becomes in Hosea's prophecy a symbol of how God transforms places of failure into doorways of hope.
12. The Eucharist (from Greek *eucharistia*, "thanksgiving") was the central act of Christian worship from the earliest period. Refraining from communion due to a sense of unworthiness, while understandable, was often addressed by the Church Fathers as a form of inverted pride—making one's sin greater than Christ's grace.
13. The "interior castle" metaphor, though here attributed to Teresa, anticipates her famous work *The Interior Castle* (*El Castillo Interior*, 1577), in which she describes the soul as a castle with seven dwelling places, with God enthroned at the center. The fictional encounter in

this narrative imagines Teresa sharing this insight before writing it down.

14. "Where I am weak, there I am strong" paraphrases 2 Corinthians 12:10: "For when I am weak, then I am strong." Paul's paradoxical declaration follows his account of the "thorn in the flesh" and God's response: "My grace is sufficient for you, for my power is made perfect in weakness" (12:9).

15. Teresa of Ávila (1515-1582) and John of the Cross (1542-1591) were Spanish Carmelite mystics and reformers. Their appearance in a fourth-century Egyptian setting is, of course, fictional—a literary device that allows the wisdom of the later Carmelite tradition to be woven into the desert father narrative. Both are Doctors of the Church, recognized for their profound contributions to Christian spirituality.

16. The "dark night of the soul" (*noche oscura del alma*) is John of the Cross's term for a period of spiritual desolation in which God withdraws the felt sense of His presence to purify the soul of attachments and deepen faith. John distinguished between the "dark night of the senses" (purification of sensory attachments) and the "dark night of the spirit" (purification of spiritual attachments).

17. Teresa's description of prayer as "intimate conversation with the One who loves us" paraphrases her famous definition in *The Life of Teresa of Jesus* (Autobiography), Chapter 8: "Mental prayer in my opinion is nothing else than an intimate sharing between friends; it means taking time frequently to be alone with Him who we know loves us."

18. The practice of *lectio divina* ("divine reading"), though systematized later by Guigo II, has roots in the desert tradition. The four movements—reading (*lectio*), meditation (*meditatio*), prayer (*oratio*), and contemplation (*contemplatio*)—represent a progression from active engagement with Scripture to receptive resting in God's presence.

19. Romans 8:26: "Likewise the Spirit helps us in our weakness. For we do not know what to pray for as we ought, but the Spirit himself intercedes for us with groanings too deep for words" (ESV). This

passage grounds the understanding that even inarticulate longing—including physical hunger during fasting—can be a form of Spirit-led prayer.
20. The *Missio Dei* ("Mission of God") concept emphasizes that mission originates in God's own nature and activity. The church does not have a mission so much as God's mission has a church. See David Bosch, *Transforming Mission: Paradigm Shifts in Theology of Mission* (Maryknoll, NY: Orbis, 1991).
21. The Greek term *politeia* (citizenship, commonwealth, way of life) appears in Philippians 3:20: "But our citizenship (*politeuma*) is in heaven." In monastic contexts, the term described the common life of the community—the shared practices, disciplines, and relationships that constituted life together in Christ.
22. The understanding of the Eucharist as "medicine for the sick" rather than "reward for the worthy" echoes Ignatius of Antioch's description of the Eucharist as "the medicine of immortality" (*pharmakon athanasias*) in his *Letter to the Ephesians* 20:2 (c. 107 AD).
23. The Benedictine tradition, founded by Benedict of Nursia (c. 480-547), emphasized stability, community, and the balanced rhythm of prayer and work (*ora et labora*). The fictional "Father Gregory" represents the ongoing influence of Benedictine spirituality in contemporary spiritual direction.
24. The distinction between "earning" and "receiving" forgiveness reflects the Protestant emphasis on justification by grace through faith (Ephesians 2:8-9), while also resonating with the Catholic and Orthodox understanding that grace is not a transaction but a participation in divine life.
25. The concept of the soul as an "interior castle" comes from Teresa of Ávila's *The Interior Castle* (1577). Teresa describes seven "dwelling places" or "mansions" through which the soul progresses toward union with God at the center. The journey inward is simultaneously a journey toward God.
26. John of the Cross (Juan de la Cruz, 1542-1591) wrote extensively about the "dark night" in his poems and commentaries, particularly

The Dark Night of the Soul and *The Ascent of Mount Carmel*. His teaching emphasizes that spiritual desolation, properly understood, is a gift that purifies the soul's attachments and prepares it for deeper union with God.

27. The book of Hosea narrates the prophet's marriage to Gomer, a woman who repeatedly returns to prostitution despite Hosea's faithful love. God commands Hosea to keep pursuing her (Hosea 3:1-3), making the marriage a living parable of God's relentless love for unfaithful Israel.

28. Chenè's approach to spiritual direction integrates psychological insight with contemplative spirituality, reflecting contemporary developments in the field. The name "Chenè" (from French, meaning "oak") suggests rootedness and strength.

29. "O Lord, open my lips, and my mouth shall declare your praise" (Psalm 51:15) is the traditional opening versicle for Morning Prayer in both Eastern and Western liturgical traditions. The prayer acknowledges that even the ability to praise God is a gift that must be received.

30. The "noon pause" or midday prayer (Sext in the Western tradition) was one of the "little hours" of the Divine Office. Its placement at the middle of the workday served as a moment of recollection and return to God's presence amid daily labor.

31. Psalm 4:8: "In peace I will both lie down and sleep; for you alone, O LORD, make me dwell in safety" (ESV). This verse, traditionally associated with Compline (Night Prayer), expresses trust in God's protection through the vulnerability of sleep.

32. The practice of nighttime confession and examination of conscience has roots in both the desert tradition and later developments like the Ignatian *Examen*. The emphasis here on confession as "agreement with reality" rather than earning forgiveness reflects a grace-centered understanding of repentance.

33. The distinction between the wound and the symptom—between the deep emptiness that drives addictive behavior and the behavior itself—reflects insights from both contemplative spirituality and

contemporary psychology. Healing requires addressing root causes, not merely managing surface behaviors.

34. The phrase "the long obedience in the same direction" comes from Friedrich Nietzsche, *Beyond Good and Evil* (1886), §188, but was popularized in Christian circles by Eugene Peterson's book *A Long Obedience in the Same Direction: Discipleship in an Instant Society* (InterVarsity Press, 1980; 2nd ed. 2000).
35. The *Book of Common Prayer*, first published in 1549 under Thomas Cranmer, contains the daily offices (Morning and Evening Prayer), the Psalter arranged for monthly reading, and collects (short prayers) for each day and season. It remains a primary resource for Anglican and Episcopal spirituality.
36. Psalm 51:10-12: "Create in me a clean heart, O God, and renew a right spirit within me. Cast me not away from your presence, and take not your Holy Spirit from me. Restore to me the joy of your salvation, and uphold me with a willing spirit" (ESV). This penitential psalm, traditionally attributed to David after his sin with Bathsheba, has been central to Christian practices of confession and renewal.
37. The concept of the Spirit's conviction versus condemnation is grounded in Romans 8:1: "There is therefore now no condemnation for those who are in Christ Jesus." The Spirit convicts of sin (John 16:8) in order to lead to repentance and restoration, not to crush or destroy.
38. The practice of fasting one day per week has ancient roots. The *Didache* (late first/early second century) instructs Christians to fast on Wednesdays and Fridays, distinguishing their practice from Jewish fasts on Mondays and Thursdays.
39. The Eucharistic formula "This is my body, broken for you" echoes 1 Corinthians 11:24. The words of institution, repeated in every celebration of the Lord's Supper, recall Jesus's self-offering at the Last Supper and make that offering present to the worshiping community.
40. The emergence of Marcus as a spiritual director to younger monks reflects the pattern of the desert tradition, where wisdom was transmitted through personal relationship rather than formal

education. The *Apophthegmata Patrum* (Sayings of the Desert Fathers) preserves this tradition of seeking a "word" from an elder.

41. Romans 8:16: "The Spirit himself bears witness with our spirit that we are children of God" (ESV). This inner testimony of the Spirit, confirming the believer's identity as God's child, is the foundation of Christian assurance.

42. John 15:1-5 presents Christ as the Vine and believers as branches. The image emphasizes that spiritual life flows from Christ into His people; apart from Him, they "can do nothing." The disciplines, in this understanding, are ways of remaining connected to the Vine so that the Life can flow.

43. The wedding ceremony's emphasis on brokenness and belovedness reflects a grace-centered understanding of marriage. The acknowledgment that both partners will fail each other—and that this is not the end but the context for ongoing grace—counters perfectionist expectations that often burden relationships.

44. The "imaginary David" who never appeared represents the false self constructed from religious performance—the idealized version of ourselves that we present to others and even to God. The death of this false self, painful as it is, makes room for the true self to emerge in relationship with God.

45. The three-year timeframe of David's transformation reflects the reality that spiritual formation is slow, gradual work. Quick fixes and instant transformations, while occasionally granted by God, are not the norm. Most growth happens incrementally, through "the long obedience in the same direction."

46. Psalm 42:7: "Deep calls to deep at the roar of your waterfalls; all your waves and your breakers have gone over me" (ESV). This verse, from the same psalm that opened the narrative, suggests that the depths of human longing correspond to the depths of divine love—and that the overwhelming waves of suffering can become the medium of encounter with God.

47. The Wedding Feast (Revelation 19:6-9) represents the eschatological consummation of God's relationship with His people. The hunger

that remains unfulfilled in this life points toward a satisfaction that will come fully only in the age to come.
48. The description of the sacred rhythms as "cups to fill... hands to open... doors to walk through" captures the receptive understanding of spiritual disciplines developed throughout the narrative. The disciplines are not achievements but postures of receiving.
49. The prayer's structure—acknowledging the false voices (accuser and excuser), turning to the Spirit's voice, and asking for transformation—models the practice of discernment developed throughout the narrative. It invites readers to apply the story's insights to their own spiritual journey.
50. The phrase "the throne room" recalls Teresa of Ávila's image of the interior castle, where God dwells at the center. The prayer asks the Spirit to guide the reader through the various rooms of the soul toward that central encounter.

II
THE DISCIPLINE RELIGION

Recovering the Ancient Practices for a Distracted Age

"Grace is opposed to earning, not to effort." — Dallas Willard, *The Spirit of the Disciplines*

The Crisis of the Untrained Soul

There is a particular kind of exhaustion that marks the modern Christian.

This is not the exhaustion of persecution or labor. We enjoy more conveniences than any generation before us. Instead, it's an exhaustion of the scattered soul: attention divided in a thousand directions, leaving nothing for the One who made us.

As Dallas Willard notes, we have embraced "the gospel of sin management" yet remain untrained in the Way of Christ. We believe the right things, attend the right services, and feel guilty about the right sins. Yet something is missing. Transformation remains out of reach. The character of Christ doesn't form in us. The joy of the Lord—our strength—feels distant.

"The disciplines are activities of mind and body purposefully undertaken to bring our personality and total being into effective cooperation with the divine order. They enable us more and more to live in a power that is, strictly speaking, beyond us, deriving from the spiritual realm itself."

— Dallas Willard, *The Spirit of the Disciplines*

The crisis we face is not primarily theological. Our doctrines are, for the most part, sound, though we need to return to careful examination and refocus on the person of Christ. The crisis is formational. We have not been trained. We have not practiced. We have inherited a Christianity of propositions and events rather than a Christianity of embodied, daily, moment-by-moment communion with the Living God.

In a culture of constant distraction—where people check their phones 96 times a day, and attention spans are under eight seconds—the ancient faith disciplines are essential for survival.

They are indispensable.

Part One: The Modern Struggle

1.1 Attention Deficit and the Scattered Soul

Consider the predicament of the contemporary Christian.

She wakes to an alarm and immediate notifications—emails, texts, social updates, news. Before her feet touch the ground or her first prayer, her attention is already colonized. Reflexively, she scrolls through the night's accumulation. By the time she sets the phone down, her mind races with tasks, anxieties, comparisons, outrage.

When she attempts morning devotions—if at all—her mind is scattered. Scripture blurs before her eyes. Her prayers feel empty. She checks the time and her phone, promising herself to do better tomorrow.

This cycle repeats, day after day, year after year.

"We have become, in significant ways, what we behold. And if we behold screens—endless, fractured, competing screens—we become screened people: shallow, distracted, reactive, unable to sustain the kind of attention that intimacy with God requires."

— John Mark Comer, *Practicing the Way*

This is not a failure of willpower, but of formation. The modern Christian has not been trained to resist the pull of distractions or to practice ways to anchor the soul. She is told to "have a quiet time," but not how to find interior quiet. She is told to pray, but not how to reach the place where prayer becomes communion.

Jim Wilder, in his work on relational neuroscience and spiritual formation, identifies what he calls "brain damage"—the literal neurological rewiring that occurs when we live in chronic distraction:

"When we do not practice returning to joy from upset emotions, when we do not develop the capacity for quiet, when we do not train our brains to rest in attachment, we become incapable of the very things spiritual growth requires. The brain shapes the soul, and a fragmented brain produces a fragmented spirituality."

— Jim Wilder

Technology is not neutral. The scroll, the ping, the feed—they are rival liturgies, forming us in inattention, impatience, comparison, and reactivity. Each hour in the feed is an hour shaped away from the stillness, presence, and sustained attention that communion with God needs.

And we wonder why we feel far from Him.

1.2 The Deficiency in Character, Formation, and Work

The consequences of this scattered spirituality, then, are visible everywhere.

We see scattered spirituality in leaders' moral failings, born of a lack of daily practices for integrity. We see it in congregations' emotional immaturity, splintering over minor issues due to a lack of Spirit-grown character. We see it in anxious believers, who lack inner resources when external supports fail.

"The problem with our souls is not that they need to try harder. The problem is that they need to be trained differently."

— Ruth Haley Barton, *Sacred Rhythms*

The Apostle Paul understood something we have forgotten: that the Christian life is a life of training. He compared himself to an athlete in rigorous preparation, to a soldier in disciplined service. "I discipline my body and keep it under control," he wrote, "lest after preaching to others I myself should be disqualified" (1 Corinthians 9:27). The Greek word he used—*hypōpiazō*—literally means "to strike under the eye," to treat oneself with the rigorous discipline of a boxer in training.

We have made grace seem opposed to effort. We emphasize salvation "not by works" so much that we miss the works we are saved *for*—the "good works...prepared beforehand" (Ephesians 2:10). Many are justified but not sanctified, forgiven but not transformed, saved but not trained.

Leonard Ravenhill, that fierce prophet of revival, put it bluntly:

"The self-made Christian claims, 'Christ did it all'—and does not do anything himself. But the Spirit-trained believer says, 'Christ did it all'—and therefore I must discipline myself to receive what He has given. Grace does not excuse us from effort; grace empowers our effort."

— Leonard Ravenhill

The early church knew this. The Desert Fathers and Mothers retreated, not to escape, but to train their souls with God. St. Anthony of Egypt spent decades in solitude confronting his passions. He emerged radiant—not from trying harder, but by surrendering to slow, hidden transformation.

"The work of soul-making is slow work. It cannot be rushed. It cannot be programmed. It requires the cooperation of time, practice, community, and the patient brooding of the Holy Spirit over the chaos of our lives."

— Henri Nouwen

This is the practice we have lost, and this is what we must now recover as we consider how to move forward. Let us take up the ancient disciplines, pursue lives formed by daily practice, seek mentors, and commit ourselves intentionally to the slow journey of spiritual transformation, beginning today.

1.3 The Need for Mentorship and Spiritual Direction

You cannot learn to pray from a book. Here, the need for something deeper becomes clear.

Our information-rich culture struggles with this: knowledge alone does not transform us. Reading about prayer doesn't make us people of prayer. Spiritual formation is not a self-help project we can accomplish with new techniques, an app, or a program.

But the ancient tradition knew better. Spiritual formation happens in relationship—specifically, between a younger soul and a more mature guide who has walked the path before them.

"Spiritual direction is, in reality, nothing more than a way of leading us to see and obey the real Director—the Holy Spirit hidden in the depths of our soul."

— Thomas Merton

In the story of Marcus and David, we saw the transformative power of mentorship. Marcus, drowning in the dark night of his soul, was sent to Teresa and Juan—two saints who had survived the same shipwreck and could guide him to shore. David, trapped in cycles of addiction and shame, was met by Roger and Chenè—wise guides who had walked through their own wildernesses and could show him the path home.

This is not optional. This is essential.

"We are not meant to journey alone. The spiritual life is inherently communal, and the guides we need are not abstract principles but flesh-and-blood persons who embody what they teach. Without elders, we have no wisdom. Without mentors, we wander in circles. Without spiritual directors, we mistake our own preferences for the voice of God."

— St. Gregory the Great, *Pastoral Rule*

In many ways, the Protestant church has abandoned spiritual direction. We have pastors who preach and counselors who diagnose. Yet we have few spiritual mothers or fathers who simply walk with us, listening for the Spirit's voice in our lives, asking the questions we avoid, and holding us accountable to a Person, not a program.

Jim Wilder describes what he calls "the maturity gap"—the absence of mature Christians who can model the kind of relational, emotionally integrated, Spirit-led life that younger believers desperately need to see:

"We learn joy from joyful people. We learn how to suffer well from people who have suffered well. We learn how to hear God's voice from people who hear God's voice. If we do not have elders who can model these capacities, we will not develop them—no matter how many books we read or sermons we hear."

— Jim Wilder

The recovery of Christian formation requires the recovery of Christian mentorship. We need Rogers and Chenès, Teresas and Juans—not celebrities on stages but ordinary saints in our midst who have learned, through long practice, how to receive the grace that transforms.

Part Two: Digesting Spiritual Truths Through Spiritual Disciplines

2.1 The Disciplines as Means of Grace

We must recover a proper understanding of what the spiritual disciplines are—and what they are not.

They are not ladders to climb toward a distant God. Marcus learned this in his twelve years of frustrated striving: you cannot earn your way into the divine presence through spiritual effort, any more than you can earn a sunrise by staying awake all night.

They are not penances to perform for past sins. David learned this in his cycles of addiction and shame: treating confession as a transaction only deepens the bondage, turning grace into a get-out-of-jail-free card rather than the transforming power it was meant to be.

The disciplines are, as Richard Foster taught us, "means of grace"—not the grace itself, but the hands cupped to receive it:

"The Disciplines are God's way of getting us into the ground; they put us where He can work within us and transform us. By themselves the Spiritual Disciplines can do nothing; they can only get us to the place where something can be done. They are God's means of grace."

— Richard Foster, *Celebration of Discipline*

This is a crucial distinction. The disciplines do not produce transformation. God produces transformation. But the disciplines position us to receive the transformation God is always offering. They clear away the obstacles. They create space. They open doors that our striving had kept shut.

Dallas Willard used the analogy of learning to speak a language:

"If I want to speak Spanish fluently, I cannot simply resolve to do so. Willpower alone will not enable me to speak a language I have not learned. But if I practice—if I study vocabulary, listen to native speakers, immerse myself in the culture—I will eventually find myself speaking Spanish without effort. The effort created the capacity; the capacity enables effortless expression. So it is with the Christian life. We practice the disciplines not to earn righteousness, but to develop the capacity to receive and express the righteousness Christ gives."

— Dallas Willard, *The Spirit of the Disciplines*

2.2 Spiritual Digestion: From Information to Transformation

The metaphor of eating runs throughout Scripture. "Taste and see that the Lord is good." "Man does not live by bread alone, but by every word that proceeds from the mouth of God." "I am the bread of life." "Your words were found, and I ate them, and your words became to me a joy and the delight of my heart."

This metaphor reveals something essential: spiritual truth must be *digested*, not merely consumed.

We live in an age of spiritual consumption. We binge on sermons, podcasts, books, and conferences. We intake massive quantities of information about God. And yet we remain malnourished, because consumption without digestion is not nutrition—it is spiritual bulimia.

"The purpose of spiritual reading is not to gather information, not to fill the mind with interesting ideas, but to let the Word sink deeply into the heart where it can do its transforming work. This requires slowness. It requires rumination. It requires what the ancients called 'lectio divina'—

divine reading—which is less like skimming a webpage and more like letting honey slowly dissolve on the tongue."

— Martin Laird, *Into the Silent Land*

The spiritual disciplines are the digestive system of the soul. Prayer is much more than talking to God—it is how we metabolize relationship with Him. Meditation is more than thinking about Scripture—it is the slow absorption of divine truth into the fabric of our being. Fasting is more than abstaining from food—it clarifies our hunger and teaches the body to crave what the soul most needs.

Watchman Nee, in his classic work on spiritual formation, described the goal of discipline as the "release of the spirit"—the breaking of the hard outer shell of self so that the life of Christ within might flow freely:

"The Spirit of God does not work directly upon our thoughts, nor directly upon our emotions, nor directly upon our will. The Spirit works upon our spirit and through our spirit reaches our thoughts, emotions, and will. The outer man must be broken so the spirit may be released. This breaking is the work of the disciplines—not to punish us, but to liberate us."

— Watchman Nee, *The Release of the Spirit*

2.3 Spiritual Direction: Discernment and Action

The disciplines, rightly practiced, develop in us three essential capacities: direction, discernment, and action.

Spiritual Direction is the capacity to know where we are going—to have a clear sense of God's calling on our lives and the path He has set before us. This requires more than individual intuition; it requires the help of wise guides who can see what we cannot, ask the questions we are afraid to ask, and hold up a mirror to our blind spots.

"Spiritual direction is the art of noticing. It is not the director who directs, but the Holy Spirit. The human director simply helps us notice what the Spirit is already doing, pointing to the movements of God we might otherwise miss in the noise of our lives."

— Ruth Haley Barton, *Sacred Rhythms*

Spiritual Discernment is the capacity to distinguish between the voices that compete for our attention—the accuser, the excuser, and the Spirit. In the story of Marcus and David, both men had to learn to recognize the three voices: the one that condemned them as hopeless, the one that excused their sin with cheap grace, and the quiet, patient voice of the Spirit that spoke neither condemnation nor excuse but truth wrapped in love.

"Discretion is the mother of all virtues. Without it, even the other virtues become vices: zeal without discretion becomes fanaticism; humility without discretion becomes self-hatred; generosity without discretion becomes waste. The discerning soul learns to tell the difference between the motions of nature, the suggestions of the enemy, and the drawings of the Holy Spirit."

— St. Gregory the Great, *Pastoral Rule*

Spiritual Action is the capacity to do what we know we should do—to close the gap between knowing and doing, between the faith we profess and the life we live. This is perhaps the hardest capacity to develop because it requires aligning desire, will, and habit. We do not act rightly simply by deciding to act rightly; we act rightly by training ourselves, through repeated practice, until righteous action becomes second nature.

"We are what we repeatedly do. Excellence, then, is not an act, but a habit."

— Aristotle

Part Three: Finding Intimacy in Sacred Rhythms

3.1 The Necessity of Rhythm

Human beings are creatures of rhythm.

Our hearts beat in rhythm. Our lungs expand and contract in rhythm. Our days are structured by the rhythm of waking and sleeping, work and rest, eating and fasting. We are not designed for the flattened, always-on, arrhythmic existence that modern technology promotes. We are designed for rhythm.

The sacred rhythms of Christian practice are not arbitrary impositions on our nature. They are aligned with our nature—and with the nature of the God who created us. When we pray morning, noon, and night, we are not following a legalistic schedule. We are joining a dance that has been going on since creation, when "the morning stars sang together, and all the angels shouted for joy" (Job 38:7).

"The rhythms of prayer are a way of weaving our lives together with the life of God. Just as we eat at regular intervals to nourish the body, so we pray at regular intervals to nourish the soul. The rhythm itself becomes a teacher, forming us into people of attention, people of return, people who are never far from the awareness of God's presence."

— Ruth Haley Barton, *Sacred Rhythms*

Justin Whitmel Earley, in his work on household rhythms, argues that the seemingly small habits of daily life are the actual substance of spiritual formation:

"We are not formed primarily by our beliefs, or by our dramatic spiritual experiences, but by our habits. The things we do every day, often without thinking, are shaping our souls more than the things we do occasionally with great intentionality. If we want to be transformed, we must transform our habits—and this happens not by willpower but by rhythm, by the patient accumulation of small practices repeated until they become second nature."

— Justin Whitmel Earley, *Habits of the Household*

3.2 Sacred Rhythms: Prayer Morning, Noon, and Night

II THE DISCIPLINE RELIGION

The practice of praying at fixed hours is ancient—older than Christianity, rooted in the Jewish tradition of Daniel, who "got down on his knees three times a day and prayed and gave thanks before his God" (Daniel 6:10). The early church inherited this practice and developed it into the Liturgy of the Hours, the Daily Office, the regular punctuation of the day with prayer.

This is not about legalism. It is about rhythm.

Morning Prayer is the consecration of the day. Before the world has intruded, before the emails and texts and notifications have colonized your attention, you give the first fruits of your consciousness to God. You say, in effect, "This day is Yours. I am Yours. Whatever comes, I begin with You."

Teresa taught Marcus: *"Morning prayer is like a lover waking beside their beloved. You do not immediately begin listing requests. You simply rest in the joy of being together."*

Noon Prayer (or a midday pause adapted to your schedule) is the return—the gathering of the scattered attention, the recollection of whose you are in the midst of the world's demands. The day pulls at us. The urgent drowns out the important. The noon pause is the shepherd calling the sheep home.

Juan taught Marcus: *"The noon pause gathers the scattered thoughts like a shepherd gathering strayed sheep. We do not beat ourselves for the straying. We simply call them home."*

Evening Prayer is the release—the surrender of the day into the hands of the One who gave it. What was accomplished is offered. What was left undone is released. What was sinned is confessed. The soul is emptied so that it might be filled again in the night's rest.

"At day's end, we do not simply stop working; we return. We remember whose we are. We offer the day—with all its beauty and all its brokenness—to the God who can redeem both."

— Ruth Haley Barton, *Sacred Rhythms*

3.3 Meditation, Silence, and Solitude in a Noisy Culture

Silence is not the absence of noise. Silence is the presence of God.

This distinction is critical. Many Christians attempt silence and find it unbearable—filled with racing thoughts, anxieties, distractions, the deafening roar of their own internal commentary. They conclude that silence is not for them, that their minds are too active, that perhaps silence is only for contemplative monks with placid temperaments.

But this misunderstands the purpose of silence. We do not enter silence because we are already quiet. We enter silence to *become* quiet—and this is the work of a lifetime.

"When we enter into solitude and silence, we quickly discover that we are not as saintly as we thought. The noise we used to blame on our environment turns out to have been coming from within. In silence, we meet our shadow side—and this is precisely the meeting we have been avoiding. But it is also the meeting that makes transformation possible."

— Henri Nouwen

Martin Laird, in his profound work on contemplative prayer, describes the layers of noise we must pass through:

"There is the noise of the environment, which we can manage. There is the noise of the body, which we can calm through stillness and breath. But then there is the noise of the mind—the endless commentary, the inner chatter, what the Desert Fathers called 'logismoi'—and this is the hardest silence of all. We do not silence the mind by force; we silence it by attention. We give our attention to something deeper than thought: the presence of God in the ground of our being. And as we attend to that Presence, the noise gradually settles, like silt drifting to the bottom of a disturbed pond."

— Martin Laird, *Into the Silent Land*

The practice is simple, though not easy. Sit. Breathe. Let the noise come—do not fight it. But do not follow it either. Gently, patiently, return your attention to the Presence. A word, a breath, a simple interior gaze toward the God who is closer to you than you are to yourself.

Chenè taught David: *"The soul is like an interior castle with many rooms. In the outer rooms, there is much noise and many visitors—including uninvited ones. But as you move inward, toward the center where Christ dwells, the noise fades. You don't get to the center by fighting the noise. You get there by gently, persistently, turning your attention inward, toward the Presence that is already waiting."*

3.4 Weekly Hunger: The Discipline of Fasting

If silence teaches us about the noise of our minds, fasting teaches us about the appetites of our bodies—and both point to the same truth: we are full of hungers that are not being directed toward their proper end.

"Fasting confirms our utter dependence upon God by finding in Him a source of sustenance beyond food. Fasting is not a rejection of the body or of God's good gift of food; it is a redirection of our hunger toward the only One who can ultimately satisfy."

— Richard Foster, *Celebration of Discipline*

Derek Prince, that powerful teacher on fasting, understood it as spiritual warfare:

"Fasting is a practice of deliberate weakness. We choose to be weak in body that we might be strong in spirit. We choose to empty ourselves of physical sustenance that we might be filled with spiritual power. In fasting, we declare to our bodies—and to the enemy—that we do not live by bread alone, but by every word that proceeds from the mouth of God."

— Derek Prince

Teresa taught Marcus: *"Weekly hunger is not God's rejection of pleasure but His invitation to deeper pleasure. We fast from bread that we might feast on the Bread of Life. The emptiness you feel in your stomach is meant to mirror the emptiness in your soul—and both are meant to be filled by the same Source."*

The practice of weekly fasting—whether from food entirely, or from a particular meal, or from a particular kind of consumption (such as screens)—trains the body in dependence and redirects the appetites toward God. It is a declaration, embodied and repeated, that our hunger is holy, that our emptiness is prayer, that we are creatures who were made for more than what the world can offer.

3.5 Giving: Passion for the Kingdom, Compassion for the Needy

If fasting teaches us to release our grip on food, giving teaches us to release our grip on possessions—and both are exercises in the same fundamental spiritual muscle: detachment.

We do not give in order to earn favor with God. We give because giving is the nature of God, and in giving, we participate in His nature. We give because possessions have a way of possessing us, and generosity is the antidote to the anxiety of accumulation. We give because there are needs in the world, and we are called to be channels through which God's provision flows.

"The discipline of simplicity and the practice of generosity are twin sisters. We simplify our lives so that we might have more to give; we give generously so that we might live more simply. Together, they loosen the grip of Mammon on our hearts and free us for the Kingdom."

— Richard Foster, *Celebration of Discipline*

Juan taught Marcus: *"When you give to the poor who wander through your desert, you are not earning favor. You are participating in the Missio Dei—God's mission to restore all things. You become a channel through which His compassion flows."*

The practice of regular, sacrificial giving—tithing as a baseline, generosity as a lifestyle—trains the soul in the economics of the Kingdom, where the one who gives receives, the one who loses finds, the last become first, and the servants become greatest.

3.6 Hymns, Psalms, and Spiritual Songs

We sing because we are made to sing.

The earliest Christian communities were singing communities. Paul instructs the Ephesians to address "one another in psalms and hymns and spiritual songs, singing and making melody to the Lord with your heart" (Ephesians 5:19). The Colossians are told to "let the word of Christ dwell in you richly, teaching and admonishing one another in all wisdom, singing psalms and hymns and spiritual songs, with thankfulness in your hearts to God" (Colossians 3:16).

This is not decorative. This is formational.

"The songs we sing shape the souls we become. When we sing the psalms, we are not merely expressing what we already feel; we are forming ourselves to feel what the psalmists felt—the whole range of human emotion brought into the presence of God. Lament becomes our lament. Praise becomes our praise. The ancient words become our words, and in singing them, we are changed."

— Ruth Haley Barton, *Sacred Rhythms*

Teresa urged Marcus: *"Sing the psalms as if for the first time. Each psalm is a door into a room of the interior castle. The hymns are not performance; they are wings. Let them carry you."*

In an age of passive consumption—where music is piped into our ears through headphones, selected by algorithms, experienced in isolation—the practice of communal singing is countercultural and essential. When we sing together, we participate in something larger than ourselves. Our voices join other voices; our stories join the great story; the Church militant on earth joins the Church triumphant in heaven in the eternal song of the Lamb.

Part Four: Not Forsaking the Gathering

4.1 The Eucharist: The Center of Christian Practice

As Peter stated, "So I will always remind you of these things, even though you know them and are firmly established in the truth you now have. I think it is right to refresh your memory as long as I live in the tent of this body, because I know that I will soon put it aside, as our Lord Jesus Christ has made clear to me. And I will make every effort to see that after my departure you will always be able to remember these things."

There is a table at the heart of Christianity.

It is not a metaphor. It is more than a symbol. It is a table where bread is broken, and wine is poured, where Christ gives Himself to be consumed by His people, where the scattered become one Body by partaking of one Bread.

"The Eucharist is not a reward for the worthy; it is medicine for the sick. Every time we refuse the Bread out of a sense of unworthiness, we are saying that our unworthiness is greater than His grace. This is pride dressed in the robes of humility."

— Teresa of Ávila (paraphrase)

Marcus had to learn this. His sense of unworthiness kept him from the Table. David had to learn it too—his shame drove him away from the very Source of his healing. But the Table is not for the cleaned-up. It is for the broken, the failing, the stumbling, the ones who come with nothing to offer but their hunger.

"In the Eucharist, we do not simply remember what Christ did two thousand years ago; we participate in it. The past becomes present. The sacrifice of Calvary becomes food for our journey. We take and eat, and in eating, we are taken into the life of God."

— Henri Nouwen

The practice of regular Eucharistic participation—weekly at minimum, daily if possible—is not optional for the Christian who would be formed into Christlikeness. The Table is where we receive what we cannot produce, where we are fed with life not our own, where the Spirit makes Christ present in bread and wine, and makes us present to one another as His Body.

4.2 Practicing Together: Small Communities and Mutual Stirring

You cannot be a Christian alone.

This is not a recommendation. It is a statement of fact. The Christian life is, by definition, a life lived in community—in the Body of Christ, where each member needs the others, where the weak support the strong and the strong protect the weak, where "if one member suffers, all suffer together; if one member is honored, all rejoice together" (1 Corinthians 12:26).

"The writer of Hebrews understood something we have forgotten: we need one another to stay faithful. 'Let us consider how to stir up one another to love and good works, not neglecting to meet together, as is the habit of some, but encouraging one another, and all the more as you see the Day drawing near.' We are not stirred up by sermons alone, or by books alone, or by private devotions alone. We are stirred up by one another—by the presence of brothers and sisters who know our struggles and walk beside us."

— Hebrews 10:24–25

The practice of small community—whether in the form of a small group, discipleship triad, covenant group, or house church—is essential to Christian formation. In small community, we are known. Our masks slip. Our secrets are shared. Our struggles are held. We receive what the sermon cannot give: the embodied presence of Christ in the flesh-and-blood people around us.

"We do not merely learn about community in the New Testament; we see it practiced. The early church met daily in homes, broke bread together, shared their possessions, and bore one another's burdens. They were not a collection of individual Christians who happened to attend the same services; they were a family, a body, a temple being built together into a dwelling place for God."
— Jim Wilder

4.3 Politeia and Missio Dei: The Common Life and the Divine Mission

The New Testament word *politeia* refers to citizenship—the common life shared by citizens of a city. Paul uses the related word *politeuma* when he writes, "Our citizenship is in heaven, and from it we await a Savior, the Lord Jesus Christ" (Philippians 3:20). Christians are citizens of another Kingdom, members of another polity, participants in another ordering of life.

This citizenship has practical implications. We do not merely believe different things; we live differently. We order our homes, our finances, our time, our relationships according to the laws of a Kingdom that has already come and is still coming. We are, in Stanley Hauerwas's phrase, "resident aliens"—present in the world but not conformed to it, participating in society while maintaining our distinctive way of life.

And this common life is oriented toward mission.

The *Missio Dei*—the Mission of God—is the great movement of redemption that flows from the Father, through the Son, in the power of the Spirit, for the healing of the nations. We do not invent this mission; we join it. We do not create programs to save the world; we participate in the program God has already initiated.

"The church does not have a mission; the church is the mission. We are sent, as Christ was sent—not to build religious institutions, but to bear witness to the Kingdom, to be salt and light, to seek justice and love mercy and walk humbly with our God."

— Henri Nouwen

The disciplines, rightly practiced, go beyond private exercises in personal piety. They equip us for mission. The prayer-formed life becomes a life of power for service. The fasting-trained soul becomes sensitive to others' needs. The community-shaped heart becomes a conduit for the love of God to flow into the world.

Juan told Marcus, *"You cannot reach heaven alone. The politeia—the common life, the citizenship in God's Kingdom—is not optional. It is the very shape of salvation."*

Part Five: The Spirit's Work and Our Cooperation

5.1 The Holy Spirit as Guide and Power

Everything we have discussed—the disciplines, the rhythms, the practices—is empty without the Holy Spirit.

The Spirit is the One who broods over our chaos, as He brooded over the waters at creation. The Spirit is the One who convicts without condemning, who woos without coercing, who pursues us through all our wandering with a love that will not let go. The Spirit is the One who hems us in, closing the doors that lead to death, opening the one door that leads to life.

"The Holy Spirit is not an optional extra for advanced Christians. He is the sine qua non—the 'without which nothing'—of the Christian life. Without Him, the disciplines are dead works. With Him, they become encounters with the living God."

— Watchman Nee, *The Release of the Spirit*

In the story of Marcus and David, the Spirit was the protagonist—not the human characters, not even the mentors who guided them. The Spirit was the One who arranged circumstances, closed doors, created divine dissatisfaction with lesser loves, spoke in the silence between the accuser and the excuser, and gently, persistently drew both men home.

Our cooperation with the Spirit is simple, though not easy: we show up. We practice. We keep returning. We keep listening for the third voice—not the one that condemns us as hopeless, not the one that excuses us with cheap grace, but the one that says, *"Beloved. Return. I have been waiting."*

5.2 The Hemming of Love

The prophet Hosea gives us one of the most poignant pictures of God's relationship with wayward humanity. God compares Himself to a husband pursuing an unfaithful wife—pursuing not with anger, but with grief-stricken love; not to punish, but to heal.

"Therefore, behold, I will hedge up her way with thorns, and I will build a wall against her, so that she cannot find her paths. She shall pursue her lovers but not overtake them, and she shall seek them but shall not find them. Then she shall say, 'I will go and return to my first husband, for it was better with me then than now.'"

— Hosea 2:6–7

This is the hemming of love. God closes the doors that lead to death—not to imprison us, but to save us. He makes the false comforts bitter in our mouths—not to deprive us, but to awaken us to the only comfort that satisfies. He leads us into the wilderness—not to abandon us, but to speak tenderly to us there.

"Therefore, behold, I will allure her, and bring her into the wilderness, and speak tenderly to her. And there I will give her her vineyards and make the Valley of Achor a door of hope."

— Hosea 2:14–15

The Valley of Achor—the Valley of Trouble—becomes a door of hope. The wilderness—the place of desolation—becomes the place of encounter. The dark night—the experience of God's absence—becomes the pathway to a presence beyond anything we could have imagined.

This is the paradox of the spiritual life: we must be emptied to be filled, stripped to be clothed, broken to be made whole. And the Spirit is the One who does the emptying, the stripping, the breaking—not as an enemy, but as the most faithful Friend, the Lover who will stop at nothing to bring us home.

The Spirit's Power in the Early Church

"The experience of the Spirit was the hallmark of the earliest Christianity—not merely doctrine about the Spirit, but living, dynamic experience of the Spirit's presence and power."
— James D. G. Dunn, *Jesus and the Spirit*

5.3 The Charismatic Foundation of Early Christian Discipline

The disciplines of the early church were not techniques for self-improvement. They were not Stoic exercises adapted for religious purposes. They were, from the beginning, rooted in the experience of the Holy Spirit—the same Spirit who had anointed Jesus, who had fallen on the disciples at Pentecost, who continued to work with power among the communities Paul planted.

James Dunn, in his magisterial study *Jesus and the Spirit*, demonstrates that the earliest Christians lived in constant awareness of the Spirit's presence. Their prayers were Spirit-empowered; their gatherings were Spirit-animated; their ethical transformation was Spirit-produced. The disciplines were not ways of manufacturing spiritual experience but ways of positioning themselves to receive what the Spirit was already eager to give.

"The Spirit for Paul was not a theological abstraction, nor merely a future hope, but a present reality of transforming power. The Christian life was life 'in the Spirit,' 'by the Spirit,' 'through the Spirit.' The Spirit was the element in which believers lived, the power by which they were transformed, the guide who led them into truth."

— James D. G. Dunn, *Jesus and the Spirit*

This has profound implications for our understanding of spiritual discipline. The disciplines are not human efforts to ascend to God; they are human openings to receive the Spirit who descends from God. They are not works of the flesh but exercises in receptivity to the Spirit.

5.4 Jesus as the Model of Spirit-Empowered Discipline

Dunn convincingly argues that Jesus Himself was the prototype of a Spirit-filled life. His baptism marked the descent of the Spirit upon Him; His ministry was conducted "in the power of the Spirit" (Luke 4:14); His miracles were Spirit-empowered; His prayer life was Spirit-animated.

"The Spirit was the source and power of Jesus' ministry. It was the Spirit who drove Him into the wilderness; the Spirit who empowered His exorcisms; the Spirit who anointed Him to preach good news to the poor. Jesus lived and moved and had His being in the Spirit."

— James D. G. Dunn, *Jesus and the Spirit*

When Jesus taught His disciples to pray, He was teaching them to enter into the same Spirit-filled relationship with the Father that He Himself enjoyed. When He fasted forty days in the wilderness, He was demonstrating Spirit-empowered resistance to temptation. When He withdrew to lonely places to pray, He was modeling the rhythm of engagement and retreat that the Spirit requires.

"Jesus' whole life was a life of prayer—not in the sense of formal religious observance, but in the sense of constant, intimate, Spirit-animated communion with the Father. 'Abba' was not a theological term for Jesus; it was a term of intimate relationship. And this intimacy was made possible by the Spirit."

— James D. G. Dunn, *Jesus and the Spirit*

5.5 The Pentecost Community: Discipline Aflame

The community that emerged after Pentecost was characterized by both spiritual power and practical discipline. Luke's description in Acts 2 is worth careful attention:

"They devoted themselves to the apostles' teaching and the fellowship, to the breaking of bread and the prayers. And awe came upon every soul, and many wonders and signs were being done through the apostles. And all who believed were together and had all things in common."

— Acts 2:42–44

Notice the structure: teaching, fellowship, Eucharist, prayer—the same disciplines we have been discussing. But these disciplines were not empty rituals; they were the channels through which the Spirit's power flowed. The "awe" and "wonders and signs" were not separate from the daily practices; they were the fruit of them.

Dunn observes:

"The earliest Christian communities did not choose between charismatic experience and ordered practice. They had both. The Spirit's power was manifest in ecstatic utterance and prophetic insight, but also in the patient work of teaching, the faithful observance of the common meal, and the regular rhythm of prayer. The disciplines were not alternatives to the Spirit's power; they were expressions of it."

— James D. G. Dunn, *Jesus and the Spirit*

5.6 Paul's Spirit-Empowered Formation

Paul, the great apostle to the Gentiles, exemplified the union of spiritual power and practical discipline. He could speak in tongues more than all the Corinthians (1 Corinthians 14:18); he had been caught up to the third heaven and heard inexpressible things (2 Corinthians 12:2–4). Yet he also disciplined his body (1 Corinthians 9:27), fasted regularly (2 Corinthians 11:27), prayed without ceasing (1 Thessalonians 5:17), and taught the churches a structured approach to community life.

"Paul's ethics were not merely ethics of obligation but ethics of transformation. The imperative was always rooted in the indicative: 'Become what you are in Christ.' And this becoming was the work of the Spirit, gradually transforming believers from glory to glory."

— James D. G. Dunn, *Jesus and the Spirit*

For Paul, the disciplines were not ways of earning the Spirit's gifts but ways of expressing the Spirit's fruit. The same Spirit who gave prophecy and tongues also produced love, joy, peace, patience, kindness, goodness, faithfulness, gentleness, and self-control (Galatians 5:22–23). And this fruit required cultivation; they did not appear automatically but grew through the patient practice of Spirit-empowered discipline.

"The fruit of the Spirit is not instant or automatic. It grows, as all fruit grows, through the slow work of seasons, through root systems that go deep, through regular nourishment. The disciplines are the cultivation of the soil in which the Spirit's fruit can grow."

— James D. G. Dunn, *Jesus and the Spirit*

5.7 The Fruit Produced: Transformation of Character

What did this combination of spiritual power and practical discipline produce? The historical evidence is striking.

It produced communities that cared for widows and orphans in an empire that largely ignored them. The early Christians established networks of mutual aid that extended across provincial boundaries. Tertullian could write: "See how they love one another! See how they are ready to die for each other!" This love was not mere sentiment; it was practical action, funded by regular giving, organized by deacons, sustained by communities that gathered weekly to receive the Eucharist and remember who they were.

It produced individuals of remarkable character. The martyrs faced death not with grim determination but with joy—singing hymns, forgiving their persecutors, testifying to the presence of Christ even in the flames. Such character is not produced by a moment of decision; it is formed through years of practice, years of prayer and fasting and communion and service.

"The character of the martyrs was the fruit of the disciplines. No one becomes ready for martyrdom overnight. The courage they displayed was the accumulated result of countless small choices: to pray when they did not feel like praying, to fast when they would rather feast, to serve when they would rather be served, to forgive when they would rather resent. The disciplines formed them into the kind of people who could face the arena without flinching."

— Rodney Stark, *The Rise of Christianity*

It produced communities that astonished the pagan world with their resilience, their generosity, and their moral transformation. When plagues struck Roman cities and the healthy fled, Christians stayed to nurse the sick—often dying themselves in the process. When emperors demanded worship, Christians refused—not with violence but with quiet steadfastness. When the culture offered endless entertainment and distraction, Christians gathered for prayer, teaching, and the breaking of bread.

5.8 The Witness of the Didache

The *Didache* (c. 50–120 AD), one of our earliest post-apostolic documents, provides a window into the practical discipline of the first-century church. It gives detailed instructions for fasting, prayer, baptism, and the Eucharist:

"Do not fast with the hypocrites, for they fast on Monday and Thursday. Rather, fast on Wednesday and Friday. And do not pray as the hypocrites do, but pray as the Lord commanded in His Gospel: 'Our Father in heaven, hallowed be Your name...' Pray this way three times a day."

— *Didache* 8:1–3

Three times daily prayer. Twice-weekly fasting. Regular Eucharist. Weekly gathering. This was not legalism; this was the rhythm of life for a community living in the power of the Spirit. The *Didache* also includes tests for distinguishing true prophets from false ones—evidence that charismatic gifts and ordered practice existed side by side from the very beginning.

5.9 The Integration We Have Lost

What the early church possessed—and what we have largely lost—was the integration of spiritual power and spiritual discipline. We tend to set these in opposition, as if enthusiasm and order, charisma and structure, the Spirit's freedom and human practice were mutually exclusive.

But Dunn's work demonstrates that this opposition is foreign to the New Testament and to the earliest church. The Spirit is not opposed to discipline; the Spirit empowers discipline. The disciplines are not opposed to the Spirit; they are openings for the Spirit's work.

"The earliest Christians knew nothing of the later dichotomy between institutional and charismatic, between structure and Spirit. For them, the Spirit worked through structure as well as against it. The regular rhythms of prayer and Eucharist were as much expressions of the Spirit's life as the ecstatic utterance of prophecy. The Spirit who gave gifts also produced fruit—and both required cultivation."

— James D. G. Dunn, *Jesus and the Spirit*

This is the recovery we need. Not spirituality without structure, which degenerates into emotionalism. Not structure without spirituality, which degenerates into dead religion. But Spirit-empowered discipline: the ordered practices of the faith, animated by the living presence of the One who still moves over the waters of chaos, still broods over the darkness of our souls, still brings forth life where there was only death.

5.10 The Fruit We Are Promised

The promise stands: if we position ourselves to receive, we will receive. If we practice the disciplines as means of grace—not ladders to climb but hands cupped to catch the rain—the Spirit will transform us. The character of Christ will be formed in us. The fruit will grow.

"For those who live according to the flesh set their minds on the things of the flesh, but those who live according to the Spirit set their minds on the things of the Spirit. For to set the mind on the flesh is death, but to set the mind on the Spirit is life and peace."

— Romans 8:5–6

The early church walked this path before us. They faced distractions as demanding as ours, cultures as hostile, temptations as relentless. And they overcame—not by superior willpower, but by the power of the Spirit working through disciplines practiced in community, sustained by the Eucharist, oriented toward mission.

They are our cloud of witnesses. They testify that the way is real, the practices work, the Spirit is faithful. If we take up the ancient path, we will find what they found: not an easier life, but a deeper life; not escape from the struggle, but power within it; not the absence of darkness, but a light that shines in the darkness and the darkness has not overcome it.

"Therefore, since we are surrounded by so great a cloud of witnesses, let us also lay aside every weight, and sin which clings so closely, and let us run

with endurance the race that is set before us, looking to Jesus, the founder and perfecter of our faith."
— Hebrews 12:1–2

Part Six: The Witness of the Fathers

Learning Discipline in the Fires of Persecution and the Demands of Empire

"Stand firm, like an anvil under the hammer. It is the mark of a great athlete to be bruised and yet win the victory."
— Ignatius of Antioch, *Letter to Polycarp*

6.1 The Urgency of the Early Church

We often imagine the early Christians as living in a simpler time—a pre-industrial age without the distractions of technology, without the frenetic pace of modern life. We assume they had leisure for prayer that we do not possess, margins for meditation that our schedules cannot accommodate.

This is a fantasy.

The early Christians lived in one of the busiest, most demanding, most overstimulated cultures in human history: the Roman Empire. They were slaves, merchants, soldiers, artisans, and laborers. They worked from dawn until dusk. They navigated the complex social obligations of Greco-Roman society—the patron-client relationships, the guild memberships, the civic religious ceremonies from which abstention could mean economic ruin or death. They lived in crowded urban centers like Rome, Antioch, Alexandria, and Ephesus, where the noise never stopped, and privacy was a luxury few could afford.

And yet they prayed. They fasted. They gathered. They studied Scripture. They practiced the disciplines that formed them into the kind of people who could face the arena singing hymns.

How?

The answer lies not in their circumstances—which were as demanding as ours—but in their understanding of what was at stake. They knew that without the disciplines, they would be formed by the empire instead of by the Kingdom. They knew that the soul, left untrained, defaults to the patterns of the surrounding culture. They knew that spiritual formation is not a luxury for the leisured but a necessity for the faithful.

"Let no one's place deceive him; let no one's rank deceive him; let no one's wealth deceive him. If we do not strip ourselves of vanity and put on humility, we cannot be disciples. For we must become learners before we become teachers."

— Clement of Rome, *First Letter to the Corinthians*

6.2 Ignatius of Antioch: Training for Martyrdom

Ignatius, the third bishop of Antioch, wrote his seven letters while being transported under armed guard to Rome, where he would be thrown to wild beasts in the Colosseum. He was an old man, tired and in chains, yet his letters burn with spiritual vitality. How was such a man formed?

The answer is decades of disciplined practice.

Ignatius understood that the moment of martyrdom was not the time to begin developing courage, patience, and trust in God. These capacities had to be cultivated long before the crisis came. The disciplines were not preparation for an easy life; they were training for the hardest moments a human being could face.

"Now I am beginning to be a disciple. May nothing visible or invisible prevent me from attaining to Jesus Christ. Fire and cross and battles with wild beasts, mutilation, mangling, wrenching of bones, crushing of the whole body, cruel tortures inflicted by the devil—let them come upon me, only let me attain to Jesus Christ."

— Ignatius of Antioch, *Letter to the Romans*

Such words are not produced by enthusiasm alone. They are produced by formation—by years of prayer that trained the heart to desire Christ above life itself, by fasting that taught the body its proper subordination to the spirit, by communal worship that wove the individual into the Body so tightly that death itself could not separate him from his Lord.

Ignatius's practical counsel to the churches reflects this understanding. To Polycarp, the young bishop of Smyrna, he writes with the specificity of a trainer preparing an athlete:

"Let not those who seem to be trustworthy yet teach strange doctrines disturb you. Stand firm, like an anvil under the hammer. It is the mark of a great athlete to be bruised and yet win the victory. For God's sake, we must endure all things, that God also may endure us. Be more diligent than you are. Understand the times. Look for Him who is above all time, the Eternal, the Invisible, who for our sake became visible."

— Ignatius, *Letter to Polycarp*

The language of athletics pervades early Christian writing. Paul spoke of running the race, fighting the fight, and training the body. The Church Fathers inherited this metaphor and expanded it. They understood that spiritual formation, like athletic training, requires daily practice, progressive challenge, competent coaching, and the willingness to endure discomfort for a greater goal.

"Let your prayers be said with regularity. Ask for larger gifts than before. Be watchful, with a spirit that never sleeps. Speak to each one as God enables you. Bear the infirmities of all, as a perfect athlete. Where the labor is great, the gain is great."

— Ignatius, *Letter to Polycarp*

6.3 Polycarp of Smyrna: Eighty-Six Years of Faithfulness

Polycarp, the recipient of Ignatius's letter, would himself face martyrdom at the age of eighty-six. When the proconsul urged him to curse Christ and save his life, Polycarp replied with words that have echoed through the centuries:

"Eighty-six years I have served Him, and He has done me no wrong. How can I blaspheme my King who saved me?"

— *The Martyrdom of Polycarp*

Eighty-six years. Not eighty-six days, not eighty-six weeks. Eighty-six years of daily prayer, weekly Eucharist, regular fasting, communal worship, Scripture meditation, and service to the poor. Eighty-six years of the sacred rhythms that form a soul into the kind of bedrock that cannot be shaken even when flames rise around it.

The *Martyrdom of Polycarp*, one of the earliest accounts of a martyrdom we possess, describes his death with remarkable detail. When the flames refused to consume him—forming, witnesses said, like a sail around his body—he was dispatched with a dagger. The account notes that he had spent the days before his arrest in prayer, "as was his custom," and that even in captivity, he prayed for "all who had ever come in contact with him, small and great, distinguished and undistinguished, and for the whole catholic Church throughout the world."

This was not heroism summoned in a moment. This was character formed across a lifetime.

"We worship Christ because He is the Son of God; but we love the martyrs as disciples and imitators of the Lord, and rightly so, because of their unsurpassable devotion to their own King and Teacher. May we also become their companions and fellow disciples."

— *The Martyrdom of Polycarp*

6.4 Clement of Alexandria: Disciplines for the Distracted City

Clement of Alexandria (c. 150–215) ministered in one of the ancient world's most cosmopolitan cities—a center of commerce, philosophy, religion, and cultural ferment that rivaled anything in our modern world. His congregants were businesspeople, scholars, government officials, and slaves. They did not have the luxury of monastic retreat. They had to practice their faith amid a noisy, demanding, pluralistic urban environment.

Clement's response was not to lower the bar but to show how the disciplines could be woven into ordinary life:

"Let us practice prayer morning, noon, and night. Let the man who works lift up his heart to God with his hands. Let the woman at her loom pause to whisper a petition. Let the merchant in the marketplace turn his thoughts heavenward between transactions. For the gnostic [Clement's term for the mature Christian] makes his whole life a prayer, conversing with God while working, eating, walking, and even sleeping."

— Clement of Alexandria, *Stromata*

This is not spiritualized escapism. This is the integration of discipline into the texture of daily existence. Clement understood that most Christians would never become monks or hermits, yet they still needed to be formed. The disciplines, adapted to their circumstances, were the means.

"Prayer is keeping company with God. The soul that is trained by prayer does not need to be told when to pray; it prays without ceasing, breathing God as naturally as the body breathes air."

— Clement of Alexandria, *Stromata*

Clement also emphasized the formational power of fasting in the midst of a culture of excess:

"The soul cannot become light and ready for the ascent to God while it is weighed down with heavy foods and the lethargy of overindulgence. Fasting is training for the soul, teaching it to be satisfied with little, to govern the body rather than be governed by it, to keep the appetites in their proper place—which is second place, after the love of God."

— Clement of Alexandria, *The Instructor*

6.5 Origen: The Discipline of the Mind

Origen (c. 185–254), perhaps the most brilliant mind of the early church, understood that intellectual work could itself be a spiritual discipline when rightly ordered. He rose before dawn to pray and study Scripture, memorizing vast portions of the Bible. He fasted rigorously, slept on the bare ground, and lived in poverty—not because he despised the body, but because he wanted nothing to distract him from the single-minded pursuit of God.

"If you seek patiently, you will find. If you ask earnestly, it will be opened to you. But do not imagine that you can understand the depths of Scripture after a single reading, or a casual glance. The Word of God is like a well: you must dig deep before you find water, and the deeper you dig, the sweeter the water becomes."

— Origen, *On First Principles*

Origen's method of Scripture meditation—reading, prayer, wrestling, re-reading, praying again—became foundational for the later tradition of lectio divina. He modeled how intellectual rigor and contemplative depth could be held together, each enriching the other.

"We must approach the sacred texts as those who hunger and thirst for righteousness. We must come not to master them but to be mastered by them, not to extract information but to be transformed by encounter."

— Origen, *Homilies on Genesis*

6.6 Cyprian of Carthage: Discipline in the Face of Persecution

Cyprian (c. 200–258), bishop of Carthage during the Decian persecution, watched his congregation face the choice between apostasy and death. Some stood firm; many fell. After the persecution lifted,

Cyprian wrestled with how to restore the fallen—and how to prevent future falls.

His answer was deeper formation through more rigorous discipline:

"Let those who have stood pray more fervently; let those who have fallen pray with more tears. Let fasting become more serious, confession more thorough, the Eucharist more precious. For we have learned that the enemy does not rest, and we must not rest either. The day of testing will come again, and we must be ready."

— Cyprian of Carthage, *On the Lapsed*

Cyprian's practical instructions for the training of catechumens (those preparing for baptism) are remarkably detailed: they included a three-year period of instruction, regular fasting, almsgiving to the poor, renunciation of morally compromised professions, and intensive prayer, culminating in an all-night vigil before baptism. The early church took formation seriously because they had seen what happened when formation was neglected.

"We are soldiers of Christ, enlisted in His service. A soldier who does not train will not be able to fight. A soldier who does not practice discipline in peacetime will fail in battle. Let us train now, while we have time, so that when the day of testing comes, we will not be found wanting."

— Cyprian, *Letters*

6.7 The Desert Fathers and Mothers: Laboratories of the Soul

In the third and fourth centuries, thousands of Christians fled to the deserts of Egypt, Syria, and Palestine—not to escape persecution (which was diminishing) but to engage in intensive spiritual training. They understood that the end of persecution was not the end of spiritual danger; the comfort and respectability that came with Constantine's legalization of Christianity brought new temptations that required new disciplines.

Anthony of Egypt (c. 251–356), the father of monasticism, spent decades in solitary combat with his own passions, his own demons, his own disordered loves. When he emerged, visitors marveled at his radiance, his joy, his profound peace. Athanasius, his biographer, records:

"Those who had known him before his withdrawal were amazed when they saw him again. His body had maintained its former condition, neither fat from lack of exercise nor lean from fasting and fighting with demons. He was altogether balanced, as one governed by reason and steadfast in that which was natural."

— Athanasius, *Life of Anthony*

The Desert Fathers and Mothers developed sophisticated wisdom about the interior life—how to recognize the movements of the soul, distinguish between different kinds of thoughts, and resist temptation while cultivating virtue. Their sayings (*Apophthegmata Patrum*) became a treasury of practical spiritual guidance:

"Abba Moses asked Abba Silvanus, 'Can a man lay a new foundation every day?' The old man replied, 'If he works hard, he can lay a new foundation every moment.'"

— *Sayings of the Desert Fathers*

"Abba Poemen said, 'To throw yourself before God, not to measure your progress, to leave behind all self-righteousness—these are the instruments of the soul's work.'"

— *Sayings of the Desert Fathers*

"Amma Syncletica said, 'In the beginning, there is struggle and much effort, but afterward, unspeakable joy. It is just like lighting a fire. First, you are troubled by the smoke and your eyes water, but afterward, you get the fire you want. So we must kindle the divine fire in ourselves with tears and effort.'"

— *Sayings of the Desert Mothers*

6.8 Evagrius Ponticus: The Discernment of Thoughts

Evagrius (345–399), a brilliant theologian who became a desert monk, developed a comprehensive analysis of the "eight thoughts" (*logismoi*) that attack the soul—the ancestors of what would later become the "seven deadly sins." His work was foundational for all later Christian psychology and spiritual direction.

"The first struggle is against gluttony; the second, against fornication; the third, against avarice; the fourth, against sadness; the fifth, against anger; the sixth, against acedia [spiritual listlessness]; the seventh, against vainglory; the eighth, against pride. Whether or not all these thoughts trouble the soul is not within our power; but whether they linger within us or stir up passions is within our power."

— Evagrius Ponticus, *Praktikos*

Evagrius understood that the goal of discipline was not merely the suppression of bad behavior but the cultivation of interior freedom—the ability to perceive thoughts clearly, to choose which to follow and which to release, to gradually become transparent to God.

"Prayer is the putting away of thoughts. When you pray, do not imagine the Divinity. Have no image in your mind. Let your intellect be simple and formless, and you will pray with truth."

— Evagrius Ponticus, *On Prayer*

6.9 John Cassian: Bringing the Desert to the West

John Cassian (c. 360–435) lived for years among the Egyptian monks before traveling to the West, where he founded monasteries in Gaul (modern France) and wrote his *Conferences* and *Institutes*—works that would profoundly shape Western monasticism, including the Rule of Benedict.

Cassian's genius was translation: he took the wisdom of the desert and made it accessible to Christians living in community, in the midst of ordinary life. His practical instructions on prayer, fasting, and the common life became the standard for Western Christian formation for a millennium:

"The aim of our profession is the Kingdom of God. But our immediate aim is purity of heart, without which it is impossible for anyone to reach that goal. We must therefore fix our gaze constantly on this aim, and if our thought should wander somewhat from it, we must restore it to its proper position, like a carpenter who smooths rough wood with a ruler."

— John Cassian, *Conferences*

"We must not measure our fasts by the quantity of food we abstain from, but by the intensity of our desire for God. A fast without prayer is useless; prayer without fasting is weak. Let the two be joined, and they will raise the soul to heaven."

— John Cassian, *Institutes*

6.10 John Chrysostom: Disciplines for the Ordinary Christian

Our dear St. John Chrysostom (c. 349–407),
of the Eastern church, was bishop of Constantinople—the imperial capital, a city of overwhelming wealth, distraction, and temptation. His congregation included emperors and slaves, aristocrats and artisans. He knew that most of them would never become monks. Yet he insisted that the disciplines were not optional extras for the spiritually elite but necessities for every Christian:

"Do you say that you cannot fast because of your work, your health, your responsibilities? Then fast from anger, from envy, from harsh speech, from judgment of your neighbor. This fast anyone can keep, and it is more pleasing to God than the abstinence of monks who fast from food but feast on gossip and contempt."

— John Chrysostom, *Homilies on the Statues*

"Let no one say, 'I have no time for prayer.' The merchant in his shop, the soldier in the field, the slave in the kitchen—all can lift their hearts to

God. Prayer does not require a special place or special hours. It requires only a heart that remembers God."

— John Chrysostom, *Homilies on Hannah*

Chrysostom was particularly insistent on the integration of prayer and action, contemplation and compassion:

"You honor the Body of Christ at the altar; do not despise it when you see it clothed in rags in the street. You cannot truly receive the Eucharist while ignoring the poor, for they are the Body of Christ as surely as the bread and wine. The liturgy continues after the dismissal; it continues in alms, in service, in works of mercy."

— John Chrysostom, *Homilies on Matthew*

6.11 Augustine of Hippo: The Restless Heart and Its Training

Augustine (354–430), perhaps the most influential theologian in the Western tradition, knew from personal experience the power of disordered desires. His *Confessions* chart his journey from enslavement to lust, ambition, and intellectual pride to freedom in Christ. And he understood that the disciplines were essential to that freedom:

"You have made us for yourself, O Lord, and our hearts are restless until they rest in you."

— Augustine, *Confessions*

This restlessness is not merely a problem to be solved but an energy to be redirected. The disciplines, for Augustine, were the means by which the restless heart is gradually trained to desire what it was made for:

"Prayer is the directing of the heart to God. It is the soul's movement toward its true home. All our disciplines aim at this: to clear away the obstacles, to quiet the distractions, to train the desires, so that the heart can finally rest where it was meant to rest."

— Augustine, *Letters*

Augustine also understood the corporate dimension of formation:

"We are the Body of Christ. In Him, we are members one of another. The discipline I receive from my brother's rebuke is as valuable as the discipline I impose on myself. The encouragement I receive in the assembly is as necessary as the encouragement of private prayer. We are not formed alone; we are formed together."

— Augustine, *Homilies on 1 John*

6.12 Basil the Great and Gregory of Nazianzus: Friendship in Formation

Basil of Caesarea (330–379) and Gregory of Nazianzus (329–390), two of the Cappadocian Fathers, modeled an essential truth: the power of spiritual friendship in formation. They studied together, prayed together, and held each other accountable. Their letters reveal a relationship of remarkable depth and honesty.

Basil's rules for monastic life emphasized the communal nature of spiritual formation:

"We are members one of another. The eye cannot say to the hand, 'I have no need of you.' Neither can the one who prays say to the one who labors, 'I have no need of your work.' Nor can the one who labors say to the one who prays, 'I have no need of your prayers.' We are formed together, in community, or we are not formed at all."

— Basil the Great, *The Longer Rules*

Gregory, reflecting on their friendship, wrote:

"We had all things in common, and one soul was in both of us. We were a test of the saying that all things are shared among friends. Our one aim and ambition was virtue, and a life of hope in the blessings to come. We tried to leave everything earthly behind and to live entirely for the life to come."

— Gregory of Nazianzus, *Oration 43*

This kind of soul-friendship—what the tradition calls *anam cara* or "soul friend"—is a discipline in itself: the willingness to be known, to be challenged, to receive correction, to journey together. The Fathers understood that we cannot see our own blind spots; we need companions who love us enough to show us what we cannot see.

Part Seven: Five Practices for the Journey

Beginning the Disciplined Life with Ancient Wisdom

"We do not think ourselves into new ways of living; we live ourselves into new ways of thinking."
— Richard Rohr

The path of spiritual discipline can feel overwhelming. Where does one begin? How does one integrate ancient practices into a modern life already crowded with demands?

The wisdom of the tradition offers this counsel: begin small, begin somewhere, and trust the Spirit to guide the growth. What follows are five practices drawn from different streams of Christian spirituality—each addressing a different dimension of the soul's need, each offering a doorway into deeper communion with God.

Do not attempt all five at once. Choose one. Practice it for a season—perhaps forty days, perhaps a liturgical season, perhaps until it becomes second nature. Then add another. The disciplines are not boxes to check but relationships to cultivate, and relationships take time.

7.1 Lectio Divina: Divine Reading

Category: Engagement with Scripture

Lectio divina—Latin for "divine reading"—is an ancient practice of prayerful engagement with Scripture that dates back to the early monasteries. Unlike study, which seeks to master the text, *lectio divina* allows the text to master us. Unlike devotional reading, which covers ground, *lectio divina* digs deep into a single passage, allowing the Spirit to speak through the living Word.

"When we read the Word of God, we should not be satisfied to skim over the surface. We must dig deep, like miners searching for gold. The gold is there—hidden, perhaps, but present. Patient, prayerful reading will discover it."
— Origen, *Homilies on Genesis*

The Practice:

Lectio divina traditionally follows four movements, though they are not rigid steps but fluid rhythms:

1. Lectio (Reading): Read a short passage of Scripture slowly, aloud if possible. Read it again. Read it a third time. Let the words wash over you without analyzing or rushing. The passage need not be long—a few verses are sufficient. The quality of attention matters more than the quantity of text.

2. Meditatio (Meditation): Notice which word or phrase catches your attention—what the tradition calls being "addressed" by the text. Sit with that word. Turn it over in your mind. Repeat it silently. Let it sink from your head to your heart. Ask: Why this word? What is the Spirit saying to me through it?

3. Oratio (Prayer): Let meditation become conversation. Speak to God about what you have heard. This is not formal prayer but intimate dialogue—the response of the heart to the Word that has addressed it. You may find yourself confessing, petitioning, thanking, lamenting, or simply resting in silence.

4. Contemplatio (Contemplation): Let the words fall away. Rest in the Presence beyond words. This is the goal toward which *lectio divina* moves: not information about God, but communion with God. You may experience nothing but silence. That is enough. The Spirit is working beneath the level of consciousness.

"In lectio divina, we are not trying to cover ground but to be covered by the Word. We are not reading the Bible; the Bible is reading us."

— Martin Laird, *Into the Silent Land*

Beginning the Practice:

Start with five to ten minutes. Choose a Gospel passage—perhaps a story of Jesus' encounter with someone. Read slowly. Notice what draws your attention. Speak to God about it. Rest in His presence. That is all. The practice will deepen over time.

7.2 The Daily Examen: Prayerful Review

Category: Self-Awareness and Discernment

The *Examen* is a practice developed by Ignatius of Loyola in the sixteenth century, though its roots reach back to the earliest Christian traditions of self-examination. It is a simple, daily review of the movements of the soul—noticing where God was present, where we responded to grace, and where we resisted it.

"The examen is not a guilt-inducing review of failures. It is a loving review of the day, conducted in the presence of the One who loves us. We are not looking for what we did wrong; we are looking for where God was at work—and how we responded."

— Dennis Linn, Sheila Fabricant Linn, and Matthew Linn, *Sleeping with Bread*

The Practice:

The traditional Examen has five movements, which can be practiced in ten to fifteen minutes at the end of each day:

1. Become Aware of God's Presence: Settle into silence. Acknowledge that you are not alone—that the Spirit is with you, eager to help you see your day through His eyes. Ask for the grace to see clearly.

2. Review the Day with Gratitude: Walk through the day in your memory, from waking to the present moment. Notice the gifts—small and large. The morning coffee. A conversation that went well. A moment of beauty. A problem solved. Let gratitude rise naturally. Thank God specifically.

3. Pay Attention to Your Emotions: As you review the day, notice your feelings. Where did you feel alive, energized, connected to God and others? Where did you feel drained, anxious, disconnected? The tradition calls the first kind of movement "consolation" and the second "desolation." Both are data; both reveal something about your soul's condition.

4. Choose One Feature of the Day and Pray About It: Select one moment—whether of consolation or desolation—and bring it to God in conversation. If it was a moment of grace, give thanks. If it was a moment of failure or struggle, ask for insight. What was happening beneath the surface? What invitation is hidden in the experience?

5. Look Toward Tomorrow: Ask the Spirit to show you what lies ahead. Is there a particular challenge you anticipate? A relationship that needs attention? A temptation you expect to face? Ask for the grace you will need. Entrust the day to come into God's hands.

"The examen teaches us to recognize God's presence in the ordinary moments of our lives—not just in the dramatic spiritual experiences, but in the daily round of work and rest, conversation and silence, success and failure."

— Ruth Haley Barton, *Sacred Rhythms*

Beginning the Practice:

Do the Examen at the same time each day—perhaps before bed, perhaps during a quiet moment in the evening. Keep a journal if that helps. Over time, patterns will emerge. You will begin to recognize the movements of the Spirit in your life—and the movements that resist Him.

7.3 Silence: The Discipline of Presence

Category: Contemplation and Interior Stillness

Silence is perhaps the most countercultural discipline in our noisy age—and perhaps the most necessary. Silence is more than the absence of sound; it is the cultivation of interior stillness and the creation of space for God to speak and for us to listen.

"God is the friend of silence. See how nature—trees, flowers, grass—grows in silence; see the stars, the moon, and the sun, how they move in silence. We need silence to be able to touch souls."

— Mother Teresa

The Desert Fathers called silence *hesychia*—a word that connotes not just quietness but peace, stillness, the settled calm of a soul at rest in God. This is not a state we achieve by effort but a gift we receive through practice.

The Practice:

Begin simply. Set a timer for five minutes. Sit in a comfortable but alert posture—not so comfortable that you fall asleep, not so rigid that you become distracted by discomfort. Close your eyes or lower your gaze.

1. Settle the Body: Take several deep breaths. Release the tension in your shoulders, your jaw, your hands. Let the body become still.

2. Acknowledge the Presence: You are not alone. The Spirit is with you—closer than your own breath. Acknowledge His presence silently. You might use a simple phrase: "Here I am, Lord" or "Come, Holy Spirit."

3. Let Thoughts Pass: The noise will come. Thoughts will arise—anxieties about tomorrow, memories of yesterday, mental to-do lists, stray ideas. Do not fight them. Notice them, as you might notice clouds passing across the sky, and let them go. Gently return your attention to the Presence.

4. Use a Sacred Word (Optional): Some find it helpful to use a single word as an anchor—a "sacred word" that represents their intention to be present to God. When distractions arise, the word can be silently repeated to refocus attention. Traditional words include "Jesus," "Abba," "Love," "Peace," or "Maranatha" (Aramaic for "Come, Lord").

5. Rest: The goal is not to produce anything—no insights, no feelings, no visions. The goal is simply to be present. To rest in the Presence that rests in you.

"In silence, we discover that we are not our thoughts. We are not our feelings. We are not our anxieties. We are, beneath all of that, children of God—held, known, loved. Silence is how we remember who we really are."
— Martin Laird, *Into the Silent Land*

Beginning the Practice:

Start with five minutes. Increase gradually—to ten minutes, then fifteen, then twenty. Do not be discouraged by the noise; it takes time for the pond to settle. The practice itself is forming you, even when you feel you are "doing it wrong." There is no wrong way to sit in silence with the One who loves you.

7.4 Fasting: The Discipline of Holy Hunger

Category: Embodied Prayer and Dependence

Fasting is the voluntary abstention from food (or other goods) for spiritual purposes. It is one of the oldest and most universal spiritual practices, found in virtually every religious tradition—and strongly emphasized in both the Old and New Testaments.

"Fasting is the soul's discipline. It teaches the body its proper place; it humbles the flesh; it creates space for the Spirit. When the stomach is empty, the soul has room to be filled."

— John Chrysostom, *Homilies on the Statutes*

Jesus assumed His followers would fast. "When you fast," He said—not "if" (Matthew 6:16). The early church fasted twice weekly, on Wednesday and Friday. The great saints of every era have testified to fasting's power to clarify the mind, intensify prayer, and break the grip of appetites that have grown too strong.

The Practice:

There are many forms of fasting. The most common include:

Complete Fast: Abstaining from all food for a set period (usually twenty-four hours), while continuing to drink water. This is the traditional Christian fast.

Partial Fast: Abstaining from certain kinds of food—often meat, sweets, or rich foods—while eating simply. The Daniel Fast (vegetables and water) is one example.

Meal Fast: Skipping one or two meals, using the time normally spent eating for prayer.

Media: Abstaining from screens, social media, news, or entertainment. In our digital age, this can be as spiritually significant as a food fast.

Beginning the Practice:

If you are new to fasting, begin with a single-meal fast. Skip lunch, and use the lunch hour for prayer and Scripture reading. Notice what happens in your body and soul. The hunger you feel is not just physical; it is the hunger of a creature made for more than bread.

As you grow in the practice, consider a weekly fast—perhaps from dinner one evening until dinner the next day, following the ancient rhythm. Or observe the traditional Wednesday and Friday fasts of the early church.

"The hunger of the body becomes a prayer the mind cannot articulate. When the stomach cries out for food, let the soul cry out for God. This is the meaning of fasting: to let the body teach the soul to long for what it truly needs."

— Derek Prince

Important Cautions:

Fasting is not for everyone in every season. Those with eating disorders, pregnant or nursing mothers, those with diabetes or other health conditions, and children should not fast from food without medical guidance. The goal of fasting is freedom, not bondage; if fasting triggers unhealthy patterns, it should be modified or set aside.

7.5 Sabbath: The Discipline of Rest

Category: Rhythm and Trust

Sabbath is the practice of intentional rest—a weekly day set apart from work, productivity, and the endless demands of accomplishment. It is rooted in the creation narrative (God rested on the seventh day) and enshrined in the Ten Commandments as a fundamental obligation of covenant life.

"Sabbath is not simply the pause that refreshes. It is the pause that transforms. It is an act of resistance against the culture of endless productivity, an act of trust in the God who provides, an act of remembrance that we are human beings, not human doings."

— Ruth Haley Barton, *Sacred Rhythms*

In an age of constant connectivity, where we carry our offices in our pockets and are never truly "off," Sabbath has become both more difficult and more necessary. It is the discipline that most directly confronts our addiction to productivity and our anxiety about falling behind.

The Practice:

Sabbath involves two movements: stopping and delighting.

Stopping: Sabbath begins with ceasing work, commerce, and the endless cycle of production and consumption. This means different things for different people. For some, it means not checking email. For others, it means not doing household chores. The specifics matter less than the intention: for one day each week, you are not defined by what you produce.

Delighting: Sabbath is not merely negative (what you don't do) but positive (what you do). It is a day for the activities that restore your soul: worship, rest, play, feasting, time with loved ones, walks in nature, naps, good food, and laughter. Sabbath is not a burden but a gift—the day God gives us to remember that we are loved apart from our usefulness.

"The Sabbath is a weekly reminder that we do not save the world by our efforts. God saved the world while we were sleeping. Our rest is not laziness; it is faith. It is the lived confession that the world is in better hands than ours."

— Walter Brueggemann, *Sabbath as Resistance*

Beginning the Practice:

Choose a twenty-four-hour period each week—traditionally from sundown to sundown, though the specifics can be adapted. Begin the Sabbath with a simple ritual: lighting a candle, sharing a meal, and offering a prayer of thanksgiving. During the Sabbath, resist the urge to work, to check devices, to be productive. Instead, rest. Play. Worship. Feast. Remember whose you are.

"If you want to change the world, take a nap. If you want to transform your soul, stop working one day a week. Sabbath is the most subversive of all the disciplines—it strikes at the root of our anxious striving and declares that we are held by a grace that does not depend on our efforts."

— John Mark Comer, *The Ruthless Elimination of Hurry*

A Note on Beginning

You do not have to master these practices. You do not have to do them perfectly. You simply have to begin.

Choose one practice. Give it a season of faithful attention. Notice what happens in your soul. Bring what you discover to a mentor, a spiritual director, or a trusted friend. Let the Spirit guide you into the next practice when the time is right.

The goal is not to accumulate disciplines but to cultivate a life of communion with God. The practices are means, not ends. They are doors, not destinations. Walk through one door, and you will find that the other doors open.

"Do not be afraid to begin. The Holy Spirit is gentle with beginners. He does not demand perfection; He invites participation. Start where you are. Use what you have. Do what you can. Grace will meet you there."

— Henri Nouwen

The Life-Giving Religion is Disciplined

"Discipline without desire is drudgery. Desire without discipline is disaster. But discipline flowing from desire is the doorway to transformation."
— Dallas Willard

We began this chapter by acknowledging a crisis: the untrained soul in a distracted age, the formational deficit that has left so many Christians believing the right things while remaining fundamentally unchanged. We have traced the ancient wisdom of the Church Fathers, explored the Spirit-empowered formation of the earliest communities, and offered practical pathways into the disciplined life.

Now we must address a final question—perhaps the most important question of all: Why? Why discipline? Why effort? Why practices and rhythms and structures in a faith that proclaims grace, freedom, and the finished work of Christ?

The answer is this: true, life-giving, spiritual religion is always disciplined—not despite grace, but because of it.

The False Dichotomy

We have inherited a false dichotomy. On one side stands "religion"—understood as dead ritual, legalistic obligation, the grinding attempt to earn God's favor through human effort. On the other side stands "relationship" or "spirituality"—understood as free, spontaneous, unstructured, and utterly dependent on grace.

The implication is clear: discipline belongs to religion, and religion is bad; freedom belongs to relationship, and relationship is good. Choose your side.

But this dichotomy is a lie.

The saints knew better. The Fathers knew better. The Scriptures know better. True spirituality—the kind that transforms sinners into saints, that produces the character of Christ, that enables ordinary people to face the arena singing hymns—has always been disciplined spirituality.

"Grace is opposed to earning, not to effort. Earning is an attitude; effort is an action. Grace is the enabling gift of God, not to earn, but to live rightly. The disciplines are the means by which we receive and express that grace."

— Dallas Willard, *The Spirit of the Disciplines*

The disciplines are not ways of earning what grace gives freely. They are ways of receiving what grace offers abundantly. They are not ladders we climb to reach a distant God; they are channels through which the near God flows into our parched souls.

The Organic Nature of Spiritual Growth

Consider how growth works in every other domain of life.

The musician who wishes to play with freedom and expression must first submit to scales and exercises. The athlete who wishes to perform with power and grace must first submit to training and practice. The writer who wishes to produce work that moves the soul must first submit to the discipline of craft—reading, writing, revising, writing again.

No one looks at a concert pianist and thinks, "What bondage! What legalism! If only she were free from all that practice, she could really express herself." We understand that the practice is what made the expression possible. The discipline created the freedom.

"The goal of a virtuous life is to become like God, so far as that is possible for human nature. This requires long habituation in the good. We do not become holy by a single act of will, but by countless small choices repeated until they become second nature."

— Gregory of Nyssa, *On the Making of Man*

Spiritual growth works the same way. The freedom to love, the capacity for joy, the strength to endure—these are not produced by wishing or by a single dramatic experience. They are cultivated through practice. They are trained into us through the patient repetition of the disciplines.

The Disciplines as Training in Receptivity

Here is the deepest truth about the spiritual disciplines: they train us to receive.

We are creatures designed for receptivity. We were made to receive life from God—to breathe His breath, to eat His bread, to drink from His river. But sin has curved us inward upon ourselves. We have become grasping, striving, anxious creatures—trying to secure for ourselves what can only be received as a gift.

The disciplines retrain us in the posture of receptivity. Prayer teaches us to receive guidance. Fasting teaches us to receive sustenance. Silence teaches us to receive presence. Sabbath teaches us to receive rest. The Eucharist teaches us to receive Christ Himself.

"The spiritual life is not about what we do for God but about what we allow God to do in us. The disciplines are not our action upon God but our opening to God's action upon us. They are the hands we cup to catch the rain that is already falling."

— Richard Foster, *Celebration of Discipline*

This is why the disciplines, rightly practiced, never feel like burden but like relief. They are not additional demands on an already overloaded life; they are the simplification of life to its essentials. They are not obligations that complicate; they are practices that liberate.

The Joy of the Disciplined Life

The great saints have always testified to the joy of the disciplined life. Not grim endurance—joy. Not teeth-gritting determination—delight.

II THE DISCIPLINE RELIGION

St. Ignatius of Antioch, on his way to martyrdom, wrote letters burning with eagerness and joy. St. Francis of Assisi, who embraced radical poverty, was famous for his laughter and his songs. St. Teresa of Ávila, who reformed the Carmelite order and lived in austere simplicity, was known for her wit and her dancing. The Desert Fathers, who fasted rigorously and slept on stone floors, were described by their visitors as radiant, peaceful, and surprisingly happy.

This is not a coincidence. The disciplines do not suppress joy; they release it. They strip away the thousand false pleasures that compete for our attention and leave us with the one true Pleasure that satisfies. They detach us from what cannot ultimately fulfill and attach us to the only One who can.

"The disciplined person is not the grim, tight-lipped person who has suppressed all desire. The disciplined person is the one whose desires have been trained and ordered, so that they flow naturally toward their proper objects. Such a person experiences more pleasure, not less—because their pleasures are real pleasures, not counterfeits."

— C. S. Lewis, *The Screwtape Letters* (adapted)

The Discipline of Love

Ultimately, the disciplines are the discipline of love.

Love is not merely a feeling. Love is a practice. Love is patient and kind; love does not envy or boast; love is not arrogant or rude; love does not insist on its own way; love is not irritable or resentful; love does not rejoice at wrongdoing but rejoices with the truth; love bears all things, believes all things, hopes all things, endures all things (1 Corinthians 13:4–7).

These are not descriptions of a spontaneous emotion. These are descriptions of a practiced virtue. They require training. They require discipline. They require the slow, patient cultivation of a heart that has been reordered by grace.

"To love at all is to be vulnerable. Love anything and your heart will be wrung and possibly broken. If you want to make sure of keeping it intact, you must give it to no one, not even an animal. Wrap it carefully round with hobbies and little luxuries; avoid all entanglements; lock it up safe in the casket of your selfishness. But in that casket—safe, dark, motionless, airless—it will change. It will not be broken; it will become unbreakable, impenetrable, irredeemable."

— C. S. Lewis, *The Four Loves*

The disciplines are how we unlock the casket. They are how we train our hearts to love—to love God with all our heart, soul, mind, and strength, and to love our neighbors as ourselves. They are how we become the kind of people for whom love is not an effort but an overflow.

The Religion That Gives Life

There is a religion that kills. It is the religion of mere performance, of external conformity, of rules without relationship. Jesus denounced it in the Pharisees. Paul warned against it in his letters. The prophets thundered against it in Israel. It is real and deadly.

But there is also a religion that gives life. It is the religion of disciplined receptivity, of practices that open the soul to grace, of rhythms that align human life with divine life. It is the religion of the Psalms, which structure daily prayer around the sun's movements. It is the religion of the prophets, who called for fasting that loosens the bonds of wickedness and lets the oppressed go free. It is the religion of Jesus, who withdrew to lonely places to pray and taught His disciples to do the same. It is the religion of the apostles, who established communities devoted to teaching, fellowship, breaking of bread, and prayers.

This religion does not oppose grace. It is grace—grace embodied, grace practiced, grace received through the hands and feet and breath and time of creatures who were made to receive it.

> "True religion is not the enemy of life; it is the shape of life lived in communion with the Source of life. The disciplines are not burdens imposed from outside; they are the natural expressions of a soul that has tasted and seen that the Lord is good."
> — Eugene Peterson, *A Long Obedience in the Same Direction*

Conclusion

We began with a crisis: the untrained soul in a distracted age.

We end with an invitation: the ancient path, still open, still lit by the Spirit, still leading home.

The disciplines are not burdens to bear but wings to fly. They are not punishments for sins but means of receiving grace for holiness. They are not ladders to climb but tables to feast at, doors to walk through, cups to fill.

Leonard Ravenhill prayed:

"O God, send us a generation of Christians who know how to pray! Who knows how to fast! Who knows how to be silent before You! Who knows how to gather in Your Name! Who knows how to live for Your Kingdom and die for Your glory! Send us, O Lord, a disciplined generation—not legalists, but lovers; not performers, but worshipers; not consumers, but participants in Your divine nature!"

And John Mark Comer reminds us:

"The goal of apprenticeship to Jesus is not to master a set of spiritual practices. The goal is to become the kind of person for whom love, joy, peace, patience, kindness, goodness, faithfulness, gentleness, and self-control are not efforts but expressions—the natural overflow of a life lived in union with Christ. The practices are the means; union is the end. And in that union, we find what we were always looking for: intimacy with God."
— John Mark Comer, *Practicing the Way*

We are Marcus in the desert and David in the city. We are lost and found, failing and rising, wandering and being hemmed in by Love. The accusing voice still speaks; the excusing voice still whispers. But beneath both, there is a third Voice—patient, persistent, gentle as breath and relentless as the tide:

Beloved. Come home. I have been waiting.

The table is set. The disciplines are the doors. The Spirit is the Guide.

All that remains is to walk through.

"And I will betroth you to me forever. I will betroth you to me in righteousness and in justice, in steadfast love and in mercy. I will betroth you to me in faithfulness. And you shall know the Lord."

— Hosea 2:19–20

Endnotes

1. Dallas Willard, *The Spirit of the Disciplines: Understanding How God Changes Lives* (San Francisco: HarperSanFrancisco, 1988), 156. Willard's distinction between grace opposing "earning" rather than "effort" has been foundational for recovering a healthy understanding of spiritual disciplines in evangelical contexts.
2. The phrase "gospel of sin management" comes from Dallas Willard, *The Divine Conspiracy: Rediscovering Our Hidden Life in God* (San Francisco: HarperSanFrancisco, 1998), 41-42. Willard critiques a Christianity focused primarily on forgiveness of sins and afterlife security rather than transformation into Christlikeness.
3. Willard, *The Spirit of the Disciplines*, 68.
4. Studies on smartphone usage vary, but research from Asurion (2019) found Americans check their phones an average of 96 times per day. Microsoft's attention span research (2015) suggested average human attention spans had declined to approximately eight seconds, though this figure has been disputed by subsequent researchers.
5. John Mark Comer, *Practicing the Way: Be with Jesus, Become Like Him, Do as He Did* (New York: WaterBrook, 2024). Comer's work synthesizes Dallas Willard's vision of spiritual formation with practical guidance for contemporary disciples.
6. Jim Wilder's work on relational neuroscience and spiritual formation appears primarily in *Renovated: God, Dallas Willard, and the Church That Transforms* (Colorado Springs: NavPress, 2020) and, with Michel Hendricks, *The Other Half of Church: Christian Community, Brain Science, and Overcoming Spiritual Stagnation* (Chicago: Moody Publishers, 2020).
7. Ruth Haley Barton, *Sacred Rhythms: Arranging Our Lives for Spiritual Transformation* (Downers Grove, IL: InterVarsity Press, 2006), 15.

8. 1 Corinthians 9:27: "But I discipline my body and keep it under control, lest after preaching to others I myself should be disqualified" (ESV). The Greek *hypōpiazō* literally means "to strike under the eye" or "to give a black eye," reflecting the intensity of athletic training.
9. Ephesians 2:10: "For we are his workmanship, created in Christ Jesus for good works, which God prepared beforehand, that we should walk in them" (ESV).
10. Leonard Ravenhill (1907-1994) was a British evangelist known for his passionate calls to prayer and revival. His books include *Why Revival Tarries* (1959) and *Revival God's Way* (1983). The quotation reflects Ravenhill's characteristic emphasis on the active cooperation with grace that genuine spirituality requires.
11. St. Anthony of Egypt (c. 251-356) is considered the father of Christian monasticism. His life is recorded in Athanasius of Alexandria's *Life of Anthony* (c. 360 AD), one of the most influential hagiographies in Christian history.
12. Henri Nouwen (1932-1996) was a Dutch Catholic priest and prolific author on spirituality. His works include *The Way of the Heart*, *The Return of the Prodigal Son*, and *Life of the Beloved*. The quotation reflects themes developed throughout his corpus.
13. Thomas Merton (1915-1968), *Spiritual Direction and Meditation* (Collegeville, MN: Liturgical Press, 1960), 16. Merton, a Trappist monk and prolific author, was instrumental in bringing contemplative spirituality to popular attention in the twentieth century.
14. Gregory the Great (c. 540-604), *Pastoral Rule* (*Regula Pastoralis*), Book I. Gregory's work became the standard manual for pastoral ministry throughout the medieval period and remains influential today.
15. Richard Foster, *Celebration of Discipline: The Path to Spiritual Growth* (San Francisco: Harper & Row, 1978; revised and expanded editions 1988, 1998). Foster's work was pivotal in recovering the spiritual disciplines for Protestant audiences in the late twentieth century.

II THE DISCIPLINE RELIGION

16. Willard, *The Spirit of the Disciplines*, 156.
17. The metaphor of eating and spiritual nourishment appears throughout Scripture: Psalm 34:8 ("Taste and see that the LORD is good"); Deuteronomy 8:3 and Matthew 4:4 ("Man shall not live by bread alone"); John 6:35 ("I am the bread of life"); Jeremiah 15:16 ("Your words were found, and I ate them").
18. Martin Laird, *Into the Silent Land: A Guide to the Christian Practice of Contemplation* (Oxford: Oxford University Press, 2006), 4. Laird, an Augustinian friar, offers one of the most accessible contemporary guides to contemplative prayer.
19. Watchman Nee (1903-1972), *The Release of the Spirit* (New York: Christian Fellowship Publishers, 1965). Nee was a Chinese church leader and Christian teacher whose works have been widely influential in both Eastern and Western Christianity.
20. Barton, *Sacred Rhythms*, 147.
21. Gregory the Great, *Pastoral Rule*, Book III, Chapter 1. Gregory's discussion of *discretio* (discernment) as the "mother of virtues" became foundational for later spiritual direction traditions.
22. The quotation "We are what we repeatedly do. Excellence, then, is not an act, but a habit" is commonly attributed to Aristotle but is actually a paraphrase by Will Durant in *The Story of Philosophy* (1926), summarizing Aristotle's thought in the *Nicomachean Ethics*, Book II.
23. Job 38:7: "when the morning stars sang together and all the sons of God shouted for joy" (ESV).
24. Barton, *Sacred Rhythms*, 145.
25. Justin Whitmel Earley, *Habits of the Household: Practicing the Story of God in Everyday Family Rhythms* (Grand Rapids: Zondervan, 2021). Earley also authored *The Common Rule: Habits of Purpose for an Age of Distraction* (2019).
26. Daniel 6:10: "When Daniel knew that the document had been signed, he went to his house where he had windows in his upper chamber open

toward Jerusalem. He got down on his knees three times a day and prayed and gave thanks before his God, as he had done previously" (ESV).

27. The Liturgy of the Hours (also called the Divine Office or Daily Office) developed from Jewish prayer practices through early Christian usage into a structured cycle of daily prayer. The classic hours include Matins (night), Lauds (dawn), Prime (first hour), Terce (third hour), Sext (sixth hour), None (ninth hour), Vespers (evening), and Compline (night).

28. Barton, *Sacred Rhythms*, 51.

29. Nouwen's discussion of silence and the encounter with one's "shadow side" appears throughout his works, particularly in *The Way of the Heart: The Spirituality of the Desert Fathers and Mothers* (San Francisco: HarperSanFrancisco, 1981).

30. Laird, *Into the Silent Land*, 15-16. The Greek term *logismoi* (λογισμοί) refers to the intrusive thoughts that the Desert Fathers identified as obstacles to prayer.

31. Foster, *Celebration of Discipline*, 48.

32. Derek Prince (1915-2003) was a Bible teacher and author whose works on prayer and fasting, including *Shaping History Through Prayer and Fasting* (1973), have been widely influential in charismatic circles.

33. Foster, *Celebration of Discipline*, 80.

34. Ephesians 5:19: "addressing one another in psalms and hymns and spiritual songs, singing and making melody to the Lord with your heart" (ESV).

35. Colossians 3:16: "Let the word of Christ dwell in you richly, teaching and admonishing one another in all wisdom, singing psalms and hymns and spiritual songs, with thankfulness in your hearts to God" (ESV).

36. Barton, *Sacred Rhythms*, 167.

37. 2 Peter 1:12-15: Peter's commitment to remind believers of essential truths "as long as I am in this body" establishes a biblical pattern for the regular rehearsal of foundational teachings.
38. The understanding of the Eucharist as "medicine for the sick" echoes Ignatius of Antioch's description of it as "the medicine of immortality" (*pharmakon athanasias*) in his *Letter to the Ephesians* 20:2.
39. Nouwen's eucharistic spirituality is developed in *With Burning Hearts: A Meditation on the Eucharistic Life* (Maryknoll, NY: Orbis Books, 1994).
40. Hebrews 10:24-25: "And let us consider how to stir up one another to love and good works, not neglecting to meet together, as is the habit of some, but encouraging one another, and all the more as you see the Day drawing near" (ESV).
41. 1 Corinthians 12:26: "If one member suffers, all suffer together; if one member is honored, all rejoice together" (ESV).
42. Philippians 3:20: "But our citizenship is in heaven, and from it we await a Savior, the Lord Jesus Christ" (ESV). The Greek *politeuma* (citizenship, commonwealth) emphasizes the political and communal dimensions of Christian identity.
43. Stanley Hauerwas and William H. Willimon, *Resident Aliens: Life in the Christian Colony* (Nashville: Abingdon Press, 1989). The book argues that the church's primary task is not to transform society directly but to be a faithful alternative community.
44. Nouwen's understanding of mission as integral to Christian identity appears throughout his works, particularly in *Compassion: A Reflection on the Christian Life* (with Donald P. McNeill and Douglas A. Morrison, 1982).
45. Nee, *The Release of the Spirit*, 9.
46. Hosea 2:6-7 (ESV).
47. Hosea 2:14-15 (ESV).

48. James D.G. Dunn, *Jesus and the Spirit: A Study of the Religious and Charismatic Experience of Jesus and the First Christians as Reflected in the New Testament* (London: SCM Press, 1975; Grand Rapids: Eerdmans, 1997). Dunn's comprehensive study remains foundational for understanding the Spirit's role in early Christian experience and formation.
49. Dunn, *Jesus and the Spirit*, 199.
50. Luke 4:14: "And Jesus returned in the power of the Spirit to Galilee, and a report about him went out through all the surrounding country" (ESV).
51. Dunn, *Jesus and the Spirit*, 67.
52. Acts 2:42-44 (ESV).
53. Dunn, *Jesus and the Spirit*, 189.
54. 1 Corinthians 14:18: "I thank God that I speak in tongues more than all of you" (ESV).
55. 2 Corinthians 12:2-4: Paul's account of being "caught up to the third heaven" and hearing "things that cannot be told, which man may not utter."
56. 1 Corinthians 9:27; 2 Corinthians 11:27; 1 Thessalonians 5:17.
57. Dunn, *Jesus and the Spirit*, 212.
58. Galatians 5:22-23: "But the fruit of the Spirit is love, joy, peace, patience, kindness, goodness, faithfulness, gentleness, self-control; against such things there is no law" (ESV).
59. Dunn, *Jesus and the Spirit*, 316.
60. Tertullian, *Apologeticus*, Chapter 39 (c. 197 AD): "See, they say, how they love one another... and how they are ready to die for each other."
61. Rodney Stark, *The Rise of Christianity: How the Obscure, Marginal Jesus Movement Became the Dominant Religious Force in the Western World in a Few Centuries* (Princeton: Princeton University Press, 1996). Stark, a sociologist of religion, argues that practical Christian

virtues—including care for the sick during epidemics—contributed significantly to Christianity's growth.
62. *The Didache* (Teaching of the Twelve Apostles), Chapter 8. This early Christian document, dated variously between 50-120 AD, provides some of our earliest evidence for post-apostolic Christian practices.
63. Dunn, *Jesus and the Spirit*, 345.
64. Romans 8:5-6 (ESV).
65. Hebrews 12:1-2 (ESV).
66. Ignatius of Antioch, *Letter to Polycarp*, Chapter 3 (c. 107-110 AD). Ignatius wrote seven letters while being transported to Rome for martyrdom.
67. Clement of Rome, *First Letter to the Corinthians*, Chapter 13 (c. 96 AD). Clement's letter is one of the earliest Christian documents outside the New Testament.
68. Ignatius, *Letter to the Romans*, Chapter 5.
69. Ignatius, *Letter to Polycarp*, Chapters 2-3.
70. *The Martyrdom of Polycarp*, Chapter 9 (c. 155-160 AD). This account is one of the earliest martyrdom narratives we possess.
71. *The Martyrdom of Polycarp*, Chapters 5, 8.
72. Clement of Alexandria, *Stromata* (Miscellanies), Book VII (c. 198-203 AD). Clement's term *gnostic* (from Greek *gnosis*, knowledge) refers to the spiritually mature Christian, not to the heretical Gnostic movements.
73. Clement of Alexandria, *Stromata*, Book VII.
74. Clement of Alexandria, *The Instructor* (*Paedagogus*), Book II.
75. Origen, *On First Principles* (*De Principiis*), Preface (c. 220-230 AD).
76. Origen, *Homilies on Genesis*, Homily 2.
77. Cyprian of Carthage, *On the Lapsed* (*De Lapsis*), Chapter 35 (c. 251 AD). Cyprian wrote this work to address the question of how to restore Christians who had apostatized during the Decian persecution.
78. Cyprian, *Letters*, Letter 73.

79. Athanasius, *Life of Anthony*, Chapter 14 (c. 360 AD).
80. *Apophthegmata Patrum* (Sayings of the Desert Fathers), Abba Silvanus 3. The alphabetical and systematic collections of desert sayings were compiled in the fifth and sixth centuries.
81. *Apophthegmata Patrum*, Abba Poemen 184.
82. *Apophthegmata Patrum*, Amma Syncletica 1.
83. Evagrius Ponticus, *Praktikos*, Chapter 6 (c. 399 AD). Evagrius's eight *logismoi* (gluttony, fornication, avarice, sadness, anger, acedia, vainglory, pride) were later condensed by Gregory the Great into the seven deadly sins.
84. Evagrius Ponticus, *On Prayer*, Chapter 67.
85. John Cassian, *Conferences*, Conference 1, Chapter 4 (c. 420-429 AD). Cassian's works transmitted desert spirituality to Western monasticism.
86. John Cassian, *Institutes*, Book 5, Chapter 6.
87. John Chrysostom, *Homilies on the Statues*, Homily 3 (387 AD). These homilies were preached during a crisis in Antioch when the populace had rioted and destroyed imperial statues.
88. John Chrysostom, *Homilies on Hannah*, Homily 4.
89. John Chrysostom, *Homilies on Matthew*, Homily 50. This passage connects eucharistic devotion with service to the poor.
90. Augustine, *Confessions*, Book I, Chapter 1 (c. 397-400 AD).
91. Augustine, *Letters*, Letter 130.
92. Augustine, *Homilies on 1 John*, Homily 10.
93. Basil the Great, *The Longer Rules* (*Regulae Fusius Tractatae*), Question 7 (c. 358-364 AD).
94. Gregory of Nazianzus, *Oration 43* (Funeral Oration for Basil), Chapter 20 (c. 382 AD).
95. The Celtic term *anam cara* (soul friend) refers to a spiritual companion or director. The concept was developed in the Irish monastic tradition and has been popularized by John O'Donohue's book *Anam Cara: A Book of Celtic Wisdom* (1997).

96. Richard Rohr, *Falling Upward: A Spirituality for the Two Halves of Life* (San Francisco: Jossey-Bass, 2011), xxi.
97. *Lectio divina* was systematized by Guigo II, a Carthusian monk, in his *Scala Claustralium* (Ladder of Monks) around 1150 AD. However, the practice has roots in Origen and the desert tradition.
98. Origen, *Homilies on Genesis*, Homily 13.
99. Laird, *Into the Silent Land*, 37.
100. The Daily Examen was developed by Ignatius of Loyola (1491-1556) as part of his *Spiritual Exercises*. It remains central to Ignatian spirituality.
101. Dennis Linn, Sheila Fabricant Linn, and Matthew Linn, *Sleeping with Bread: Holding What Gives You Life* (Mahwah, NJ: Paulist Press, 1995), 1.
102. The terms "consolation" and "desolation" are technical vocabulary in Ignatian spirituality. Consolation refers to movements toward God, peace, and life; desolation refers to movements away from God toward anxiety, isolation, and despair.
103. Barton, *Sacred Rhythms*, 117.
104. Mother Teresa of Calcutta (1910-1997). The quotation reflects her consistent teaching on the necessity of silence for hearing God's voice.
105. The Greek term *hesychia* (ἡσυχία) refers to stillness, quietness, and inner peace. It became central to the Eastern Christian hesychast tradition of contemplative prayer.
106. Laird, *Into the Silent Land*, 45.
107. Centering Prayer, developed by Thomas Keating, Basil Pennington, and William Meninger in the 1970s, uses a "sacred word" as an anchor for contemplative prayer. The practice draws on the fourteenth-century anonymous English mystical text *The Cloud of Unknowing*.
108. Laird, *Into the Silent Land*, 3.

109. Matthew 6:16: "And when you fast, do not look gloomy like the hypocrites..." (ESV). Jesus's use of "when" rather than "if" assumes fasting as a normal practice for His followers.
110. John Chrysostom, *Homilies on the Statutes*, Homily 3.
111. Derek Prince, *Shaping History Through Prayer and Fasting* (New Kensington, PA: Whitaker House, 1973), 87.
112. Barton, *Sacred Rhythms*, 77.
113. Walter Brueggemann, *Sabbath as Resistance: Saying No to the Culture of Now* (Louisville: Westminster John Knox Press, 2014), 45.
114. John Mark Comer, *The Ruthless Elimination of Hurry: How to Stay Emotionally Healthy and Spiritually Alive in the Chaos of the Modern World* (New York: WaterBrook, 2019), 178.
115. Nouwen's guidance on beginning spiritual practices appears throughout his works, particularly in *Spiritual Direction: Wisdom for the Long Walk of Faith* (with Michael J. Christensen and Rebecca J. Laird, 2006).
116. Willard, *The Spirit of the Disciplines*, 156.
117. 1 Corinthians 13:4-7 (ESV).
118. C.S. Lewis, *The Four Loves* (London: Geoffrey Bles, 1960), 169.
119. Foster, *Celebration of Discipline*, 7.
120. Eugene Peterson, *A Long Obedience in the Same Direction: Discipleship in an Instant Society* (Downers Grove, IL: InterVarsity Press, 1980; 2nd ed. 2000), 17.
121. Leonard Ravenhill, *Why Revival Tarries* (Minneapolis: Bethany House, 1959), adapted from various passages.
122. Comer, *Practicing the Way*, 23.
123. Hosea 2:19-20 (ESV).

III

THE GROANING AND THE GLORY

A Story of Omar and Michelle

Part One: The Return

I.

The airplane touched down at 11:47 PM, and Omar Whitfield pressed his forehead against the cold window, watching the tarmac lights blur into streaks of orange and white. Three months. Ninety-two days in the villages outside Port-au-Prince, holding the hands of dying children, praying over mass graves from the earthquake's aftermath, preaching hope while his own soul hemorrhaged somewhere beneath his ribs.

He should feel something. Joy, perhaps. Relief. The anticipation of holding Michelle, of meeting his son—*his son*—born seven weeks ago while Omar was 1,600 miles away, cradling someone else's child as she took her last breath.

Instead, there was only the static. That white noise that had settled into his chest somewhere around week six and never left. He watched himself from a great distance now, like a man observing his own life through a window smeared with Vaseline.

"The Lord is my shepherd," he whispered to himself, a reflex more than a prayer. The words fell flat against the sealed cabin air.

And yet—something stirred. Faint as a half-remembered dream. A warmth at the edge of his consciousness, like a hand reaching through fog. *I am still here,* the warmth seemed to say. *Even when you cannot feel Me.*

Omar closed his eyes. He wanted to believe it. He wasn't sure he could.

Michelle stood at the arrivals gate with baby Elijah strapped to her chest, her hair unwashed, her smile practiced. She had rehearsed this moment in the bathroom mirror that morning, had coached herself through the appropriate expressions: *joy, relief, gratitude.* But when she saw Omar emerge through the sliding doors—thinner now, his eyes carrying something she didn't recognize—the performance collapsed.

He looked haunted.

And she was too exhausted to pretend she wasn't.

"Hey," she said.

"Hey." He reached for her, and she let him fold her into an embrace that felt like two strangers bumping into each other on a crowded street. Elijah stirred between them, a small warm comma of need.

"He's beautiful," Omar said, looking down at his son.

"He doesn't sleep," Michelle replied. "Neither do I."

They walked to the car in silence.

But as Michelle buckled Elijah into his car seat, she felt something she couldn't explain—a gentle nudge, almost physical, like a hand pressing lightly against her back. *Be patient with him,* something whispered. *He is carrying more than you know.*

She shook her head, dismissing it as exhaustion. She had her own burdens to carry.

II.

The first week home, Omar preached twice—once at the Wednesday night service, once at Sunday morning worship. Both times, he stood behind the pulpit and delivered words that seemed to come from someone else's mouth, someone who still believed them. The congregation wept. They praised God for Brother Omar's faithfulness. They had no idea that he had spent the previous night sitting on the edge of the bathtub, staring at his razor, wondering if anyone would miss him if he simply... stopped.

The thought horrified him. And yet it kept returning, unbidden, like a stray dog that had caught his scent.

Dark night of the soul. He knew the term. He'd read St. John of the Cross in seminary, had preached about spiritual desolation with the confident authority of a man who had never actually walked through it. Now he understood. The dark night wasn't merely the absence of God's felt presence—it was the terrifying suspicion that perhaps there had never been a presence at all, that he had spent his life talking to an empty room.

On the third night, unable to sleep, Omar wandered into the living room and found his Bible on the coffee table. He hadn't opened it in weeks—not for himself, only for sermon preparation, the words becoming tools rather than bread. But something made him pick it up now. His hand fell open to Romans 8, and his eyes landed on a verse he had read a hundred times:

"Likewise the Spirit helps us in our weakness. For we do not know what to pray for as we ought, but the Spirit himself intercedes for us with groanings too deep for words."

Omar stared at the page. *Groanings too deep for words.* That was exactly it—the pain that had no language, the despair that couldn't be articulated. And here was Paul saying the Spirit was already praying it, already interceding, already carrying what Omar could not carry himself.

He didn't feel anything change. But he sensed, dimly, that he was not as alone as he had believed.

III.

Michelle had her own darkness.

It had started three weeks after Elijah's birth—the crying jags that came without warning, the crushing weight on her chest that made it hard to breathe, the intrusive thoughts that whispered *you're a terrible mother* and *he deserves better* and *you should never have had a child*. She knew the clinical term: postpartum depression. But knowing the name didn't make the demon any smaller.

And then there was the other thing. The thing she hadn't told anyone, not even Omar.

Pastor David Mercer.

Her mentor for eight years. The man who had discipled her through college, officiated her wedding, ordained her husband. The man who had texted her at 2 AM to "check in on her spiritual growth." The man who had hugged her a beat too long, commented on her appearance in ways that felt wrong but were never quite wrong enough to name. The man who had once put his hand on her knee during a counseling session and let it linger there, his thumb tracing small circles on her thigh, while he talked about "emotional intimacy with Christ."

She had worshipped that man. She had trusted him with her soul.

And now, lying awake at 3 AM while Elijah screamed and Omar stared at the ceiling like a corpse, she finally understood what it had been. All of it. The special attention. The late-night calls. The way he'd isolated her from other mentors, made her feel like she was uniquely chosen, uniquely spiritual, uniquely *his*.

Grooming. The word made her sick.

The realization had come to her three weeks ago, sudden and devastating, while she was nursing Elijah in the dark. It wasn't a logical deduction—it was more like a veil being lifted, a light being turned on in a room she hadn't known was dark. One moment she was remembering Pastor David's "mentoring," and the next moment she *saw* it, saw it for what it had always been.

She had gasped aloud, startling Elijah. And then she had wept—for hours, for days, a grief that seemed bottomless.

This is the Spirit, some part of her knew. *The Spirit of truth, showing you what you couldn't see before.* But the knowing didn't make the pain any less. If anything, it made it worse. Because now she had to live with the truth.

IV.

The fights began in week three.

Omar came home late from a deacon meeting—the second one that week—and found Michelle in the nursery, rocking Elijah with a ferocity that bordered on violence, tears streaming down her face.

"You're never here," she said.

"I'm here now."

"No. You're not." She looked at him with something that might have been hatred. "You're somewhere else. You've been somewhere else since you got back. Where are you, Omar? Because you're not with me. You're not with your son."

He felt the wall go up, brick by brick, the familiar fortress he'd learned to build as a child when his father's rage filled the house. *Don't engage. Don't react. Go inside, where it's safe.*

"I'm tired," he said, his voice flat. "I just need some time to readjust."

"Time?" Michelle laughed, but there was no humor in it. "You had three months in Haiti. I had three months alone, pregnant, terrified, while you played savior to strangers. And now you need *time*?"

"That's not fair."

"None of this is fair, Omar!"

Elijah started crying. Omar turned and walked out of the room.

Behind him, Michelle shouted: "That's right! Walk away! Just like every other man in my life!"

He went to the garage and sat in his car for forty-five minutes, engine off, staring at the concrete wall. Somewhere deep in his chest, beneath the static, something was screaming. But he couldn't reach it. He couldn't reach anything anymore.

And then—faint, almost imperceptible—a thought that didn't feel like his own: *She is not your enemy. She is wounded, like you. Go back.*

Omar gripped the steering wheel. He didn't want to go back. Going back meant feeling, and feeling meant pain.

Go back.

He sat for another ten minutes, wrestling. Then, slowly, he opened the car door.

He found Michelle on the kitchen floor, sobbing. He didn't say anything. He just sat down beside her and put his hand on her back—awkwardly, uncertainly, but *present*.

They stayed that way for a long time.

Part Two: The Demon Dialogues

V.

Dr. Susan Tucker had been practicing cognitive behavioral therapy for twenty-three years, and she recognized dissociation when she saw it. The man sitting across from her—Pastor Omar Whitfield, thirty-four, referred by his primary care physician—was present in body only. His eyes had that particular glassiness, that subtle disconnect, that told her his mind had learned to vacate the premises when things got too painful.

"Tell me about Haiti," she said.

Omar's hands tightened on his knees. "It was... difficult."

"Difficult how?"

Silence. Then: "There was a little girl. Esther. She was seven." His voice was mechanical, like a news anchor reading a teleprompter. "She had cholera. I held her for three days while she died. I prayed for healing. I believed—" He stopped. Swallowed. "I believed God would save her."

"And He didn't."

"And He didn't."

Dr. Tucker waited.

"After that," Omar continued, "something... broke. I kept doing the work. I kept preaching, kept praying, kept showing up. But I wasn't... there. I was watching myself from far away, like a movie I'd already seen. And I started thinking—" He stopped again.

"What did you start thinking, Omar?"

The silence stretched. When he finally spoke, his voice was barely a whisper.

"That it would be easier if I just... wasn't here anymore."

Dr. Tucker nodded slowly, her face betraying nothing but compassion. "I'm glad you told me that. And I want you to know that what you're experiencing—the dissociation, the depression, the thoughts of suicide—these are symptoms. They're not who you are. They're not the truth about you. They're your mind's way of trying to cope with more pain than it knows how to hold."

Omar looked at her, and for a moment, she saw the man behind the mask—exhausted, terrified, utterly alone.

"Can you help me?" he asked.

"I can. But I need you to commit to this work. It's going to be hard. We're going to have to go to some places that hurt. Are you willing?"

He nodded.

"Good. Then let's begin."

VI.

Pastor Terrence Nix had been Omar's spiritual director for five years—a quiet, silver-haired man in his sixties who had survived his own dark night decades ago and emerged with a faith both gentler and fiercer than before. He met with Omar every Thursday evening at a small coffee shop near the seminary, and he listened without flinching as Omar confessed the full extent of his spiritual collapse.

"I don't know if I believe anymore," Omar said. "I stand up there on Sunday mornings and say the words, and they feel like ash in my mouth. What kind of pastor am I?"

Pastor Nix took a long sip of his black coffee. "Do you remember Job?" he asked.

"Of course."

"Do you remember what God said to him at the end? After all the suffering, all the questioning, all the anguished why's?"

Omar frowned. "He showed him the leviathan. The vastness of creation."

"Yes. But notice what God *didn't* say. He didn't explain. He didn't justify. He didn't give Job a theological treatise on the problem of evil." Pastor Nix leaned forward. "He simply showed him that there was more—more than Job could see, more than Job could understand, more than Job could hold in his finite human mind. And Job's response wasn't 'Now I understand.' His response was 'Now I have *seen* you.'"

"I don't feel like I'm seeing anything except darkness."

"I know. And that's why we call it a dark night, Omar—not a dark *afternoon*. The night is long. But morning comes." He paused. "Can I tell you something the Spirit has been pressing on my heart for you?"

Omar looked up.

"The Spirit is not absent in your darkness. He is *working* in it. The very fact that you're sitting here, that you haven't given up, that you're still reaching out for help—that's not your strength. That's His. He's interceding for you with groanings too deep for words, remember? Even when you can't pray, He's praying through you."

Omar's eyes filled with tears—the first he'd cried since Esther died.

"But," Pastor Nix continued, his voice growing firm, "you cannot walk this road alone. And you cannot walk it while your marriage is crumbling. Michelle needs you, Omar. Not the Omar who performs wellness while dying inside—the *real* Omar, even in his brokenness. I need you to be zealously committed to your own transformation. Not for the church. Not for the ministry. For *you*. For her. For that little boy. The Spirit is calling you to this work. Will you answer?"

"I don't know how."

"Then let's figure it out together."

VII.

The demon dialogues came for them on a Tuesday night.

Michelle had found a text on Omar's phone—innocent, professional, a female colleague asking about a sermon schedule—and something in her snapped. She knew, even as the accusations poured out of her mouth, that she was being irrational. She knew Omar wasn't Pastor David. She *knew*.

But she couldn't stop.

"Who is she?" Michelle demanded, her voice rising to a pitch that made Elijah stir in his crib. "How long has this been going on? Do you think I'm stupid?"

Omar felt the familiar shutdown begin—the walls going up, the emotions retreating to somewhere unreachable. "Michelle. It's a work email. Calm down."

"*Don't tell me to calm down!*" She was crying now, that ugly desperate crying that came from somewhere deeper than anger. "You're never here! You're always at church, always with other people, always somewhere I can't reach you! And now there's some woman texting you at nine o'clock at night—"

"You're being paranoid."

The word hit her like a slap. *Paranoid.* That's what Pastor David had called her, the one time she'd tried to set a boundary. *You're being paranoid, Michelle. I'm just trying to help you grow.*

"Get out," she said.

"This is my house."

"I said *get out!*"

Omar grabbed his keys and walked to the front door. He paused, his hand on the knob, and turned back to her. His face was stone.

"You know what?" he said quietly. "I spent three months watching children die. I came home to a wife who can barely look at me and a God who feels like a stranger. And now you want to accuse me of cheating because a coworker sent me an email about Sunday's announcements?" He laughed, a hollow sound. "I can't do this, Michelle. I don't have anything left."

He walked out.

Michelle sank to the kitchen floor and sobbed.

VIII.

Omar drove for an hour, nowhere in particular, the radio off, the silence pressing against him like a weight. He ended up at the church—empty now, dark except for the emergency exit signs casting their red glow over the sanctuary.

He sat in the back pew and stared at the cross on the wall.

"I don't know what to do," he said aloud. His voice echoed in the empty space. "I don't know how to love her. I don't know how to feel anything. I don't even know if You're real anymore."

Silence.

And then—not audibly, but unmistakably—a response. Not words, exactly. More like a knowing that settled into his chest, bypassing his mind entirely.

III THE GROANING AND THE GLORY

She is fighting a battle you cannot see. Ask her about Pastor David.

Omar frowned. Pastor David Mercer? Michelle's old mentor? He hadn't thought about the man in years. Why would—

Ask her.

He sat with it for a long time. The knowing didn't fade. If anything, it grew stronger, more insistent.

Finally, he drove home.

Michelle was still on the kitchen floor, though the sobbing had quieted to a kind of hollow stillness. Omar sat down beside her, his back against the cabinets, and waited.

"Michelle," he said finally. "I need to ask you something."

She didn't respond.

"What happened with Pastor David?"

Her whole body went rigid. For a long moment, he thought she wouldn't answer. Then, in a voice so small he could barely hear it:

"How did you know?"

"I don't know. I just... knew." He paused. "Tell me."

And she did. All of it. The grooming she'd only recently recognized. The manipulation. The violation of trust so profound she hadn't even been able to name it until a few weeks ago. The shame that made her feel like everything was her fault—like she was dirty, complicit, damaged beyond repair.

Omar listened. He didn't interrupt. He didn't try to fix it or explain it or minimize it. He just listened.

When she finished, the silence stretched between them—but it was a different kind of silence now. Less like a wall, more like a space.

"I'm so sorry," Omar said finally. "I'm so sorry that happened to you."

Michelle looked at him—really looked, for the first time in weeks.

"I've been taking it out on you," she whispered. "Haven't I? All my fear, all my suspicion—I've been treating you like you're him."

"I think so. But I understand why."

"No. You don't get to just understand." She shook her head. "I've been hurting you. I've been cruel. And you've been carrying your own darkness, and I've been too wrapped up in mine to even see it." She started crying again. "What's wrong with us, Omar? What's happening to us?"

He reached for her hand. "I don't know. But I think... I think we need help. Real help. More than we can give each other right now."

"Okay," she said.

"Okay?"

"Okay. Let's get help."

It wasn't healing. Not yet. But it was the first step toward it.

Part Three: The Work

IX.

They started seeing Dr. Tucker together, in addition to Omar's individual sessions. And Pastor Nix began meeting with them as a couple, integrating the therapeutic work with spiritual direction.

"What you're caught in," Dr. Tucker explained during one of their early sessions, "is what attachment researchers call a 'demon dialogue.' It's a cycle—a dance—that couples fall into when their attachment bonds are threatened."

She drew a diagram on her whiteboard: two circles, connected by arrows that formed a loop.

"Michelle, when you feel abandoned or unsafe, you *pursue*. You push harder, demand answers, test Omar's commitment. It's not because you're trying to be difficult—it's because your nervous system is screaming *danger!* and the only way it knows to respond is to pursue proof that you're loved."

Michelle nodded slowly.

"And Omar, when you feel criticized or inadequate, you *withdraw*. You shut down, go silent, retreat into yourself. Not because you don't care, but because the pain of engagement feels unbearable. You're protecting yourself the only way you know how."

Omar stared at the diagram.

"The tragedy is that each of your responses triggers the other's deepest fear. Michelle pursues, which makes Omar feel overwhelmed, so he withdraws. His withdrawal makes Michelle feel abandoned, so she pursues harder. Around and around you go, each trying to cope, each making things worse."

"How do we stop?" Michelle asked.

"You learn to recognize the cycle. You learn to name it when it's happening—*We're doing the dance again*. And then, slowly, you learn to step out of the cycle and reach for each other in a new way. Not from your defenses, but from your vulnerability."

Pastor Nix leaned forward. "This is where the Spirit's work becomes essential. Your natural instincts will always be to protect yourselves—to pursue or withdraw, to attack or hide. But the Spirit offers a different way. *'The fruit of the Spirit is love, joy, peace, patience, kindness, goodness, faithfulness, gentleness, self-control.'* Notice how many of those are about how we treat *others*. The Spirit's work isn't just internal transformation—it's relational transformation. He's teaching you to love each other the way Christ loves the church."

Michelle felt something stir in her chest—that same gentle nudge she'd felt at the airport, the night Omar came home. *This is the path. Walk it.*

X.

The cognitive behavioral work was unglamorous, tedious, and surprisingly effective. Dr. Tucker taught Omar to notice the thoughts that preceded his dissociative episodes—the familiar lies that whispered *you're worthless, you're a fraud, everyone would be better off without you.* She taught him to challenge those thoughts, to examine the evidence, to replace the lies with statements that were true, or at least *truer*.

"The thought comes: 'I'm a terrible husband,'" she would say. "What's the evidence for that thought?"

"I shut down. I withdraw. I can't give Michelle what she needs."

"And what's the evidence against that thought?"

Omar struggled. "I... I'm still here. I haven't left. I'm trying."

"Good. So a more balanced thought might be: 'I'm struggling to connect with Michelle right now, but I'm committed to working on our marriage.'"

It felt clunky, artificial. But slowly, over weeks, Omar began to notice something shifting. The thoughts still came—but they no longer felt like absolute truth. They felt like *thoughts*. Distortions. Lies his wounded mind told itself to make sense of pain it couldn't process.

One evening, during his quiet time, Omar felt a sudden clarity—one of those moments when Scripture seems to leap off the page and speak directly to his situation. He was reading 2 Corinthians 10:5: *"We destroy arguments and every lofty opinion raised against the knowledge of God, and take every thought captive to obey Christ."*

Take every thought captive. That was exactly what the CBT work was teaching him—but now he saw the deeper dimension. This wasn't just psychological hygiene. This was spiritual warfare. The lies that tormented him—*you're worthless, you're a fraud*—those weren't just cognitive distortions. They were accusations from the Enemy, the one Scripture called *the accuser of the brethren.*

And the Spirit was teaching him to fight back.

XI.

Michelle began her own therapy that spring—a referral from Dr. Tucker to a colleague who specialized in religious trauma. For the first time, she told someone the full story of Pastor David Mercer.

The telling felt like vomiting up poison. She shook for hours afterward.

But something loosened in her chest. Some coiled thing that had been living there for years, feeding on shame and silence, began to lose its grip.

"What he did to you was abuse," her therapist said, plainly and without drama. "Not physical abuse, not sexual abuse in the traditional sense, but abuse nonetheless. Spiritual abuse. Emotional manipulation. A systematic violation of the trust you placed in him as your pastor."

"But I let him," Michelle said. "I wanted his attention. I—"

"You were twenty-two. He was your authority. He used his position to exploit your faith and your need for guidance. Whatever you felt, whatever you did or didn't do—*he was the adult. He was the pastor. The responsibility was his.*"

Michelle wept.

That night, she couldn't sleep. She found herself in the nursery, rocking Elijah even though he was already asleep, staring out the window at the dark backyard.

I'm so ashamed, she prayed—the first real prayer she'd offered in months. *I feel so dirty. So broken. I don't know how to be free of this.*

The response came not as words but as an image—sudden, vivid, almost tactile. She saw herself standing in a river, the water rising around her, dark and cold. And then she saw a hand reaching down from above, not pulling her out but joining her in the water, holding her steady, keeping her from being swept away.

I am with you in the flood, the image seemed to say. *I will not let you drown.*

Michelle gripped the arms of the rocking chair and wept—but this time, the tears felt different. Less like despair. More like release.

XII.

Pastor Nix met with them together in his small office, the three of them crowded around a coffee table stacked with theology books and half-empty mugs.

"I want to read something to you," he said, opening his worn Bible. "Colossians 1. Listen carefully."

He read slowly, letting each phrase settle:

"I am glad, because it gives me a chance to complete in my own sufferings something of the untold pains for which Christ suffers on behalf of his body, the Church... And the secret is simply this: Christ in you! Yes, Christ in you bringing with him the hope of all glorious things to come."

He closed the book.

"Paul wrote this from prison," he said. "He was suffering. His churches were a mess. His friends had abandoned him. And yet he talks about *gladness*. About *hope*. About a secret hidden for ages and now revealed."

"I don't feel very hopeful," Michelle admitted.

"Neither did Paul, I suspect. Not in the way we think of hope—that bubbly optimism that says everything will turn out fine." Pastor Nix leaned back. "Biblical hope is different. It's a stubborn trust that God is doing something, even when all the evidence suggests otherwise. It's Corrie ten Boom, forgiving the Nazi guard who had beaten her sister to death. It's Job, sitting in the ash heap, saying 'Though He slay me, yet will I trust Him.'"

Omar shifted uncomfortably. "I've been thinking about Corrie ten Boom lately, actually."

"Oh?"

"Her sister, Betsie—she died in Ravensbrück. And her last words to Corrie were 'There is no pit so deep that God's love is not deeper still.'" Omar's voice cracked. "I want to believe that. But I've been in some pretty deep pits lately, and I'm not sure I felt God's love at all."

"But you're here," Pastor Nix said quietly. "You're still breathing. You're still fighting for your marriage, your faith, your life. Where do you think that strength comes from?"

Omar was silent.

"The Spirit doesn't always announce Himself with thunder and fire. Sometimes He works so quietly we don't even recognize Him—a thought that comes from nowhere, a decision we didn't know we could make, a moment of grace in the middle of darkness." He paused. "The Spirit has been carrying you, Omar. Both of you. Even when you couldn't feel it."

Michelle reached for Omar's hand.

"Now," Pastor Nix continued, "the question is: will you cooperate with His work? Will you be zealously committed to the transformation He's offering? It won't be easy. It won't be quick. But if you surrender to the process—if you let Him remake you from the inside out—you'll find something you never expected."

"What?" Michelle asked.

"Glory. Not the cheap glory of easy success, but the deep glory of redemption. The glory of a marriage that has walked through fire and come out refined. The glory of *Christ in you*—two broken people becoming one flesh, reflecting the mystery of Christ and the church."

Part Four: The Turning

XIII.

In May, Dr. Tucker referred them to a weekend intensive for couples—a program based on attachment research and emotionally focused therapy.

"It's concentrated work," she explained. "Two and a half days of going deep into your attachment patterns and learning new ways of connecting. I think you're ready."

The retreat center was an old farmhouse two hours north of the city, surrounded by rolling hills and ancient oaks. Nine other couples gathered in the main room that Friday evening, each carrying their own particular cargo of hurt and hope.

The facilitators began by explaining the program's foundation: that human beings are wired for connection, that secure attachment is our deepest need, and that most marital conflict is really a desperate attempt to maintain that attachment in the face of perceived threat.

"We're not going to teach you communication techniques," the facilitator said. "We're going to help you understand the *why* beneath your conflicts—the attachment fears and needs that drive your behaviors. And then we're going to help you reach for each other from those vulnerable places."

Omar felt Michelle's hand slip into his. He held it.

XIV.

On Saturday morning, they worked on recognizing their cycle—the demon dialogue they'd been trapped in for months. They mapped the triggers, the reactions, the escalations. Seeing it on paper was revelatory. It wasn't about the email. It wasn't about the late nights at church. It was about the dance—a dance they both hated but neither knew how to stop.

During a break, Michelle walked outside and stood by an old oak tree, watching clouds drift across the April sky. She felt drained, exposed, like a wound that had been opened for cleaning.

Lord, she prayed silently, *I don't know if I can do this. I'm so tired.*

The response came as a sudden memory—a verse she hadn't thought about in years. Isaiah 43: *"When you pass through the waters, I will be with you; and through the rivers, they shall not overwhelm you."*

I am with you, the Spirit seemed to say. *Keep going.*

She took a deep breath and walked back inside.

XV.

The afternoon session focused on what the facilitators called "raw spots"—the attachment wounds that made certain interactions so painful.

"What's the raw spot?" the facilitator asked. "The wound underneath the reaction?"

Michelle went first. Her voice trembled.

"I think... I think my raw spot is *I'm not safe*. I learned from a young age that the people who were supposed to protect me would hurt me. My father left. My mentor—" She couldn't finish. "I learned that love is dangerous. That trusting someone means they'll eventually use you and discard you."

Omar's turn.

"Mine is... *I'm not enough*. That I'll never be able to give people what they need. That I'll always disappoint them. And when Michelle accuses me, when she seems angry and unsatisfied—it's like confirmation of everything I already believe about myself. That I'm a failure. That I'm worthless."

They looked at each other, really looked, maybe for the first time since he'd come home from Haiti.

"I didn't know," Michelle whispered. "I didn't know that's what you were feeling."

"I didn't tell you."

"Why not?"

"Because I was afraid that if you saw how broken I was, you'd leave."

She took his face in her hands. "Omar. I'm not leaving. I'm *here*."

And in that moment, Omar felt something shift—a crack in the fortress he'd built around his heart. Not a demolition, not yet. But a beginning.

XVI.

That night, back in their room at the retreat center, they lay in the dark and talked for hours. Really talked—not about logistics or responsibilities, but about fears and longings, wounds and hopes.

"I've been so angry," Michelle said. "At Pastor David. At the church. At you, even though you didn't do anything wrong. I think I've been angry at God, too."

"For letting it happen?"

"For letting me be so blind. For not protecting me." She paused. "But today, during the session, I felt... something. Like God was there, in the middle of all the pain. Not fixing it, not explaining it—just *present*."

Omar nodded slowly. "I've been feeling that too. Not all the time. Not even most of the time. But sometimes—these moments of *knowing*. Like the Spirit is speaking, but not in words. More like... nudges. Directions."

"Like when you asked me about Pastor David."

"Yes. Exactly like that."

Michelle rolled onto her side to face him. "Do you think that's real? The Spirit speaking to us?"

"I didn't used to believe it was so... immediate. So personal. I thought the Spirit worked through Scripture and the church, but not through direct communication." He was quiet for a moment. "But I can't explain some of the things that have happened any other way. The knowing. The timing. The way things have unfolded."

"Maybe that's part of the mystery," Michelle said. "The beauty of mystery in God. Not understanding everything, but trusting that He's present, even when we can't see how."

Omar reached for her hand in the darkness.

"Pastor Nix says our marriage is supposed to reflect the gospel," he said. "Christ and the church. A mystery, Paul calls it. I used to think that meant we were supposed to be perfect—a shining example for others. But maybe it's more like... we reflect the gospel in our *need* for redemption. In our brokenness and our healing. In the way we keep reaching for each other even when it hurts."

Michelle squeezed his hand.

"Christ in us," she whispered. "The hope of glory."

They fell asleep holding on to each other.

XVII.

The final session of the retreat focused on forgiveness and bonding—the slow, ongoing work of rebuilding trust.

"Forgiveness isn't a one-time event," the facilitator explained. "It's a process. Sometimes it takes years. But it begins with a willingness—a willingness to see your partner's pain beneath their offense, and to choose connection over resentment."

During a couples exercise, Michelle turned to Omar.

"I need to tell you something," she said. "I've been holding onto anger—not just at Pastor David, but at you. For not being there when I was pregnant. For coming home broken when I needed you to be strong. For all of it."

Omar nodded. "I know."

"And I'm choosing to let it go. Not because I've stopped feeling it—I don't think feelings work that way. But because I don't want to carry it anymore. Because I want us to have a future more than I want to punish you for the past."

Omar's eyes filled with tears.

"I forgive you too," he said. "For the accusations. For the suspicion. For all the ways you've pushed me away." He paused. "But honestly? I think what you really need is forgiveness for yourself. For the shame you've been carrying. For believing the lies about your worth."

Michelle looked down.

"That's harder," she admitted.

"I know. But maybe we can work on it together."

XVIII.

They drove home on Sunday afternoon, the late spring sun warming their faces through the windshield. Something had shifted between them—not a dramatic transformation, but a turning. A new direction.

"I'm not healed," Michelle said as they merged onto the highway. "I know that. There's still so much to work through."

"Me neither. But I feel... different. More present. More *here*."

"The Spirit is doing something," Michelle said. "I can feel it. Not finished—but begun."

Omar reached over and took her hand.

"'He who began a good work in you will be faithful to complete it,'" he quoted softly.

"Philippians 1:6."

"Yeah."

They drove in comfortable silence for a while. Then Michelle spoke again:

"Pastor Nix talked about being zealously committed to our transformation. I've been thinking about what that means. I think it means... not expecting it to be easy. Not giving up when it's hard. Trusting that the work is worth it, even when we can't see the results."

"Like Corrie ten Boom," Omar said. "Forgiving the guard. Not because she felt like it—because she chose to ask God for what she couldn't manufacture herself."

"Yeah." Michelle paused. "I'm not there yet. With Pastor David, I mean. But I'm willing to start asking."

Omar squeezed her hand.

"We'll ask together."

III THE GROANING AND THE GLORY

Part Five: The Slow Healing

XIX.

Healing is not linear. Anyone who tells you otherwise is selling something.

The months after the retreat were a patchwork of progress and regression, breakthrough and breakdown. Omar still had days when the darkness descended without warning, when the static returned and his soul felt a thousand miles away. Michelle still had nights when the suspicion clawed its way back, when she found herself interrogating Omar about innocent texts and everyday interactions.

But something had shifted.

Now, when Omar felt himself withdrawing, he could name it. "I'm going into protective mode," he would say to Michelle. "I need a minute, but I'm not leaving."

And when Michelle felt the old paranoia rising, she could pause. *This isn't about Omar,* she would remind herself. *This is Pastor David's voice. This is the wound, not the truth.*

They built what Dr. Tucker called "repair rituals"—small ways of returning to each other after ruptures. A hand on the arm. A quiet "I'm sorry." A walk around the block together while Elijah slept in the stroller.

The demon dialogues didn't disappear entirely. But they lost their power. They became recognizable, nameable, something to step around rather than something to be swallowed by.

XX.

The Spirit's work became more visible as the months passed—not in dramatic interventions, but in small accumulating graces.

There was the morning Omar woke from a dream about Esther—but instead of the usual grief and guilt, he felt a strange peace. He had dreamed that she was alive, laughing, running through a field of yellow flowers. And when he woke, he sensed—not knew, but *sensed*—that she was okay. That somehow, beyond all his understanding, she was held in hands larger than his own.

There was the afternoon Michelle was praying in the kitchen, halfheartedly, while doing dishes, and felt a sudden warmth spread through her chest—like being hugged from the inside. She stood there, hands in soapy water, and wept. Not from sadness. From something closer to relief.

There was the evening they were fighting—a real fight, the old cycle rising up again—and in the middle of it, Omar stopped and said: "Wait. Can we pray?"

Michelle stared at him.

"Right now?"

"Right now. Before we say anything else we'll regret."

They stood in the kitchen, hands linked, and prayed aloud—awkwardly, haltingly, but together. And something shifted. The anger didn't disappear, but it loosened. They were able to talk instead of attack, to hear instead of defend.

Afterward, Michelle said: "That was the Spirit, wasn't it? Prompting you to stop."

"I think so. I didn't plan it. It just... came."

"We should do that more often."

"Yeah. We should."

XXI.

Pastor Nix continued meeting with them, his presence a steady anchor as they navigated the slow work of transformation.

"I want to tell you something about the nature of spiritual growth," he said one evening. "It's not like climbing a ladder, where you start at the bottom and work your way up. It's more like a spiral. You keep coming back to the same issues, the same struggles, the same wounds—but each time, you engage them from a slightly higher vantage point. You're not failing when you revisit old patterns. You're deepening."

"That's encouraging," Michelle said wryly. "I thought I was just failing."

"No. You're sanctifying." He smiled. "There's a difference."

He opened his Bible to a passage he'd shared with them before.

"In ever-deepening devotion to Him," he read from a commentary, "our hearts begin and continue to swell with life, and hope, and peace, and joy, and pleasure not only in our perfection but in our *perfecting*."

He looked up.

"The joy isn't waiting at the end, after you're fully healed. The joy is in the journey—in the daily work of becoming who God made you to be. The groaning and the glory, remember? They accompany one another. The tension serves to develop and deepen a real devotion in and to our communion with God."

Omar thought about that for a long moment.

"So the pain isn't something to be escaped," he said slowly. "It's something to be... transformed? Redeemed?"

"Yes. Exactly." Pastor Nix leaned forward. "This is what Paul means when he talks about completing in his sufferings 'something of the untold pains for which Christ suffers on behalf of his body, the Church.' Our suffering, when surrendered to God, becomes part of His redemptive work. It doesn't just hurt us—it heals the world. Mysteriously. Incomprehensibly. But really."

Michelle felt tears prick her eyes.

"Even what Pastor David did to me?"

"Even that. Not that God caused it—never that. But that God can take the worst things done to us and, through His Spirit, turn them into sources of ministry and compassion. Corrie ten Boom's suffering became her greatest message. Your suffering—both of your suffering—can become part of your calling."

XXII.

There was the day Michelle finally wrote the letter.

Not a letter to send—she had no desire to contact Pastor David, and her therapist had advised against it. But a letter to *write*. To put words to what had been done to her, to name it, to release it onto the page.

She sat at the kitchen table while Elijah napped, pen in hand, and let the words pour out. The anger. The grief. The betrayal. The shame. Page after page, unfiltered, uncensored.

And then, at the end, something she hadn't planned:

I forgive you. Not because you deserve it. Not because what you did was okay. But because I don't want to carry this poison anymore. Because holding onto hatred is destroying me more than it's punishing you. Because Jesus forgave me, and He asks me to forgive others.

This doesn't mean I trust you. It doesn't mean I want to see you. It doesn't mean there won't be consequences for what you did.

But I release you. I give you to God. I choose to be free.

She signed her name, folded the letter, and walked outside to the fire pit.

Omar was waiting there—she'd asked him to be present for this.

She dropped the letter into the flames and watched it burn.

"How do you feel?" Omar asked.

Michelle watched the paper curl and blacken.

"Not finished," she said. "But... lighter. Like something heavy just shifted."

"The Spirit's work," Omar said.

"Yeah." She turned to him. "The Spirit's work."

XXIII.

Elijah turned one in September.

They threw him a small party—just a few friends, some cake, a lot of photos. Omar stood in the kitchen doorway, watching Michelle bounce their son on her hip while laughing at something her sister said, and he felt something he hadn't felt in a very long time.

Hope.

Not the naive hope he'd carried before Haiti—the assumption that everything would work out because God was good and good things happened to good people. That hope had died in the villages, had been buried alongside Esther and a dozen others.

This was a different hope. A hope that had walked through darkness and come out the other side, scarred but alive. A hope that could hold both the groaning and the glory, the pain and the promise. A hope that expected suffering and chose to trust anyway.

Later that night, after the guests had left and Elijah was asleep, Omar and Michelle sat on the back porch, watching the stars.

"Do you remember what Pastor Nix said about Corrie ten Boom?" Michelle asked. "About asking God for forgiveness she couldn't manufacture herself?"

"I remember."

"I think I'm starting to understand what that means. Not just for Pastor David—for everything. For you. For myself. For this whole broken mess of a life." She leaned her head against his shoulder. "I can't fix myself, Omar. I can't heal myself. I can't make myself into the wife or the mother or the Christian I'm supposed to be. All I can do is show up and ask God to give me what I don't have."

"Me too," Omar said. "Every single day."

They sat in silence for a while, the late summer air cool against their skin.

"I love you," Michelle said finally. "Not the you I want you to be. Not the you I'm afraid you might be. Just... you. The real you. Even when you're a mess."

"I love you too," Omar replied. "The real you. Especially when you're a mess."

He kissed her forehead, and she pressed closer, and somewhere in the vast darkness beyond the porch light, the Spirit of God moved over the chaos like He'd done since the beginning of time, bringing order out of disorder, light out of darkness, life out of death.

They were still broken. They would always be broken.

But they were being healed.

Epilogue: The Gospel in Miniature

XXIV.

Two years later, Omar stood before his congregation on a Sunday morning in late autumn, Elijah playing in the nursery down the hall, Michelle sitting in the third row with her eyes full of something that might have been pride.

He had thought long and hard about what to say. In the end, he decided on the truth.

"Marriage is hard," he began. "Some of you know that from experience. Some of you are in the middle of it right now—the fights, the distance, the feeling that you and your spouse are speaking different languages about completely different things."

He paused.

"A few years ago, Michelle and I almost lost each other. Not because either of us was unfaithful or abusive or fundamentally incompatible. We almost lost each other because we were both broken people trying to protect ourselves from more pain. I built walls. She tested them. We fell into patterns that nearly destroyed us."

The congregation was silent.

"What saved us wasn't willpower or communication techniques or even good theology. What saved us was grace. The Holy Spirit, working through a wise spiritual director, a skilled therapist, a weekend retreat that taught us to reach for each other instead of running away. The Spirit, speaking through Scripture at just the right moments, prompting us to pray when we wanted to fight, giving us strength we didn't have on our own."

He looked at Michelle.

"I've been thinking lately about how marriage reflects the gospel. Not because marriage is easy—it's not. But because the same dynamics are at play. We come to God broken, wounded, full of patterns and defenses that keep us from real intimacy. And God, like a patient spouse, keeps reaching for us. Keeps pursuing. Keeps offering Himself, even when we pull away."

He opened his Bible.

"Paul says in Colossians that there's a mystery hidden for ages and now revealed. And the mystery is this: *Christ in you, the hope of glory.* Not Christ beside you. Not Christ above you. Christ *in* you—living, breathing, transforming you from the inside out."

He closed the book.

"That's what Michelle and I have learned. The hope of glory isn't something that comes after all the pain is over. The hope of glory is present *in* the pain—Christ in us, working through us, making something beautiful out of our mess. The groaning and the glory. The tension of a maturing faith. The slow, hard, holy work of becoming who we were meant to be."

He smiled.

"If you're struggling in your marriage today, I want you to know: there is hope. Not easy hope. Not painless hope. But real, blood-bought, resurrection hope. The same power that raised Jesus from the dead is available to you. It can raise your marriage from the dead. It can raise *you* from the dead."

He stepped back from the pulpit.

"As Paul wrote from his prison cell: 'I am glad, because it gives me a chance to complete in my own sufferings something of the untold pains for which Christ suffers on behalf of his body, the Church... And the secret is simply this: Christ in you! Yes, Christ in you bringing with him the hope of all glorious things to come.'"

The organist began to play.

And in the third row, Michelle Whitfield bowed her head, a prayer of gratitude rising from her healing heart, her hand finding her husband's across the space between them—a small, holy gesture of reaching, of staying, of choosing love one more time.

The mystery, revealed.

Christ in them.

The hope of glory.

THE END

III THE GROANING AND THE GLORY

Endnotes

1. The 2010 Haiti earthquake, which struck on January 12, 2010, killed an estimated 220,000-316,000 people and displaced 1.5 million, making it one of the deadliest natural disasters in recorded history. Cholera outbreaks in the aftermath claimed additional thousands of lives.
2. Romans 8:26: "Likewise the Spirit helps us in our weakness. For we do not know what to pray for as we ought, but the Spirit himself intercedes for us with groanings too deep for words" (ESV). This verse is central to the narrative's title and theme, suggesting that the Spirit's intercessory work continues even when human prayer fails.
3. The "dark night of the soul" (*noche oscura del alma*) is a term from the sixteenth-century Spanish mystic John of the Cross (1542-1591). In his poem and commentary of the same name, John describes a period of spiritual desolation in which God withdraws the felt sense of His presence to purify the soul and deepen faith. See John of the Cross, *The Collected Works of St. John of the Cross*, trans. Kieran Kavanaugh and Otilio Rodriguez, 3rd ed. (Washington, DC: ICS Publications, 2017).
4. Suicidal ideation in clergy is more common than often acknowledged. Studies suggest that clergy experience depression and burnout at rates comparable to or exceeding the general population, while facing unique barriers to seeking help due to professional expectations and fear of stigma.
5. Postpartum depression affects approximately 10-15% of new mothers and can manifest through persistent sadness, anxiety, intrusive thoughts, and difficulty bonding with the infant. It is distinct from the more common "baby blues" in its severity and duration.
6. Spiritual abuse refers to the misuse of religious authority to control, manipulate, or harm others. Grooming in religious contexts involves a pattern of boundary violations, special attention, isolation from other

relationships, and gradual normalization of inappropriate behavior. See Diane Langberg, *Redeeming Power: Understanding Authority and Abuse in the Church* (Grand Rapids: Brazos Press, 2020).

7. The sudden recognition of past abuse, sometimes called "delayed disclosure" or "recovered awareness," often occurs when victims encounter new information, reach developmental milestones, or experience triggers that allow previously suppressed or minimized experiences to be seen clearly.

8. Jesus's promise that the Spirit would "guide you into all the truth" (John 16:13) suggests the Spirit's ongoing work of illumination—revealing what was hidden, clarifying what was confused, and bringing believers into deeper understanding of reality.

9. Dissociation is a psychological defense mechanism in which a person disconnects from their thoughts, feelings, surroundings, or sense of identity. It often develops as a response to trauma and can range from mild detachment to more severe disconnection from reality.

10. Cognitive behavioral therapy (CBT), developed primarily by Aaron Beck in the 1960s, is an evidence-based therapeutic approach that focuses on identifying and challenging distorted thought patterns and developing healthier cognitive and behavioral responses. It has demonstrated effectiveness for depression, anxiety, and trauma-related conditions.

11. The book of Job addresses the problem of innocent suffering through the story of a righteous man who loses everything. Notably, God's response from the whirlwind (Job 38-41) does not explain Job's suffering but reveals the vastness of divine wisdom and the limitations of human understanding. Job's final response—"I had heard of you by the hearing of the ear, but now my eye sees you" (Job 42:5)—suggests that encounter with God transcends explanation.

12. The concept of the Spirit "interceding" and "carrying" believers reflects Paul's teaching in Romans 8:26-27 that the Spirit's prayers continue

even when human prayer fails. This understanding offers comfort to those experiencing spiritual desolation, suggesting that their inability to pray does not mean they are abandoned.

13. "Demon dialogues" is a term coined by Dr. Sue Johnson, the developer of Emotionally Focused Therapy (EFT), to describe the destructive interaction patterns that couples fall into when their attachment bonds are threatened. Johnson identifies three primary demon dialogues: "Find the Bad Guy" (mutual blame), "The Protest Polka" (pursue-withdraw cycle), and "Freeze and Flee" (mutual withdrawal). See Sue Johnson, *Hold Me Tight: Seven Conversations for a Lifetime of Love* (New York: Little, Brown, 2008).

14. Attachment theory, developed by John Bowlby and Mary Ainsworth, proposes that humans have an innate need for close emotional bonds and that early attachment experiences shape patterns of relating throughout life. In adult relationships, attachment fears—of abandonment or engulfment—drive much of what appears as conflict. See John Bowlby, *Attachment and Loss*, 3 vols. (New York: Basic Books, 1969-1980).

15. The pursue-withdraw cycle is one of the most common and destructive patterns in distressed couples. Research suggests that approximately 80% of couples seeking therapy exhibit this pattern, with one partner (often the woman) pursuing connection through criticism or demands while the other (often the man) withdraws emotionally or physically.

16. The "knowing" that Omar experiences—receiving specific guidance about Michelle's history with Pastor David—reflects the biblical pattern of spiritual discernment and prophetic insight. The Spirit's communication often bypasses rational deduction, providing understanding that could not have been acquired through natural means. See 1 Corinthians 12:8-10 on the "word of knowledge" as a spiritual gift.

17. Galatians 5:22-23: "But the fruit of the Spirit is love, joy, peace, patience, kindness, goodness, faithfulness, gentleness, self-control; against such things there is no law" (ESV). The relational nature of these qualities suggests that Spirit-formed character is expressed primarily in how we treat others.

18. 2 Corinthians 10:5: "We destroy arguments and every lofty opinion raised against the knowledge of God, and take every thought captive to obey Christ" (ESV). This verse provides biblical grounding for the cognitive restructuring work of CBT, reframing thought management as spiritual warfare.

19. The title "accuser of the brethren" for Satan comes from Revelation 12:10: "the accuser of our brothers has been thrown down, who accuses them day and night before our God." The accusatory "voices" that torment those struggling with depression and shame can be understood as having both psychological and spiritual dimensions.

20. Religious trauma refers to the psychological harm caused by harmful religious experiences, including spiritual abuse, authoritarian leadership, shame-based teaching, or other misuses of religious authority. Treatment often requires addressing both the psychological wounds and the theological distortions that accompanied them. See Laura Anderson, *When Religion Hurts You: Healing from Religious Trauma and the Impact of High-Control Religion* (Grand Rapids: Brazos Press, 2023).

21. Colossians 1:24 (J.B. Phillips translation): "I am glad because it gives me a chance to complete in my own sufferings something of the untold pains for which Christ suffers on behalf of his body, the Church." This mysterious verse suggests that believers' sufferings participate in Christ's redemptive work—not adding to the atonement, but extending its effects through the church.

22. Colossians 1:27 (J.B. Phillips translation): "And the secret is simply this: Christ in you! Yes, Christ in you bringing with him the hope of all

III THE GROANING AND THE GLORY

glorious things to come." The phrase "Christ in you, the hope of glory" encapsulates the mystical union between Christ and believers that is central to Pauline theology.

23. Corrie ten Boom (1892-1983) was a Dutch Christian who, along with her family, helped hide Jews during the Nazi occupation of the Netherlands. After being arrested and imprisoned in the Ravensbrück concentration camp—where her sister Betsie died—Corrie spent the rest of her life speaking about forgiveness and God's love. Her memoir *The Hiding Place* (1971) became one of the most influential Christian books of the twentieth century.

24. Betsie ten Boom's words "There is no pit so deep that God's love is not deeper still" were reportedly spoken to Corrie shortly before Betsie's death in Ravensbrück. The phrase has become one of the most quoted expressions of Christian hope in the face of extreme suffering.

25. The famous story of Corrie ten Boom encountering and forgiving the Nazi guard who had been cruel to her and Betsie at Ravensbrück is recounted in her book *Tramp for the Lord* (1974). Corrie describes being unable to raise her hand to shake the former guard's hand until she prayed for God's strength, at which point she felt a current of warmth flow through her arm.

26. Isaiah 43:2: "When you pass through the waters, I will be with you; and through the rivers, they shall not overwhelm you; when you walk through fire you shall not be burned, and the flame shall not consume you" (ESV). God's promise is not protection from suffering but presence within it.

27. The image of Christ joining Michelle in the flood rather than pulling her out reflects the incarnational theology of Emmanuel ("God with us"). The doctrine of divine impassibility has been challenged by theologians who emphasize God's solidarity with human suffering through the cross.

28. Weekend intensives for couples, often based on Emotionally Focused Therapy (EFT), typically involve 12-20 hours of concentrated work over 2-3 days. Research suggests these intensive formats can achieve results comparable to months of traditional weekly therapy. See Sue Johnson and Brent Bradley, *The Practice of Emotionally Focused Couple Therapy: Creating Connection*, 3rd ed. (New York: Routledge, 2019).
29. "Raw spots" is EFT terminology for the attachment wounds that make certain interactions particularly painful. These wounds, often formed in childhood or previous relationships, are activated by present-day triggers that symbolically resemble the original injury.
30. The concept of "attachment fears" underlying marital conflict is central to EFT. Common fears include fear of abandonment ("You'll leave me"), fear of inadequacy ("I'll never be enough for you"), and fear of engulfment ("You'll control or consume me").
31. Philippians 1:6: "And I am sure of this, that he who began a good work in you will bring it to completion at the day of Jesus Christ" (ESV). This verse grounds Christian hope not in human effort but in divine faithfulness.
32. The integration of psychological healing with spiritual formation reflects a growing recognition that human beings are whole persons whose psychological, relational, and spiritual dimensions are interconnected. See Curt Thompson, *The Soul of Shame: Retelling the Stories We Believe About Ourselves* (Downers Grove, IL: InterVarsity Press, 2015).
33. The spiral model of spiritual growth—returning to the same issues at progressively higher levels—contrasts with linear models that view repeated struggles as failure. This understanding is consistent with the classical Christian teaching on sanctification as a lifelong process.
34. The quotation about "ever-deepening devotion" and finding pleasure "not only in our perfection but in our perfecting" reflects the

understanding that sanctification itself is a gift to be enjoyed, not merely a goal to be achieved.

35. The practice of writing letters to abusers (without sending them) is a recognized therapeutic technique for processing trauma and working toward forgiveness. The ritual of burning the letter can provide symbolic closure and release.
36. Forgiveness in the Christian tradition is understood not as excusing or minimizing harm, but as releasing the offender from personal vengeance while trusting God for justice. This does not require reconciliation with the abuser or the absence of consequences. See L. Gregory Jones, *Embodying Forgiveness: A Theological Analysis* (Grand Rapids: Eerdmans, 1995).
37. The distinction between forgiveness as a choice and forgiveness as a feeling reflects the reality that emotional healing often lags behind the decision to forgive. Corrie ten Boom testified that she had to pray repeatedly for the grace to forgive her former captors, and that feelings of resentment sometimes returned even after she had genuinely forgiven.
38. The concept of hope that "holds both the groaning and the glory" reflects Paul's teaching in Romans 8:18-25, where present sufferings coexist with future glory, and the entire creation "groans" while awaiting redemption.
39. Marriage as a reflection of the gospel derives from Ephesians 5:31-32: "'Therefore a man shall leave his father and mother and hold fast to his wife, and the two shall become one flesh.' This mystery is profound, and I am saying that it refers to Christ and the church" (ESV).
40. The phrase "Christ in you, the hope of glory" (Colossians 1:27) serves as the theological center of the narrative, suggesting that transformation occurs not through human effort but through the indwelling presence of Christ, working through the Spirit, even amid ongoing struggle and pain.

IV

THE PERSEVERING RELIGION

On Enduring the Dark Night and Finding God in the Shadows

When the Lights Go Out

There is a moment in the life of faith when everything you thought you knew about God collapses into ash. This is not a sign of failure, but a crucial part of persevering faith: when darkness comes, enduring and seeking God in uncertainty is what leads to deeper, honest spirituality.

It comes differently for different people. For some, it arrives in a moment: the death of a child, the betrayal of a spouse, or a life-altering diagnosis. For others, it creeps in slowly—their certainty erodes, the divine presence fades. One morning, you may realize you've been praying to an empty room for months.

Mystics have called this season the dark night of the soul. For many contemporary believers, the experience is unnamed. They may assume that something is wrong, that their faith was never genuine, or that God has left them for unfathomable reasons. Externally, they smile on Sunday while internally they diminish, week by week.

What if the darkness signals not failed faith, but a call to deeper faith—stripping away old comforts for something truer?

Consider Omar, returning from Haiti with his soul in fragments. He had held a dying child in his arms for three days, praying for healing that never came. He had watched cholera sweep through villages while he proclaimed a God of love and power. And something in him had broken—not his theology exactly, but something deeper: the felt connection between his beliefs and his experience, the sense that the universe was fundamentally safe because God was in control.

He came home to a wife he couldn't reach, a son he didn't know how to father, and a calling that felt as a merciless joke. He stood in the pulpit and preached words that tasted like cardboard. He sat on the edge of the bathtub at night and contemplated the razor with a detachment that terrified him.

This is not the experience of a man without faith. This is the experience of a man whose faith is being tested in the crucible—burned down to its essential elements so that what remains might be gold instead of straw.

The Theology of Lament

The modern church has largely forgotten how to grieve.

We have become so enamored with the language of victory—the triumphant resurrection, the conquering King, the abundant life—that we have lost our capacity to sit with loss. When darkness comes, we immediately reach for the light switch. We quote Romans 8:28 before the body is cold. We rush past Good Friday in our hurry to reach Easter morning.

But the biblical witness tells a different story. Nearly one-third of the Psalms are laments—cries of anguish, accusations against God, desperate pleas for relief. The book of Lamentations gives voice to grief so deep it threatens to swallow the griever whole. Job stands at the center of wisdom literature, refusing to provide the easy answers we crave.

As Christopher Ash writes in his masterful commentary on Job: "The book of Job stands as a rebuke to every simplistic theology that ties suffering neatly to sin, or promises that faith will always deliver prosperity. Job's friends were certain they understood how God works. They were wrong. And their wrongness should give us pause when we are tempted to explain someone else's suffering."

Job's friends—Eliphaz, Bildad, Zophar, and even young Elihu—show the religious impulse at its worst: the urge to make sense of suffering, to fit it into a neat theological framework, to defend God against the accusations of reality. They said many true things. Their theology was orthodox. But at the end, God's anger burned against them because they "have not spoken of me what is right, as my servant Job has."

What had Job spoken? Accusations. Complaints. Demands for an audience with the Almighty. Wild swings between hope and despair. Raw, unfiltered grief that refused to be domesticated by religious propriety.

And this, somehow, was more pleasing to God than his friends' careful defenses.

The Ministry of Presence

Paul David Tripp, in his profound work on suffering, reminds us that "suffering is not a puzzle to be solved but a reality to be endured in relationship with God and with others who will sit with us in the ashes."

This is what Job's friends got wrong. They came, initially, with the right instinct. For seven days, they sat with him in silence, simply present in his pain. It was only when they opened their mouths to explain that they became agents of further harm.

There is a ministry of presence that the church desperately needs to recover. It is the ministry of sitting shiva, of bearing witness, of refusing to flee from suffering even when we have no words. It is the ministry Jesus practiced when he wept at Lazarus's tomb—even knowing he was about to raise his friend. The tears were not a failure of faith. They were an act of solidarity with the grieving.

Omar found this ministry in his spiritual director, Pastor Terrence Nix—a man who had walked through his own dark night decades earlier and emerged with a faith both gentler and fiercer than before. Nix didn't try to fix Omar. He didn't offer platitudes or premature hope. He simply sat with him, week after week, and bore witness to the unraveling.

"The Spirit is not absent in your darkness," Nix told him once. "He is *working* in it. The very fact that you're sitting here, that you haven't given up, that you're still reaching out for help—that's not your strength. That's His."

This is the persevering religion: doubt remains, but endurance persists. Suffering does not disappear, but we refuse to suffer alone. Embrace this journey—see doubts as paths to deeper understanding and endure in community, not isolation. Walk with others in their struggles, find strength in shared journeys, and witness faith transformed through endurance.

Learning to Lament

Rebekah Eklund, in her essential work *Practicing Lament*, argues that "lament is not the opposite of faith but its expression in the minor key. To lament is to bring our grief to God rather than nursing it in isolation. It is an act of trust—the trust that God can handle our anger, our confusion, our accusations."

The Psalms of Lament follow a surprising pattern. They begin by addressing God—acknowledging that even in anger, the psalmist speaks to the One who can change things. Next comes complaint, often raw and uncomfortably honest. Then comes a petition, a request for God to act. Most end with a statement of trust or praise, however fragile.

This structure matters. Lament is not mere venting or expressing negative emotion. It is a *liturgical act*—a form of prayer that takes suffering seriously while refusing to let go of God.

N.T. Wright has written extensively on the importance of lament for Christian spirituality: "The Psalms of lament teach us that faith is not about pretending everything is fine. It is about bringing our true selves—our angry, grieving, confused selves—into the presence of God and trusting that He will meet us there. A faith that cannot accommodate lament is a faith too small for the real world."

Consider how Omar learned to lament. In the early weeks after his return from Haiti, he couldn't pray at all—not in the sense of the confident, articulate prayers he had offered before. But he found himself returning, almost against his will, to the Psalms. Not the praise psalms. The dark ones. Psalm 88, which ends without resolution: "You have taken from me friend and neighbor—darkness is my closest friend." Psalm 22, which begins with the cry Jesus quoted from the cross: "My God, my God, why have you forsaken me?"

These words gave him permission to feel what he was feeling. They assured him that he was not the first to walk this road, that the people of God had been crying out from the darkness for millennia, that his experience—however isolating—was part of a long tradition.

Slowly, almost imperceptibly, lament became a form of connection. It was not the warm, fuzzy connection he'd known before, but something rawer and more honest. He stopped pretending with God and sat in the silence of his own vulnerability. In those moments of raw honesty, unshielded by pretense, he allowed himself to simply be present with God. It was only then, in that place of openness and surrender, that he found a different kind of intimacy.

The Gift of Unanswered Questions

The ending of Job has troubled readers for centuries. After thirty-seven chapters of anguished questioning, God finally speaks—but He doesn't answer Job's questions. Instead, He asks His own:

IV THE PERSEVERING RELIGION

"Where were you when I laid the foundation of the earth? Tell me, if you have understanding."

God takes Job on a tour of creation—the wild donkey and ostrich, the behemoth and leviathan, the storehouses of snow, the dwelling of light. It displays power and mystery, complexity beyond human comprehension. Job's response is not "Now I understand." Instead, he says, "Now I have *seen* you."

Christopher Ash reflects on this remarkable ending: "God's answer to Job is not an explanation but a revelation. He does not solve the problem of suffering; He overwhelms it with His presence. Job wanted to understand why. God gave him something better: Himself."

This is the most counterintuitive truth of the persevering religion: answers are not always what we need. We want explanations. We ask why—the child died, the marriage failed, the prayers went unanswered. But even if we had explanations, they would not heal us. Only presence can do that.

C.S. Lewis, in the raw pages of *A Grief Observed*, written after the death of his wife Joy, captures this truth with devastating honesty:

"When I lay these questions before God, I get no answer. But a rather special sort of 'No answer.' It is not the locked door. It is more like a silent, certainly not uncompassionate, gaze. As though He shook His head not in refusal but in waving the question aside. Like, 'Peace, child; you don't understand.'"

Lewis goes on to reflect on how his image of God had to be shattered before a truer knowledge could emerge:

"My idea of God is not a divine idea. It has to be shattered again and again. He shatters it Himself. He is the great iconoclast. Could we not almost say that this shattering is one of the marks of His presence?"

This shattering is what Omar experienced in Haiti, what Michelle experienced in the slow revelation of her mentor's abuse. Their comfortable images of God—the God who protects the innocent, the God who honors those who serve Him faithfully, the God who would never allow His children to be harmed—had to be broken. And the breaking was agonizing.

But what emerged from the rubble was not atheism, not cynicism, not the abandonment of faith. What emerged was a God who was bigger than their categories, more mysterious than their systems, more present in darkness than they had ever imagined.

The Witness of the Fathers and Mothers

The early church knew suffering in ways that most Western Christians today can barely imagine. Persecution was not a theoretical possibility but a daily reality. Martyrdom was not metaphorical but literal. And yet it was precisely in this context of suffering that the church grew most rapidly and produced some of its most profound theology.

Our dear St. John Chrysostom, was exiled twice for his faithfulness, dying on a forced march in 407 AD. From exile, he wrote: "In the furnace the gold is made pure. The soul in affliction is cleansed, the spirit refined, the heart enlarged. Suffering is the school of virtue and the test of faith."

Our good friend, Gregory of Nazianzus, lost most of his family to death within a short span of years. His reflections on grief remain remarkably relevant: "The soul that has never known sorrow cannot know the heights of joy. We are deepened by what we lose. Our capacity for God grows in proportion to our experience of emptiness without Him."

And the desert mothers and fathers, those wild saints who fled to the wilderness to do battle with their demons, understood that the spiritual life was not a smooth ascent but a brutal struggle. Amma Syncletica taught: "In the beginning there is struggle and a lot of work for those who come near to God. But after that, there is indescribable joy. It is just like building a fire: at first it's smoky and your eyes water, but later you get the desired result."

The metaphor is apt. The dark night produces smoke. Our eyes water. We question whether this spiritual endeavor is worth the effort. But the early Christians knew what we have often forgotten: that the struggle is not a sign of failure but of engagement. The smoke comes before the fire.

Perseverance as Participation

There is a strange and difficult passage in Colossians where Paul claims to "complete in my sufferings what is lacking in Christ's afflictions for the sake of his body, the church." The language is startling. What could possibly be *lacking* in Christ's afflictions? Was His sacrifice insufficient?

The Church Fathers wrestled with this passage and concluded that it speaks not of deficiency but of participation. Christ's work is complete in itself, but the application of that work continues through His body. We are called not just to receive His suffering but to participate in it—to carry in our own bodies the dying of Jesus so that His life is revealed in us.

This is the mystery of persevering faith: when we surrender our suffering to God, it becomes part of redemption. We do not just endure pain; in some way, we complete something. Our dark nights contribute to the coming dawn.

Corrie ten Boom understood this perhaps better than anyone. She had watched her sister Betsie die in Ravensbrück, a Nazi concentration camp. She had known suffering that should have destroyed her faith entirely. And yet she spent the rest of her life traveling the world, testifying that "there is no pit so deep that God's love is not deeper still."

When Corrie stood face to face with one of her former guards—a man who had participated in the brutal treatment of the prisoners—she found that she could not forgive. Her arm would not move to shake his extended hand. The hatred was too deep, the wound too fresh.

So she prayed, "Jesus, I cannot forgive this man. Give me your forgiveness."

And in that moment of surrendered inability, she felt what she described as a current passing through her arm—warmth, love, healing that was not her own. She took his hand. She spoke the words. And something broke free in her soul.

This is participation. This is the suffering that completes something. Corrie's forgiveness was not a human achievement but a divine gift flowing through a human vessel. Her wound became a window through which grace could enter the world.

Paul's Theology of Pressing On

The Man Who Knew Suffering

If anyone in the early church had credentials to speak about perseverance, it was the apostle Paul.

This was no armchair theologian spinning theories about suffering from the comfort of a study. This was a man who had been beaten with rods three times, whipped with thirty-nine lashes on five separate occasions, stoned and left for dead, shipwrecked three times, and spent a night and a day adrift in the open sea. He had known hunger and thirst, cold and exposure, the constant anxiety of caring for the churches he had planted, and the peculiar pain of being abandoned by those he had poured his life into.

And yet—and this is the astonishing thing—Paul's letters are not characterized by bitterness or despair. They overflow with joy. They pulse with hope. They radiate the kind of confidence that can only come from someone who has discovered a secret the comfortable will never learn: that suffering, when surrendered to God, becomes a doorway into deeper communion with Christ.

"I want to know Christ," Paul wrote to the Philippians, "and the power of his resurrection and the fellowship of sharing in his sufferings, becoming like him in his death, and so, somehow, attaining to the resurrection from the dead."

Notice the order. The power of resurrection comes *with* the fellowship of suffering, not instead of it. Paul does not seek to bypass the cross on his way to glory. He understands that the cross *is* the way to glory—that the path of Christ is the path of descent before ascent, of death before resurrection, of losing one's life in order to find it.

Pressing On: Philippians 3

The third chapter of Philippians contains some of the most intensely personal writing in all of Paul's letters. Here the apostle drops his guard and allows us to see the inner dynamics of his spiritual life—the struggle, the longing, the relentless forward motion that characterized his walk with Christ.

"Not that I have already obtained this or am already perfect," Paul admits, "but I press on to make it my own, because Christ Jesus has made me his own. Brothers, I do not consider that I have made it my own. But one thing I do: forgetting what lies behind and straining forward to what lies ahead, I press on toward the goal for the prize of the upward call of God in Christ Jesus."

The Greek verb translated "press on" is *diōkō*—a word that carries connotations of intense pursuit, even persecution. It is the same word used for a hunter chasing prey or an athlete straining toward the finish line. Paul is not strolling toward spiritual maturity. He is *running*. He is *chasing*. He is pouring every ounce of energy into the pursuit of Christ.

And yet crucially—this pursuit is grounded not in anxiety but in assurance. Paul presses on "because Christ Jesus has made me his own." The initiative belongs to Christ. The security belongs to Christ. Paul's striving is not an attempt to earn what he does not have but a response to having already been grasped by divine love. He runs not to win acceptance but from acceptance—propelled by grace, not driven by fear.

This distinction matters enormously for those in the dark night. The temptation in seasons of suffering is to believe that our experience of God's absence reflects His actual absence—that we have somehow fallen out of His favor, that we must earn our way back through religious performance. Paul's theology cuts against this lie. We are held by Christ. We have been made His own. And from that secure foundation, we press on—not to secure what we already possess, but to experience more fully the depths of what has already been given.

"Forgetting what lies behind" is equally crucial. Paul had much to forget—both his pre-conversion life as a persecutor of the church and his post-conversion failures and disappointments. The past, whether glorious or shameful, can become a prison that prevents forward motion. But Paul refuses to be defined by yesterday. He strains forward. He reaches. He presses on.

For Omar, this Pauline vision became a lifeline. His past contained both the corpses of children he could not save and the rubble of a faith he thought was unshakeable. He could have spent the rest of his life sifting through that wreckage, cataloging his failures, mourning what was lost. Instead, slowly, painfully, he learned to forget what lay behind and strain toward what lay ahead. Not denial—he did not pretend the past hadn't happened. But release. A refusal to let yesterday's darkness determine tomorrow's direction.

Afflicted but Not Crushed: 2 Corinthians 4

If Philippians 3 gives us the inner experience of perseverance, 2 Corinthians 4 gives us its outer manifestation. Here Paul describes the paradoxical reality of apostolic ministry—and, by extension, the paradoxical reality of all Christian existence in a fallen world:

"We are afflicted in every way, but not crushed; perplexed, but not driven to despair; persecuted, but not forsaken; struck down, but not destroyed—

always carrying in the body the death of Jesus, so that the life of Jesus may also be manifested in our bodies."

The structure is poetic, almost liturgical. Four pairs of contrast, each following the same pattern: something terrible happens, but the ultimate consequence is averted. Afflicted, but not crushed. Perplexed, but not despairing. Persecuted, but not abandoned. Struck down, but not destroyed.

This is not the language of immunity from suffering. Paul does not claim that faith protects us from affliction, perplexity, persecution, or being struck down. These things happen to believers. They happened to Paul constantly. They may be happening to you right now.

But—and here is the gospel—they do not have the final word. There is a "but not" that follows every blow. The affliction is real, but it does not crush. The perplexity is genuine, but it does not spiral into despair. The persecution is painful, but it does not mean abandonment. The striking down is brutal, but it is not destruction.

What accounts for this resilience? Paul tells us: "We have this treasure in jars of clay, to show that the surpassing power belongs to God and not to us." The treasure is the gospel, the light of the knowledge of the glory of God in the face of Jesus Christ. And it is contained in jars of clay—fragile, ordinary, easily broken vessels. The contrast is deliberate. God has placed infinite treasure in finite containers precisely so that when the containers survive what should destroy them, everyone will know the power is divine.

This is the theology of perseverance in a single image. We are clay pots. We crack and chip and sometimes shatter entirely. But we carry within us something that transcends our fragility—the very life of Christ, the resurrection power of God. And that treasure, not our own strength, is what enables us to be afflicted without being crushed.

Michelle found this passage during one of her darkest nights. She had been awake since 3 AM, nursing Elijah, her mind spinning with intrusive thoughts about her worthlessness as a mother and the contamination she felt from Pastor David's abuse. She was perplexed—could not make sense of what God was doing or why He had allowed such harm to come to her. She felt persecuted—not by external enemies, but by her own memories, her own shame, her own relentless inner critic.

And then the words of Paul came to her, unbidden: *Perplexed, but not driven to despair.*

She was perplexed. She could not deny it. But despair was not inevitable. There was a "but not" available to her, a grace that held the line even when her own resources were exhausted. She did not have to figure everything out. She only had to trust that the treasure within her—Christ Himself—was sufficient to keep her from being crushed.

The Weight of Glory: Eternal Perspective

Later in the same chapter, Paul offers one of his most remarkable statements about suffering and its relationship to future hope:

"So we do not lose heart. Though our outer self is wasting away, our inner self is being renewed day by day. For this light momentary affliction is preparing for us an eternal weight of glory beyond all comparison, as we look not to the things that are seen but to the things that are unseen. For the things that are seen are transient, but the things that are unseen are eternal."

"Light momentary affliction." The words seem almost absurd coming from a man who had endured what Paul had endured. Beatings, imprisonment, shipwreck, constant danger—and he calls it *light*? *Momentary*?

But Paul is not minimizing his suffering. He is *relativizing* it. Compared to the eternal weight of glory that awaits, even the most severe suffering in this life is light. Compared to the endless ages of communion with God, even a lifetime of affliction is momentary. Paul has gained a perspective that allows him to see his present trials in light of future hope—and from that vantage point, the math changes entirely.

This is not escapism. Paul does not retreat into thoughts of heaven to avoid engaging with earthly reality. His letters are full of practical instruction, concrete counsel, engaged concern for the churches. But he holds his earthly engagement within an eternal frame. He knows that this world is not all there is, that the sufferings of the present time are not worth comparing with the glory that will be revealed.

C.S. Lewis, reflecting on this Pauline theme, wrote in his sermon "The Weight of Glory": "If we consider the unblushing promises of reward and the staggering nature of the rewards promised in the Gospels, it would seem that Our Lord finds our desires not too strong, but too weak. We are half-hearted creatures, fooling about with drink and sex and ambition when infinite joy is offered us, like an ignorant child who wants to go on making mud pies in a slum because he cannot imagine what is meant by the offer of a holiday at the sea."

The persevering religion is sustained by this eternal perspective. We do not lose heart because we know that our present suffering is producing something—not just endurance, not just character, but an "eternal weight of glory beyond all comparison." The darkness is real, but it is not final. The night is long, but morning is coming. And when morning comes, we will discover that every tear, every wound, every moment of anguished faith has been woven into something beautiful beyond imagination.

Power Made Perfect in Weakness: 2 Corinthians 12

Perhaps nowhere is Paul's theology of perseverance more personally revealed than in his account of the "thorn in the flesh" in 2 Corinthians 12. Scholars have debated endlessly what this thorn actually was—a physical ailment, a spiritual struggle, a persistent opponent. Paul never tells us, and perhaps that ambiguity is intentional. Whatever your thorn is, you can find yourself in this passage.

"To keep me from becoming conceited because of the surpassing greatness of the revelations, a thorn was given me in the flesh, a messenger of Satan to harass me, to keep me from becoming conceited. Three times I pleaded with the Lord about this, that it should leave me."

Three times. This is not a casual prayer, a quick request tossed heavenward. This is sustained, desperate, agonized pleading. Paul wanted the thorn removed. He believed God could remove it. He asked repeatedly for deliverance.

And God said no.

Or rather, God said something more profound than either yes or no:

"My grace is sufficient for you, for my power is made perfect in weakness."

This is one of the most counterintuitive statements in all of Scripture. We expect power to be made perfect in strength—in resources, in capacity, in ability. But God works differently. His power is made perfect precisely in our weakness, in our inability, in the places where we have reached the end of ourselves.

Paul's response to this revelation is equally counterintuitive:

"Therefore I will boast all the more gladly of my weaknesses, so that the power of Christ may rest upon me. For the sake of Christ, then, I am content with weaknesses, insults, hardships, persecutions, and calamities. For when I am weak, then I am strong."

Content with weaknesses. Content with insults. Content with hardships, persecutions, calamities. This is not masochism, not some perverse delight in suffering for its own sake. This is the contentment of a man who has discovered that his weakness is the very condition for experiencing divine power. As long as he was strong, he relied on his own strength. Now that he is weak, he has no choice but to rely on Christ. And Christ, it turns out, is more than sufficient.

Omar found himself returning to this passage again and again during his recovery. His weakness had been exposed—the depression, the dissociation, the suicidal ideation. Everything he had believed about his own spiritual strength had been revealed as illusion. He was not the competent pastor, the faithful missionary, the man who had it together. He was a jar of clay, cracked and leaking, barely holding on.

And it was precisely there, in that place of exposed weakness, that he began to experience a power that was not his own. The Spirit who intercedes with groanings too deep for words. The grace that is sufficient even when—especially when—we are not. The strength that shows up after we have exhausted our own.

"I used to think God was disappointed in my weakness," Omar told Pastor Nix one evening. "Like I was failing Him by not being stronger. But now I'm starting to see it differently. My weakness is the very thing that makes room for His power. If I were strong enough on my own, I wouldn't need Him. But I'm not. And so I do. And somehow, that's exactly how it's supposed to work."

Comfort in Affliction: 2 Corinthians 1

Paul begins his second letter to the Corinthians with a remarkable meditation on the purpose of suffering:

"Blessed be the God and Father of our Lord Jesus Christ, the Father of mercies and God of all comfort, who comforts us in all our affliction, so that we may be able to comfort those who are in any affliction, with the comfort with which we ourselves are comforted by God. For as we share abundantly in Christ's sufferings, so through Christ we share abundantly in comfort too."

Here Paul reveals something essential about the economy of suffering in God's kingdom: it is never wasted. The comfort we receive in our affliction is not meant to terminate in our own relief. It is meant to flow through us to others who are afflicted. Our suffering qualifies us for a ministry that the comfortable can never perform.

REDEEMING RELIGION

This is not to say that suffering is good or that God causes it for instrumental purposes. Paul is clear that the comfort comes from God; he does not say the affliction does. But in the mysterious providence of divine redemption, even the wounds inflicted by a fallen world can become sources of healing for others.

Corrie ten Boom's ministry was possible only because of Ravensbrück. Her authority to speak about forgiveness, about the presence of God in the pit, about the love that is deeper than the deepest darkness—this authority was forged in the concentration camp. She would never have chosen that path. But having walked it, she was able to guide others through their own valleys of shadow.

Michelle began to experience this transformative dynamic as her own healing progressed. The shame she had carried from Pastor David's abuse, once processed and surrendered, became a bridge to other women carrying similar shame. She found herself able to say things that no one who hadn't been there could say: "I know. I understand. I've walked that road. And there is hope."

Her wound had become a ministry. Her suffering had become a source of comfort. Not because the abuse was good—it was evil, a violation that grieved the heart of God. But because the God of all comfort had met her in her affliction and was now using that very affliction to bring comfort to others.

The Fellowship of His Sufferings

We return, finally, to Philippians 3 and that strange phrase Paul uses: "the fellowship of sharing in his sufferings."

Fellowship—*koinōnia*—is one of Paul's favorite words. It speaks of partnership, participation, communion. And Paul applies it not only to the joyful aspects of life in Christ but also to the painful ones. There is a fellowship of suffering, a communion in pain, a participation in the cross that believers share with their Lord.

This fellowship is not something we seek for its own sake. But when it comes—as it inevitably does in a fallen world—we discover that we are not alone. Christ has walked this road before us. His sufferings were not merely historical events in first-century Israel; they are ongoing realities in which His body participates through every age.

"Now I rejoice in my sufferings for your sake," Paul writes in Colossians, "and in my flesh I am filling up what is lacking in Christ's afflictions for the sake of his body, that is, the church."

What could possibly be lacking in Christ's afflictions? Nothing, in terms of their saving efficacy—the cross was complete, the atonement finished. But the *application* of those sufferings continues through His body. We carry in our mortal flesh the dying of Jesus so that His life might be manifested. We participate in His redemptive suffering, not adding to it but extending it, bringing it to bear in places and times and relationships where only embodied presence can reach.

This is the deepest meaning of the persevering religion. We endure not merely for our own sakes, not merely to develop character or prove our faith, but for the sake of Christ's body. Our perseverance is participation in His ongoing work of redemption. Our suffering, surrendered to God, becomes part of the cosmic drama of salvation.

Omar came to understand this only gradually. His initial experience of the dark night was entirely personal—his own faith, his own doubt, his own despair. But as he began to emerge from the darkness, he discovered that something had been forged in the crucible that had value for others. His congregation, who had watched their pastor suffer publicly and recover slowly, found in his journey a template for their own. His marriage, which had nearly collapsed under the weight of mutual woundedness, became a testimony to the persevering grace of God.

"I wouldn't wish this on anyone," he told Michelle one evening, reflecting on the road they had walked. "But I also wouldn't trade what we've learned. We know things now that we couldn't have known any other way. We've met God in places we never would have gone voluntarily. And somehow—I don't fully understand how—our suffering has become part of our calling."

Paul's Perseverance as Pattern

The apostle Paul did not merely teach perseverance. He embodied it. His life was a living demonstration of what it means to press on toward the goal, to be afflicted without being crushed, to carry the dying of Jesus so that His life might be made manifest.

At the end of his life, facing execution in Rome, Paul could write to Timothy with a confidence that transcended his circumstances:

"I have fought the good fight, I have finished the race, I have kept the faith. Henceforth there is laid up for me the crown of righteousness, which the Lord, the righteous judge, will award to me on that day, and not only to me but also to all who have loved his appearing."

This is the voice of perseverance completed. Not the absence of struggle—Paul had struggled until the very end. Not the absence of suffering—he was writing from prison, awaiting death. But the presence of faithfulness, sustained over decades of hardship, resulting in a finish that honored the Lord who had called him.

We are invited into this same race. Not Paul's race exactly—our circumstances differ, our callings vary. But the same kind of race: the long obedience in the same direction, the pressing on toward the goal, the refusal to let affliction crush us or perplexity drive us to despair.

The persevering religion is not for the faint of heart. But it is for the weak, because God's power is made perfect in weakness. It is for the afflicted, because the God of all comfort meets us in our affliction. It is for the perplexed, because even when we cannot trace His hand, we can trust His heart.

And it is for all who have discovered, in the depths of their own dark night, that the light shines in the darkness—and the darkness has not overcome it.

The Practices of Endurance

If the dark night is an invitation rather than a failure, how do we respond to that invitation? What practices sustain us when the familiar markers of faith have disappeared?

First, we keep showing up. This sounds almost insultingly simple, but it is the foundation of perseverance. We return to prayer even when prayer feels like talking to a wall. We attend worship even when the songs stick in our throats. We read Scripture even when the words seem foreign and distant. We practice what might be called "the obedience of despair"—doing the right things even when we feel nothing, trusting that the feelings may eventually follow.

Omar learned this in his first months home from Haiti. He didn't want to pray. He didn't feel capable of prayer. But his spiritual director encouraged him to sit in silence for fifteen minutes each morning—no striving, no performing, just being present to the absence. "The Spirit is praying through you," Nix reminded him, "even when you have no words."

Second, we tell the truth. The persevering religion is not the pretending religion. It does not require us to fake wellness or suppress doubt. God can handle our honesty; what He cannot work with is our performance. In this journey, we must ask ourselves: What truth am I avoiding right now? This introspective question can open the space needed for a transformative self-dialogue, inviting us to confront what we hide from even ourselves.

Michelle had to learn this truth in her therapy sessions, as she finally spoke aloud the reality of her mentor's abuse. The telling was excruciating.

She shook for hours afterward. But something loosened in her chest—some coiled thing that had been feeding on shame and silence began to lose its grip. The truth, however painful, was the beginning of freedom.

Third, we accept help. The dark night cannot be traversed alone. We need companions—spiritual directors, therapists, friends who will sit with us in the ashes without rushing to explain or fix. The myth of the solitary spiritual hero is just that: a myth. Even Jesus brought Peter, James, and John with Him to Gethsemane.

Hope is not a feeling that sweeps over us in dark moments. Hope is a choice—a decision to trust that God is working even when all the evidence suggests otherwise. Optimism focuses on the expectation that things will turn out well; hope rests on the trust that God is present regardless of outcome. While optimism would have failed at Ravensbrück, hope sustained Corrie ten Boom.

Against Escapism

The Comfortable Gospel

There is a version of Christianity circulating in our time that would have been unrecognizable to the apostles.

It promises health to the sick, wealth to the poor, and success to the struggling—if only they have enough faith. It treats prayer as a transaction and God as a cosmic vending machine. It proclaims victory without the cross, resurrection without death, glory without the preceding shame. And when suffering comes—as it inevitably does—it blames the sufferer for insufficient belief.

This is not the faith once delivered to the saints. It is a domesticated religion for a consumer culture, a spirituality designed to make us comfortable rather than holy. And it is, in the end, a betrayal of the gospel it claims to proclaim.

The apostles knew nothing of such escapism. They had walked with a Messiah who was crucified. They had learned that the path to glory ran through Gethsemane. They had been scattered by persecution, imprisoned, beaten, and martyred. And in their letters—those precious documents that have shaped the church for two millennia—they consistently taught that tribulation is not an interruption of the Christian life but its essential texture.

"Through many tribulations we must enter the kingdom of God," Paul and Barnabas told the new believers in Lystra and Iconium. Not *might* enter. *Must* enter. The tribulations are not detours around the kingdom but doorways into it.

Spiritual Bypassing: The Modern Disease

Before we turn to the apostolic witness, we must name a phenomenon that has become endemic in contemporary Christianity: spiritual bypassing.

The term was coined by psychologist John Welwood to describe the use of spiritual practices and beliefs to avoid dealing with painful emotions, unresolved wounds, and developmental needs. In Christian contexts, it manifests as the deployment of religious language to short-circuit genuine engagement with suffering.

"Just give it to God." "Have more faith." "Everything happens for a reason." "God is in control." These phrases, which contain kernels of truth, become tools of avoidance when used to suppress rather than process pain. They allow us to maintain a veneer of spiritual maturity while the unaddressed wounds fester beneath the surface.

Michelle encountered this bypassing repeatedly in the early weeks after realizing the truth about Pastor David. Well-meaning friends quoted Romans 8:28 as if it were an anesthetic. Church members encouraged her to "forgive and move on" before she had even begun to grieve what had been done to her. The implicit message was clear: good Christians don't dwell on pain. Real faith moves quickly to victory.

But this is not faith. It is denial dressed in religious clothing. And it produces not healing but deeper woundedness—the original trauma now compounded by the shame of not being "spiritual enough" to simply let it go.

The apostles offer a different model entirely. Their letters do not bypass suffering; they walk straight through it. They do not promise escape from tribulation; they promise the presence of Christ within it. And they insist, with uncomfortable clarity, that the refining fire of affliction is essential to the formation of genuine faith.

Peter: The Apostle of Fiery Trials

Peter had learned about suffering the hard way.

He had watched Jesus arrested, tried, and crucified. He had denied his Lord three times and wept bitterly in the aftermath. He had been restored by grace and commissioned to feed Christ's sheep. And he had spent the subsequent decades being persecuted for the faith he once abandoned.

When Peter writes to the scattered believers of Asia Minor, he writes as one who knows the cost of discipleship. And his message is not escape but endurance:

"Beloved, do not be surprised at the fiery trial when it comes upon you to test you, as though something strange were happening to you. But rejoice insofar as you share Christ's sufferings, that you may also rejoice and be glad when his glory is revealed."

Do not be surprised. The fiery trial is not an aberration. It is not a sign of God's displeasure or your lack of faith. It is the normal Christian experience in a fallen world. To be surprised by suffering is to have been formed by a false gospel—a gospel that promised immunity rather than presence, escape rather than endurance.

IV THE PERSEVERING RELIGION

Peter continues: "If you are insulted for the name of Christ, you are blessed, because the Spirit of glory and of God rests upon you."

Here is a calculus that makes no sense to the prosperity gospel. Insult equals blessing? Suffering equals glory? But Peter is not speaking paradoxically for rhetorical effect. He is describing spiritual reality. The Spirit rests in a particular way upon those who suffer for Christ's name. There is a glory available in affliction that the comfortable will never know.

Earlier in the same letter, Peter had explained the purpose of trials:

"In this you rejoice, though now for a little while, if necessary, you have been grieved by various trials, so that the tested genuineness of your faith—more precious than gold that perishes though it is tested by fire—may be found to result in praise and glory and honor at the revelation of Jesus Christ."

Faith must be tested. There is no other way to prove its genuineness. Gold is refined by fire; so is trust in God. The prosperity gospel, which promises a faith that protects from fire, produces a faith that cannot survive fire. It is fool's gold—impressive in appearance, worthless under pressure.

Peter goes further still, grounding the call to suffering in the example of Christ Himself:

"For to this you have been called, because Christ also suffered for you, leaving you an example, so that you might follow in his steps."

Called to suffering. The language is unavoidable. This is not an unfortunate side effect of Christian faith but its essential shape. We follow a suffering Savior. His path is our path. His cross prefigures our own.

The comfortable gospel has no category for this. It cannot accommodate a God who calls His beloved children into pain. And so it must either ignore these passages or reinterpret them beyond recognition—claiming that such suffering was for the apostolic age only, or that it refers to some metaphorical suffering rather than the actual hardship of embodied existence.

But Peter was writing to real people facing real persecution—exile, economic hardship, social ostracism, and sometimes death. He was not speaking in metaphors. He was preparing them for the fiery trial that was even then kindling around them.

James: Joy in the Midst of Trials

James, the brother of Jesus and leader of the Jerusalem church, opens his letter with a command that must have seemed outrageous to his first readers:

"Count it all joy, my brothers, when you meet trials of various kinds, for you know that the testing of your faith produces steadfastness. And let steadfastness have its full effect, that you may be perfect and complete, lacking in nothing."

Count it all joy. Not "grit your teeth and endure." Not "pretend it doesn't hurt." But *joy*—the deep gladness that comes from knowing that the trial is producing something, that the pain has purpose, that the fire is refining rather than destroying.

This is the opposite of spiritual bypassing. James does not tell his readers to deny the reality of their trials or to claim a victory they have not yet experienced. He tells them to *reframe* their trials—to see them through the lens of divine purpose. The testing of faith produces steadfastness. Steadfastness, given its full effect, produces maturity and completeness.

Without the testing, there is no steadfastness. Without steadfastness, there is no completion. The trial is not an obstacle to spiritual growth; it is the very means of spiritual growth.

James later returns to this theme, invoking the example of the prophets and of Job:

"As an example of suffering and patience, brothers, take the prophets who spoke in the name of the Lord. Behold, we consider those blessed who remained steadfast. You have heard of the steadfastness of Job, and you have seen the purpose of the Lord, how the Lord is compassionate and merciful."

The prophets suffered. Job suffered. And we call them blessed—not because their suffering was pleasant, but because they remained steadfast through it. The purpose of the Lord, which was hidden during the trial, became visible afterward. God's compassion and mercy were revealed not by removing the suffering but by meeting His servants within it and bringing them through to the other side.

James also offers a crucial corrective to those who would manipulate faith for personal gain:

"You ask and do not receive, because you ask wrongly, to spend it on your passions."

Prayer is not a mechanism for getting what we want. Faith is not a lever for manipulating divine favor. The prosperity gospel, which treats God as a means to human ends, has inverted the proper order. We exist for God's purposes, not He for ours. And sometimes His purposes include suffering that we would never choose and cannot understand.

John: Overcoming Through Endurance

The apostle John, writing in his old age to churches under pressure, sounds the same note of costly discipleship.

"Do not be surprised, brothers, that the world hates you," he writes in his first letter. The echo of Peter is unmistakable. Suffering at the hands of the world is not surprising but expected. To be hated by the world is, in a strange way, a validation of authentic faith. Jesus had warned His disciples: "If the world hates you, know that it has hated me before it hated you."

John also warns against the seduction of worldly comfort:

"Do not love the world or the things in the world. If anyone loves the world, the love of the Father is not in him. For all that is in the world—the desires of the flesh and the desires of the eyes and pride of life—is not from the Father but is from the world. And the world is passing away along with its desires, but whoever does the will of God abides forever."

The comfortable gospel loves the world. It baptizes worldly desires—for wealth, for health, for success, for ease—and calls them spiritual blessings. But John is clear: the love of the world and the love of the Father are mutually exclusive. We cannot serve God and mammon. We cannot pursue comfort and carry our cross.

This does not mean that physical blessings are evil or that God never provides material abundance. But it does mean that such things cannot be the measure of spiritual health or the goal of Christian faith. When they become so, we have exchanged the eternal for the temporal, the imperishable for the perishing.

John's first letter also includes a crucial warning about discernment:

"Beloved, do not believe every spirit, but test the spirits to see whether they are from God, for many false prophets have gone out into the world."

The spirits must be tested. Not every teaching that claims divine authority actually possesses it. And the prosperity gospel, with its promises of escape from suffering and its manipulation of faith for material gain, fails the test. It does not align with the apostolic witness. It does not bear the marks of cruciform faith. It is, whatever its intentions, a false prophecy that leads God's people away from the path of genuine discipleship.

Revelation: The Letters to the Seven Churches

Nowhere is the apostolic critique of comfortable Christianity more vivid than in the letters to the seven churches in Revelation. These messages, dictated by the risen Christ to the apostle John, offer a divine assessment of actual congregations—their strengths, their failures, their path forward.

To Smyrna, the suffering church, Christ says: "I know your tribulation and your poverty (but you are rich)... Do not fear what you are about to suffer. Behold, the devil is about to throw some of you into prison, that you may be tested, and for ten days you will have tribulation. Be faithful unto death, and I will give you the crown of life."

The church at Smyrna was poor by worldly standards but rich in Christ's estimation. And Christ's word to them is not "I will remove your suffering" but "Do not fear what you are about to suffer." More tribulation is coming. Be faithful unto death. The crown comes after the cross, not instead of it.

To Pergamum, Christ acknowledges that they dwell "where Satan's throne is" and yet have held fast to His name. But He also warns against those who hold to false teaching—the teaching of Balaam, who "taught Balak to put a stumbling block before the sons of Israel." False teaching leads to compromise, and compromise leads to destruction.

To Thyatira, Christ commends their love, faith, service, and patient endurance. But He also rebukes them for tolerating "Jezebel"—a false prophetess who seduces God's servants into sexual immorality and the eating of food sacrificed to idols. The call is to hold fast "until I come."

To Sardis, the rebuke is devastating: "I know your works. You have the reputation of being alive, but you are dead." Sardis looked healthy from the outside. They had a name for spiritual vitality. But Christ saw through the performance to the emptiness beneath. "Wake up, and strengthen what remains and is about to die, for I have not found your works complete in the sight of my God."

This is the diagnosis for much of comfortable Christianity. We have a reputation for being alive. Our churches are full, our programs impressive, our worship polished. But beneath the surface, something is dying—or already dead. We have substituted activity for intimacy, performance for presence, the appearance of faith for its reality.

To Philadelphia, Christ offers commendation without rebuke: "I know that you have but little power, and yet you have kept my word and have not denied my name... Because you have kept my word about patient endurance, I will keep you from the hour of trial that is coming on the whole world, to try those who dwell on the earth."

Note the phrase: "my word about patient endurance." Christ has a word about patient endurance. It is central to His teaching. And Philadelphia has kept it. Their little power is not a deficiency but a credential—they have learned to rely on Christ's strength rather than their own.

To Laodicea, finally, comes the most famous and most damning assessment: "I know your works: you are neither cold nor hot. Would that you were either cold or hot! So, because you are lukewarm, and neither hot nor cold, I will spit you out of my mouth. For you say, I am rich, I have prospered, and I need nothing, not realizing that you are wretched, pitiable, poor, blind, and naked."

Laodicea is the prosperity gospel made flesh. They are rich. They have prospered. They need nothing—not even, it seems, God Himself. And this self-sufficient wealth has made them blind to their true condition. They are wretched, pitiable, poor, blind, and naked. The very blessings they celebrate have become the barriers to genuine faith.

Christ's counsel to Laodicea is not "continue to prosper" but "buy from me gold refined by fire, that you may be rich, and white garments so that you may clothe yourself and the shame of your nakedness may not be seen, and salve to anoint your eyes, so that you may see."

Gold refined by fire. The image returns again. True spiritual wealth is not the absence of fire but the presence of refining. It is not ease that makes us rich in Christ but the trial that burns away everything false, leaving only what is genuine.

The Manipulation of Faith

The prosperity gospel is, at its heart, an attempt to manipulate faith for human ends.

It treats God as a formula: sufficient faith plus positive confession equals desired outcome. It transforms prayer from communion with a Person into a technique for acquiring things. It measures spiritual health by material prosperity and blames the suffering for their own affliction.

But faith cannot be manipulated. God is not a vending machine. And the attempt to use spiritual means for carnal ends is as old as Simon Magus, who offered money for the power of the Holy Spirit and was told, "May your silver perish with you, because you thought you could obtain the gift of God with money!"

James warned against this manipulation in his letter: "You ask and do not receive, because you ask wrongly, to spend it on your passions." And he exposed the folly of presumptuous planning: "Come now, you who say, 'Today or tomorrow we will go into such and such a town and spend a year there and trade and make a profit'—yet you do not know what tomorrow will bring... Instead you ought to say, 'If the Lord wills, we will live and do this or that.'"

The prosperity gospel says, "I will live and prosper because I have claimed it in faith." The apostolic gospel says, "If the Lord wills." The difference is not mere semantics. It is the difference between a faith that submits to God's sovereignty and a faith that attempts to override it.

Omar encountered this manipulative faith during his crisis. Well-meaning believers told him that his depression was a result of insufficient faith—that if he would only believe more strongly, confess more positively, the darkness would lift. The implicit accusation was crushing: not only was he suffering, but his suffering was his own fault.

But this counsel was not wisdom. It was cruelty dressed in religious language. And it contradicted everything the apostles taught about the normalcy of suffering in the Christian life. Paul had a thorn in the flesh that God declined to remove. Peter was crucified upside down. James was beheaded by Herod. John was exiled to Patmos. Not one of them escaped suffering through superior faith. They endured suffering through the grace of a God who was present in the fire.

The Way of the Lamb

In the book of Revelation, there is a recurring phrase that describes the followers of Christ. They are called "those who follow the Lamb wherever he goes."

Wherever the Lamb goes. Not just to green pastures and still waters, but to Gethsemane and Golgotha. Not just to resurrection morning, but through the valley of the shadow of death. The Lamb was slain. Those who follow Him must be willing to share His fate.

"They have conquered him by the blood of the Lamb and by the word of their testimony," John writes of the faithful martyrs, "for they loved not their lives even unto death."

They loved not their lives even unto death. This is the disposition that the comfortable gospel cannot produce. It loves life too much. It clings too tightly. It has not learned the secret that Jesus taught: "Whoever would save his life will lose it, but whoever loses his life for my sake will find it."

The comfortable gospel produces Christians who are unprepared for suffering. When the fiery trial comes—and it always comes—they have no category for it. They feel betrayed by the God they thought had promised them protection. Their faith, untested by fire, proves to be the fool's gold that cannot survive the refiner's furnace.

But the apostolic gospel produces Christians who are ready. They do not seek suffering, but they do not run from it. They know that the path to glory runs through the cross. They have counted the cost and found Christ worth any price. And when the trial comes, they discover what the comfortable never learn: that the presence of Christ in the fire is better than the absence of fire without Him.

IV THE PERSEVERING RELIGION

Recovering the Apostolic Vision

What would it mean to recover the apostolic vision of suffering for contemporary Christianity?

It would mean, first, telling the truth. The truth that suffering is normal. The truth that faith does not exempt us from pain. The truth that the refining fire is not a sign of divine displeasure but of divine investment—gold is refined because it is valuable, not because it is worthless.

It would mean, second, rejecting the manipulation of faith. God is not a technique. Prayer is not a formula. We come to God as children to a Father, not as consumers to a vendor. And sometimes the Father's answer is no—not because our faith is insufficient, but because His wisdom exceeds our understanding.

It would mean, third, embracing the way of the Lamb. Following Christ wherever He goes, even when He goes to places we would not choose. Losing our lives in order to find them. Taking up our cross daily and discovering that the burden is lighter than we feared, because He carries it with us.

It would mean, fourth, practicing genuine engagement rather than spiritual bypassing. Facing our pain rather than suppressing it. Doing the hard work of grief and healing rather than covering our wounds with religious Band-Aids. Trusting that God is big enough to handle our honest emotions and present enough to meet us in our darkest nights.

And it would mean, finally, recovering the eschatological hope that sustained the apostles. They endured because they knew that the sufferings of the present time are not worth comparing with the glory that will be revealed. They pressed on because they saw, by faith, a city whose builder and maker is God. They were faithful unto death because they knew that death was not the end—that the Lamb who was slain is also the Lamb who lives forever, and that those who share His sufferings will share His glory.

This is the persevering religion. It is not comfortable. It is not easy. It does not promise escape from tribulation but endurance through it. And it produces a faith that has been tested by fire and found genuine—more precious than gold, resulting in praise and glory and honor at the revelation of Jesus Christ.

"Through many tribulations we must enter the kingdom of God."

Not around them. Not over them. Through them.

And on the other side, waiting with nail-scarred hands extended in welcome, stands the One who walked the road before us—the Lamb who was slain, the Lord who conquered death, the faithful witness who calls us to follow wherever He goes.

The Morning Comes

There is no formula for the ending of the dark night. It comes differently for each person, sometimes gradually, sometimes suddenly, sometimes not fully in this life at all. But the witness of Scripture and tradition is that morning does come. Joy does return. The presence that seemed so absent reveals itself to have been there all along, hidden in the darkness, working unseen.

May your morning come with the gentle light that unveils hope, joy, and presence anew. May the resilience built through your night guide your steps into the dawn, as the shadows give way to the realized promise of enduring love and peace.

Omar's morning came in stages. There was the night he dreamed of Esther—the little girl who had died in his arms—and woke not with grief but with peace. There was the moment in therapy when he realized the suicidal thoughts had faded, replaced by something that seemed nearly like desire for life. There was the Sunday morning when the words of the hymn suddenly caught in his throat, not because they were meaningless but because they were overwhelmingly true.

Michelle's morning came differently—in the slow release of bitterness toward Pastor David, in the growing capacity to trust Omar even when old suspicions clawed at her heart, in the gradual rediscovery of a God who was not her abuser, who had been grieved by what was done to her, who was even now bringing beauty from ashes.

Neither of them would call themselves "healed" in any complete sense. The wounds remain, though they no longer bleed. The memories persist, though they no longer dominate. They have learned to live with scars, to find in those scars a strange credential—a qualification to sit with others in their own dark nights, to say with authority: "I know. I've been there. And there is hope."

This is the fruit of persevering faith: suffering is not eliminated but redeemed. We do not return to innocence, but arrive at something better—a tested faith, proven hope, and love refined by trials.

As Christopher Ash concludes his meditation on Job: "The book does not promise us an explanation. It promises us something better. It promises us that the God who made the behemoth and the leviathan, who commands the morning and walks in the recesses of the deep—this God is with us. And in the end, His presence is enough."

The Persevering God

Finally, we must remember that perseverance is not primarily something we do. It is something we receive.

The God who calls us to endure is Himself an enduring God. He has not abandoned His creation, though millennia of human rebellion might justify such abandonment. He has not given up on His people, though our faithlessness has been staggering in its consistency. He perseveres with us, year after year, generation after generation, bearing with our slowness and stupidity, never letting go.

The cross is the ultimate proof of divine perseverance. There, in the darkness of Golgotha, the Son of God endured what we cannot imagine so that we might be brought home. He did not call down legions of angels. He did not escape. He persevered—to the end, through the end, and out the other side into resurrection morning.

And now He invites us into that same perseverance. Not as an achievement but as a participation. Not in our own strength but in His. The Spirit who raised Jesus from the dead dwells in us, and He is the Spirit of endurance—the one who intercedes with groanings too deep for words, who helps us in our weakness, who carries what we cannot carry ourselves.

"In ever-deepening devotion to Him," one ancient writer observed, "our hearts begin and continue to swell with life, and hope, and peace, and joy, and pleasure not only in our perfection but in our *perfecting*. Now, of course, this life, and hope, and peace, and joy, and pleasure aren't void of the pain, and suffering, and decay, and the groan for the awaited and coming redemption. But though they accompany one another, the tension serves to develop and deepen a real devotion in and to our communion with God."

The tension does not resolve—not fully, not in this age. We groan with all creation, awaiting the redemption of our bodies. We hope for what we do not see and wait for it with patience. We walk by faith, not by sight.

But we do not walk alone. The persevering God walks with us. And in His company, we discover that we can endure more than we ever imagined—that the dark night, far from destroying us, has become the forge in which something unbreakable is being made.

This is the persevering religion. It is not for the faint of heart. But it is, finally, for the honest. For those who have stopped pretending. For those who have learned to lament. For those who have discovered that the God who seems absent in the darkness has been there all along—closer than our breath, more faithful than our doubts, persevering with us until the morning comes.

The Rewards of Overcoming: Promises to the Faithful

The God Who Rewards

Lest we think the Christian life is nothing but suffering without consolation, Scripture is replete with promises to those who endure.

The author of Hebrews reminds us that "whoever would draw near to God must believe that he exists and that he rewards those who seek him." Our God is a rewarder. He is not indifferent to faithfulness. He sees the secret struggles, the quiet endurance, the choices to trust when doubt would be easier. And He promises that none of it is in vain.

This is not the prosperity gospel's transactional reward—faith as investment, blessing as return. It is something far deeper: the eschatological promise that those who share in Christ's sufferings will share in His glory, that the light momentary affliction is preparing an eternal weight of glory beyond all comparison.

"Blessed is the man who remains steadfast under trial," James writes, "for when he has stood the test he will receive the crown of life, which God has promised to those who love him."

The crown comes after the test. The reward follows the perseverance. And the reward is not mere compensation for suffering endured but participation in the very life of God—a life that death cannot touch, that sorrow cannot diminish, that will endure when all else has passed away.

The Promises to the Overcomers

In the letters to the seven churches, the risen Christ attaches a specific promise to each congregation—a reward for those who overcome. Taken together, these promises form a breathtaking vision of what awaits those who persevere through tribulation.

To Ephesus: "To the one who overcomes I will grant to eat of the tree of life, which is in the paradise of God."

The tree of life, from which Adam and Eve were barred after the fall, will be restored to the faithful. What was lost in Eden will be regained in the new creation. The curse will be reversed. Death itself will be swallowed up in life.

To Smyrna: "The one who overcomes will not be hurt by the second death."

Physical death may claim the martyrs—Christ has just told them to be faithful "unto death." But the second death, the final judgment, holds no terror for those who belong to Christ. They may die once, but they will live forever.

To Pergamum: "To the one who overcomes I will give some of the hidden manna, and I will give him a white stone, with a new name written on the stone that no one knows except the one who receives it."

Hidden manna—the bread of heaven, the sustenance that never fails. And a white stone with a new name—a symbol of acquittal, of intimacy, of identity known fully by God and received as pure gift. The overcomer will be nourished and named by the One who knows them completely.

To Thyatira: "The one who overcomes and who keeps my works until the end, to him I will give authority over the nations, and he will rule them with a rod of iron, as when earthen pots are broken in pieces, even as I myself have received authority from my Father. And I will give him the morning star."

Authority and the morning star—participation in Christ's reign and possession of Christ Himself, who elsewhere identifies as "the bright morning star." The faithful will not merely observe the kingdom; they will help administer it. And they will possess the One whose coming signals the end of night.

To Sardis: "The one who overcomes will be clothed thus in white garments, and I will never blot his name out of the book of life. I will confess his name before my Father and before his angels."

White garments of purity and victory. Permanent inscription in the book of life. And—perhaps most staggering—Christ's personal acknowledgment before the Father: "This one is mine." The overcomer will be publicly claimed by the Son of God in the presence of the heavenly court.

To Philadelphia: "The one who overcomes, I will make him a pillar in the temple of my God. Never shall he go out of it, and I will write on him the name of my God, and the name of the city of my God, the new Jerusalem, which comes down from my God out of heaven, and my own new name."

A pillar in God's temple—permanent, load-bearing, essential. The overcomer will never be cast out, never displaced, never made to wander again. And upon them will be inscribed the threefold name: the name of God, the name of the city, and Christ's own new name. They will belong utterly, irrevocably, eternally.

To Laodicea: "The one who overcomes, I will grant him to sit with me on my throne, as I also overcame and sat down with my Father on his throne."

The final promise is almost too much to bear. The overcomer will share Christ's throne. Not merely serve in His presence, not merely worship at His feet, but sit *with* Him in the place of honor and authority. "As I overcame"—Christ's victory becomes the template and the ground of our own. His throne becomes our throne. His glory becomes our inheritance.

Crowns

Again Paul, cataloging his sufferings to the Corinthians, arrived at this remarkable conclusion:

"For this light momentary affliction is preparing for us an eternal weight of glory beyond all comparison, as we look not to the things that are seen but to the things that are unseen. For the things that are seen are transient, but the things that are unseen are eternal."

The arithmetic of eternity transforms everything. Suffering that seems unbearable in the moment is revealed as "light" when weighed against infinite glory. Trials that feel endless prove to be "momentary" when measured against everlasting life. The calculus only works if the glory is real—but Paul was convinced it was, and the apostolic witness agrees.

Peter speaks of "an inheritance that is imperishable, undefiled, and unfading, kept in heaven for you." Paul tells Timothy that "there is laid up for me the crown of righteousness, which the Lord, the righteous judge, will award to me on that day, and not only to me but also to all who have loved his appearing."

Crowns appear throughout the New Testament as symbols of the overcomer's reward: the crown of life promised to those who endure trial, the crown of righteousness for those who love Christ's appearing, the crown of glory for faithful shepherds, the imperishable crown for those who exercise self-control in the race of faith. These crowns are not mere decorations but signifiers of victory—the athlete's laurel, the monarch's diadem, awarded to those who have fought and finished and kept the faith.

The Final Vision

The book of Revelation concludes with a vision of what awaits the overcomers—a vision so beautiful it strains the capacity of human language:

"Then I saw a new heaven and a new earth, for the first heaven and the first earth had passed away, and the sea was no more. And I saw the holy city, new Jerusalem, coming down out of heaven from God, prepared as a bride adorned for her husband. And I heard a loud voice from the throne saying, 'Behold, the dwelling place of God is with man. He will dwell with them, and they will be his people, and God himself will be with them as their God. He will wipe away every tear from their eyes, and death shall be no more, neither shall there be mourning, nor crying, nor pain anymore, for the former things have passed away.'"

Every tear wiped away. Death abolished. Mourning and crying and pain—the constant companions of earthly existence—banished forever. The former things, including all the suffering that characterized them, will have passed away entirely.

And in their place: the presence of God. God Himself. Not mediated through temple or priest, not glimpsed through a glass darkly, but immediate, intimate, face to face. "They will see his face, and his name will be on their foreheads... And they will reign forever and ever."

This is what the overcomers inherit. This is what awaits on the other side of tribulation. Not merely the absence of suffering but the presence of glory—the fullness of communion with God for which we were created and toward which all our longing has been reaching.

Present Suffering, Future Glory

The apostle Paul, summarizing the relationship between present suffering and future reward, wrote:

"For I consider that the sufferings of this present time are not worth comparing with the glory that is to be revealed to us. For the creation waits with eager longing for the revealing of the sons of God... And not only the creation, but we ourselves, who have the firstfruits of the Spirit, groan inwardly as we wait eagerly for adoption as sons, the redemption of our bodies. For in this hope we were saved."

We groan now. Creation groans with us. The Spirit Himself intercedes for us with groanings too deep for words. But the groaning is not the end of the story. It is the birth pang that precedes the new creation. It is the labor that brings forth glory.

Omar and Michelle learned to hold this hope during their darkest nights. The suffering was real—they did not minimize it or pretend it away. But they came to see it within an eternal frame. The present darkness would not last forever. Morning was coming. And when it came, every tear would be answered, every wound healed, every faithful choice vindicated.

"If we endure," Paul wrote to Timothy, "we will also reign with him."

The endurance comes first. The reigning follows. And the One who has prepared such rewards for His overcomers is faithful—He will not abandon us in the trial but will bring us through to the glory He has promised.

The persevering religion is costly. But the reward is beyond all calculation: the tree of life, the crown of glory, the morning star, the throne shared with Christ, the eternal weight of glory, and—best of all—the face of God Himself, seen at last without veil or shadow.

"Be faithful unto death," Christ says to His suffering church, "and I will give you the crown of life."

The crown is coming. The morning is near. Hold fast. Persevere.

IV THE PERSEVERING RELIGION

Endnotes

1. The phrase "dark night of the soul" (*noche oscura del alma*) originates with the sixteenth-century Spanish mystic John of the Cross (1542-1591), who described a period of spiritual desolation in which God withdraws the felt sense of His presence to purify the soul and deepen faith. See John of the Cross, *The Collected Works of St. John of the Cross*, trans. Kieran Kavanaugh and Otilio Rodriguez, 3rd ed. (Washington, DC: ICS Publications, 2017).
2. The cholera epidemic following the 2010 Haiti earthquake killed an estimated 10,000 people and infected over 800,000. The outbreak was later traced to a United Nations peacekeeping base, adding layers of moral complexity to the disaster.
3. Approximately one-third of the 150 Psalms are classified as laments, including individual laments (Psalms 3, 22, 42-43, 88, etc.) and communal laments (Psalms 44, 74, 79, 80, etc.). This proportion suggests that honest expression of grief and complaint was central to Israelite worship.
4. Christopher Ash, *Job: The Wisdom of the Cross*, Preaching the Word (Wheaton, IL: Crossway, 2014). Ash's commentary is notable for its pastoral sensitivity and its emphasis on Job as a book that refuses easy answers to the problem of suffering.
5. Job 42:7: "After the LORD had spoken these words to Job, the LORD said to Eliphaz the Temanite: 'My anger burns against you and against your two friends, for you have not spoken of me what is right, as my servant Job has'" (ESV). The divine vindication of Job's raw honesty over his friends' orthodox theology is one of the most startling elements of the book.
6. Paul David Tripp, *Suffering: Gospel Hope When Life Doesn't Make Sense* (Wheaton, IL: Crossway, 2018). Tripp, a pastor and counselor,

emphasizes the relational dimension of suffering and the importance of presence over explanation.

7. John 11:35: "Jesus wept." This shortest verse in the English Bible carries profound theological weight, demonstrating that grief is not incompatible with faith—even faith that knows resurrection is imminent.

8. Romans 8:26: "Likewise the Spirit helps us in our weakness. For we do not know what to pray for as we ought, but the Spirit himself intercedes for us with groanings too deep for words" (ESV).

9. Rebekah Eklund, *Practicing Lament: A Practical Theological Exploration* (Eugene, OR: Wipf & Stock, forthcoming). Eklund's work explores how the practice of lament can be recovered for contemporary Christian worship and spiritual formation.

10. The structure of lament psalms typically includes: (1) address to God, (2) complaint, (3) confession of trust, (4) petition, and (5) vow of praise or statement of assurance. This structure maintains relationship with God even while expressing anguish.

11. N.T. Wright has addressed the theology of lament in numerous works, including *Evil and the Justice of God* (Downers Grove, IL: IVP Books, 2006) and various sermons and lectures. Wright emphasizes that lament is a form of faith, not its opposite.

12. Psalm 88 is unique among the lament psalms in that it contains no resolution, no turn toward praise. It ends in darkness: "You have caused my beloved and my friend to shun me; my companions have become darkness" (v. 18, ESV). Its inclusion in the canon validates the experience of unresolved grief.

13. Psalm 22:1: "My God, my God, why have you forsaken me?" (ESV). Jesus quoted this psalm from the cross (Matthew 27:46; Mark 15:34), identifying His own suffering with the psalmist's experience of divine abandonment.

14. Job 38:4: "Where were you when I laid the foundation of the earth? Tell me, if you have understanding" (ESV). God's response to Job's questioning takes the form of counter-questions that reveal the vast difference between divine and human perspective.
15. Job 42:5: "I had heard of you by the hearing of the ear, but now my eye sees you" (ESV). Job's final response suggests that encounter with God transcends explanation—that presence is ultimately more healing than answers.
16. Ash, *Job: The Wisdom of the Cross*, 412.
17. C.S. Lewis, *A Grief Observed* (London: Faber and Faber, 1961). Lewis wrote this raw journal of grief after the death of his wife, Joy Davidman, in 1960. Originally published under a pseudonym, it remains one of the most honest accounts of bereavement in Christian literature.
18. Lewis, *A Grief Observed*, 52.
19. Lewis, *A Grief Observed*, 66. The image of God as "iconoclast"—one who shatters idols, including our idolatrous images of Him—suggests that the dark night may serve to destroy false conceptions of God so that truer ones can emerge.
20. John Chrysostom (c. 349-407), Archbishop of Constantinople, was exiled twice for his outspoken preaching against corruption in the imperial court. He died during a forced march to a more remote place of exile, his last words reportedly being "Glory to God for all things."
21. Gregory of Nazianzus (329-390), one of the Cappadocian Fathers, lost his father, brother, and sister in quick succession. His theological orations and personal letters reveal a faith tested and deepened by profound grief.
22. *Apophthegmata Patrum* (Sayings of the Desert Fathers), Amma Syncletica 1. The fire and smoke metaphor captures the reality that

spiritual growth often begins with discomfort before yielding its benefits.

23. Colossians 1:24: "Now I rejoice in my sufferings for your sake, and in my flesh I am filling up what is lacking in Christ's afflictions for the sake of his body, that is, the church" (ESV). This difficult verse does not suggest deficiency in Christ's atoning work but rather the ongoing participation of His body in redemptive suffering.

24. Corrie ten Boom (1892-1983), *The Hiding Place* (Washington Depot, CT: Chosen Books, 1971). Ten Boom's testimony of faith forged in Ravensbrück concentration camp has become one of the most influential Christian narratives of the twentieth century.

25. Betsie ten Boom's words "There is no pit so deep that God's love is not deeper still" were spoken shortly before her death in Ravensbrück and have become one of the most quoted expressions of Christian hope in extremity.

26. The story of Corrie ten Boom's encounter with the former Ravensbrück guard and her struggle to forgive him is recounted in *Tramp for the Lord* (Fort Washington, PA: CLC Publications, 1974). Her testimony that forgiveness came as a gift when she prayed for what she could not produce illustrates the Spirit's work in sanctification.

2 Corinthians 11:24-27: Paul's catalogue of sufferings includes "five times I received at the hands of the Jews the forty lashes less one. Three times I was beaten with rods. Once I was stoned. Three times I was shipwrecked; a night and a day I was adrift at sea" (ESV).

27. Philippians 3:10-11: "that I may know him and the power of his resurrection, and may share his sufferings, becoming like him in his death, that by any means possible I may attain the resurrection from the dead" (ESV).

IV THE PERSEVERING RELIGION

28. Philippians 3:12-14 (ESV). The Greek verb *diōkō* (press on, pursue) appears in verse 12 and 14, conveying intense, purposeful pursuit.
29. The distinction between striving from acceptance versus striving for acceptance is crucial to understanding Paul's spirituality. His effort flows from security in Christ, not anxiety about his standing. See Michael J. Gorman, *Cruciformity: Paul's Narrative Spirituality of the Cross* (Grand Rapids: Eerdmans, 2001).
3   Corinthians 4:8-10 (ESV). The fourfold structure of affliction/not crushed, perplexed/not despairing, persecuted/not forsaken, struck down/not destroyed creates a poetic pattern that emphasizes the consistent "but not" of divine preservation.
30. 2 Corinthians 4:7: "But we have this treasure in jars of clay, to show that the surpassing power belongs to God and not to us" (ESV). The "treasure" is "the light of the knowledge of the glory of God in the face of Jesus Christ" (v. 6).
31. 2 Corinthians 4:16-18 (ESV). Paul's phrase "light momentary affliction" (*to parautika elaphron tēs thlipseōs*) relativizes even severe suffering when viewed from an eternal perspective.
32. C.S. Lewis, "The Weight of Glory," a sermon preached at the Church of St. Mary the Virgin, Oxford, on June 8, 1941. Published in *The Weight of Glory and Other Addresses* (New York: Macmillan, 1949).
33. 2 Corinthians 12:7-8 (ESV). The identity of Paul's "thorn in the flesh" has been debated throughout church history, with suggestions including chronic illness, persecution, spiritual temptation, or a speech impediment.
34. 2 Corinthians 12:9 (ESV): "My grace is sufficient for you, for my power is made perfect in weakness."

215

35. 2 Corinthians 12:9-10 (ESV). Paul's contentment with weakness represents a complete inversion of worldly values and demonstrates the paradoxical logic of the cross.
36. 2 Corinthians 1:3-5 (ESV). The Greek word *paraklēsis* (comfort, encouragement) appears ten times in these three verses, emphasizing the theme of consolation that flows from God through believers to others.
37. Philippians 3:10: "the fellowship of sharing in his sufferings" (*tēn koinōnian pathēmatōn autou*). The term *koinōnia* indicates participation and partnership, suggesting that believers' sufferings are united with Christ's.
38. 2 Timothy 4:7-8: "I have fought the good fight, I have finished the race, I have kept the faith. Henceforth there is laid up for me the crown of righteousness" (ESV). This is Paul's final self-assessment, written shortly before his execution in Rome.
39. The phrase "long obedience in the same direction" comes from Friedrich Nietzsche but was adopted as a description of Christian discipleship by Eugene Peterson in *A Long Obedience in the Same Direction: Discipleship in an Instant Society* (Downers Grove, IL: InterVarsity Press, 1980; 2nd ed. 2000).
40. John 1:5: "The light shines in the darkness, and the darkness has not overcome it" (ESV). The Greek verb *katelaben* can mean either "overcome" or "comprehend," suggesting that darkness neither defeats nor understands the light.
41. John Welwood coined the term "spiritual bypassing" in his article "Principles of Inner Work: Psychological and Spiritual" (1984) and developed the concept in *Toward a Psychology of Awakening: Buddhism, Psychotherapy, and the Path of Personal and Spiritual Transformation* (Boston: Shambhala, 2000). The phenomenon

IV THE PERSEVERING RELIGION

describes using spiritual practices to avoid dealing with psychological wounds.

42. Romans 8:28: "And we know that for those who love God all things work together for good, for those who are called according to his purpose" (ESV). While theologically true, this verse is often misused to short-circuit the grieving process rather than to provide long-term hope.

43. 1 Peter 4:12-13: "Beloved, do not be surprised at the fiery trial when it comes upon you to test you, as though something strange were happening to you. But rejoice insofar as you share Christ's sufferings, that you may also rejoice and be glad when his glory is revealed" (ESV).

44. 1 Peter 4:14: "If you are insulted for the name of Christ, you are blessed, because the Spirit of glory and of God rests upon you" (ESV).

45. 1 Peter 1:6-7: "In this you rejoice, though now for a little while, if necessary, you have been grieved by various trials, so that the tested genuineness of your faith—more precious than gold that perishes though it is tested by fire—may be found to result in praise and glory and honor at the revelation of Jesus Christ" (ESV).

46. 1 Peter 2:21: "For to this you have been called, because Christ also suffered for you, leaving you an example, so that you might follow in his steps" (ESV).

47. James 1:2-4: "Count it all joy, my brothers, when you meet trials of various kinds, for you know that the testing of your faith produces steadfastness. And let steadfastness have its full effect, that you may be perfect and complete, lacking in nothing" (ESV).

48. James 5:10-11: "As an example of suffering and patience, brothers, take the prophets who spoke in the name of the Lord. Behold, we consider those blessed who remained steadfast. You have heard of

the steadfastness of Job, and you have seen the purpose of the Lord, how the Lord is compassionate and merciful" (ESV).

49. James 4:3: "You ask and do not receive, because you ask wrongly, to spend it on your passions" (ESV).

50. 1 John 3:13: "Do not be surprised, brothers, that the world hates you" (ESV). Compare John 15:18: "If the world hates you, know that it has hated me before it hated you."

51. 1 John 2:15-17 (ESV). John's warning against loving "the world" (*kosmos*) refers not to creation but to the system of values opposed to God's kingdom.

52. 1 John 4:1: "Beloved, do not believe every spirit, but test the spirits to see whether they are from God, for many false prophets have gone out into the world" (ESV).

53. Revelation 2:8-11 contains Christ's letter to the church in Smyrna, a congregation facing intense persecution but receiving no rebuke—only encouragement to remain faithful.

54. Revelation 2:10: "Be faithful unto death, and I will give you the crown of life" (ESV).

55. Revelation 2:12-17 contains Christ's letter to the church in Pergamum, which is commended for faithfulness despite dwelling "where Satan's throne is" (v. 13)—likely a reference to the prominent imperial cult in that city.

56. Revelation 2:18-29 contains Christ's letter to the church in Thyatira. The "Jezebel" mentioned is likely a symbolic name for a false prophetess rather than her actual name.

57. Revelation 3:1-6 contains Christ's letter to the church in Sardis. The devastating assessment "you have the reputation of being alive, but you are dead" (v. 1) warns against spiritual complacency.

IV THE PERSEVERING RELIGION

58. Revelation 3:7-13 contains Christ's letter to the church in Philadelphia. The phrase "my word about patient endurance" (v. 10) suggests that endurance is a central theme of Christ's teaching.
59. Revelation 3:14-22 contains Christ's letter to the church in Laodicea. The city was known for its banking, textile, and medical industries—making the references to being "poor, blind, and naked" particularly pointed.
60. Acts 8:18-20: Simon Magus attempted to purchase the power to impart the Holy Spirit, prompting Peter's rebuke: "May your silver perish with you, because you thought you could obtain the gift of God with money!" The term "simony"—the buying and selling of ecclesiastical offices—derives from this incident.
61. James 4:13-15: "Come now, you who say, 'Today or tomorrow we will go into such and such a town and spend a year there and trade and make a profit'—yet you do not know what tomorrow will bring... Instead you ought to say, 'If the Lord wills, we will live and do this or that'" (ESV).
62. Revelation 14:4: "It is these who follow the Lamb wherever he goes" (ESV). The image of following the Lamb "wherever he goes" encompasses both His path of suffering and His ultimate triumph.
63. Revelation 12:11: "And they have conquered him by the blood of the Lamb and by the word of their testimony, for they loved not their lives even unto death" (ESV).
64. Matthew 16:25: "For whoever would save his life will lose it, but whoever loses his life for my sake will find it" (ESV).
65. Hebrews 11:6: "And without faith it is impossible to please him, for whoever would draw near to God must believe that he exists and that he rewards those who seek him" (ESV).

66. James 1:12: "Blessed is the man who remains steadfast under trial, for when he has stood the test he will receive the crown of life, which God has promised to those who love him" (ESV).
67. Revelation 2:7: "To the one who conquers I will grant to eat of the tree of life, which is in the paradise of God" (ESV). The tree of life, barred to humanity after the fall (Genesis 3:22-24), is restored in the new creation (Revelation 22:2).
68. Revelation 2:11: "The one who conquers will not be hurt by the second death" (ESV). The "second death" is identified in Revelation 20:14 as "the lake of fire."
69. Revelation 2:17 (ESV). The significance of the "white stone" has been variously interpreted as a token of acquittal, an admission ticket to a banquet, or a symbol of intimate friendship.
70. Revelation 2:26-28 (ESV). The "morning star" is identified with Christ Himself in Revelation 22:16: "I am the root and the descendant of David, the bright morning star."
71. Revelation 3:5 (ESV). The "book of life" appears throughout Revelation (13:8, 17:8, 20:12, 15, 21:27) as the register of those who belong to God.
72. Revelation 3:12 (ESV). The threefold inscription—God's name, the city's name, and Christ's new name—signifies complete belonging and identification with the divine.
73. Revelation 3:21: "The one who conquers, I will grant him to sit with me on my throne, as I also conquered and sat down with my Father on his throne" (ESV). This promise of co-regency with Christ represents the climax of the overcomer promises.
74. 2 Corinthians 4:17-18 (ESV).
75. 1 Peter 1:4: "to an inheritance that is imperishable, undefiled, and unfading, kept in heaven for you" (ESV).
76. 2 Timothy 4:8 (ESV).

77. The New Testament mentions several "crowns" (*stephanoi*) as rewards: the crown of life (James 1:12; Revelation 2:10), the crown of righteousness (2 Timothy 4:8), the crown of glory (1 Peter 5:4), and the imperishable crown (1 Corinthians 9:25).
78. Revelation 21:1-4 (ESV). This vision of the new creation represents the ultimate reversal of the fall and the fulfillment of God's redemptive purposes.
79. Revelation 22:4-5: "They will see his face, and his name will be on their foreheads. And night will be no more. They will need no light of lamp or sun, for the Lord God will be their light, and they will reign forever and ever" (ESV).
80. Romans 8:18-24 (ESV). Paul's vision of cosmic redemption includes not only humanity but all of creation, which "waits with eager longing for the revealing of the sons of God" (v. 19).
81. 2 Timothy 2:12: "if we endure, we will also reign with him" (ESV).

V

THE MYSTERY OF RELIGION

On Marriage, Sacrament, and the Hiddenness of God

The Secret Hidden for Ages

There is a moment in Paul's letter to the Ephesians where the apostle seems almost to lose his breath. He has been writing about marriage—the ordinary, sometimes tedious reality of husbands and wives learning to live together—when suddenly the language shifts:

"This mystery is profound, and I am saying that it refers to Christ and the church."

Mystery. The Greek word *mysterion* does not mean what we usually think of as a mystery today. We see mysteries as puzzles to solve or problems to figure out. For Paul, a mystery is a reality hidden in God before the foundation of the world, now revealed in Christ, yet still beyond our full comprehension.

Marriage, Paul says, is such a mystery. It points beyond itself to something infinite. The love between husband and wife goes beyond social contract, biological arrangement, or emotional bond. It is an icon—a window into the very heart of God.

Ray Ortlund, in his luminous study *Marriage and the Mystery of the Gospel*, captures this truth with characteristic clarity:

"Your marriage is more than your marriage. It is a living parable of the love between Christ and His church. Every moment of tenderness, every act of forgiveness, every choice to stay when leaving would be easier—these are not mere domestic duties. They are gospel proclamations. You are telling the story of God's love with your lives."

This vision of marriage—as mystery, as sacrament, as participation in divine love—anchors the central thesis: that the deepest truths of faith are encountered in mystery, not mastered by intellect. In our therapeutic age, we risk reducing marriage to a contract, a partnership for fulfillment, or a lifestyle easily abandoned. In doing so, we lose sight of the profound truth that binding ourselves to another touches something eternal, revealing the heart of God's ways with the world.

The God Who Hides Himself: The Prophetic Witness to Mystery
The Hidden God

Long before Paul wrote of mysteries hidden for ages, the prophets of Israel grappled with a God who refused to be domesticated by human understanding.

Isaiah, standing in the courts of a fallen kingdom, declared what generations of the faithful had discovered through painful experience: "Truly, you are a God who hides himself, O God of Israel, the Savior."

Deus absconditus. The hidden God. This is a glory of the divine nature. God hides Himself because He is too present, too vast, and too utterly other to be contained by finite minds. As the sun blinds the eye that looks directly at it, so the full revelation of God would overwhelm creatures made from dust.

The prophet continues, speaking on behalf of a God whose ways confound human expectation:

"For my thoughts are not your thoughts, neither are your ways my ways, declares the LORD. For as the heavens are higher than the earth, so are my ways higher than your ways and my thoughts than your thoughts."

This is not anti-intellectualism. God does not dismiss thinking or theology. Instead, He emphasizes that the gap between Creator and creature is infinite. Our highest thoughts about God fall far short of the reality, and even our best theology is like a child's drawing compared to the masterpiece it tries to represent.

The implications for how we approach mystery are immediate. We are not to approach the hidden things of God with the presumption that sufficient cleverness will crack the code. We are to approach with humility—the humility appropriate to creatures standing before their Creator, to the finite confronting the infinite.

Moses, the great lawgiver, codified this principle for Israel: "The secret things belong to the LORD our God, but the things that are revealed belong to our children and to us forever, that we may do all the words of this law."

There are secret things. They belong to God. We cannot grasp, demand, or wrest them from heaven by intellect or prayer. There are also revealed things—truths God has disclosed, commands He has given, promises He has made. These belong to us. Our task is to faithfully live the truths God has revealed, rather than try to penetrate the mysteries He keeps hidden.

This posture of reverent humility runs throughout Scripture. God is truly knowable, but never fully comprehensible. We can know Him without knowing everything about Him. We can trust Him without understanding all His ways.

Daniel and the Revealer of Mysteries

The book of Daniel introduces a phrase that will echo through later revelation: God is the "revealer of mysteries."

When Nebuchadnezzar demands that his wise men tell him both his dream and its interpretation—an impossible task by human reckoning—Daniel turns to the God of heaven. And God responds:

"He reveals deep and hidden things; he knows what is in the darkness, and the light dwells with him."

V THE MYSTERY OF RELIGION

Daniel's prayer of thanksgiving establishes the fundamental biblical posture toward mystery:

"Blessed be the name of God forever and ever, to whom belong wisdom and might. He changes times and seasons; he removes kings and sets up kings; he gives wisdom to the wise and knowledge to those who have understanding; he reveals deep and hidden things; he knows what is in the darkness, and the light dwells with him."

Notice the careful balance. God reveals—but He reveals what He chooses, when He chooses, to whom He chooses. The mysteries are His to keep or disclose. Human wisdom, however impressive, cannot storm the gates of heaven and seize what God has not given. But what God gives, He gives generously to those who ask in humility.

Later in the same book, an angel tells Daniel about visions that concern the distant future: "But you, Daniel, shut up the words and seal the book, until the time of the end. Many shall run to and fro, and knowledge shall increase."

Some mysteries are sealed—not forever, but until their appointed time. The prophets themselves did not always understand what they prophesied. Peter would later write that they "searched and inquired carefully, inquiring what person or time the Spirit of Christ in them was indicating when he predicted the sufferings of Christ and the subsequent glories." Even the angels, Peter adds, "long to look into these things."

Even prophets and angels do not fully understand the mysteries of God. We, with our finite and fallen nature, should approach them with humility.

Ecclesiastes: Living with What Cannot Be Known

The Preacher of Ecclesiastes, that most enigmatic voice in the wisdom literature, wrestled with mystery throughout his meditation on life "under the sun."

"He has made everything beautiful in its time. Also, he has put eternity into man's heart, yet so that he cannot find out what God has done from the beginning to the end."

Here is the human predicament in a single verse. God has placed eternity in our hearts—a longing for transcendence, a sense that there must be more, an intuition that the visible world is not all there is. And yet we cannot find out what God has done from beginning to end. We are creatures designed for infinity but limited to finitude. We hunger for answers that exceed our capacity to discover.

The Preacher's conclusion is not despair but trust:

"I perceived that whatever God does endures forever; nothing can be added to it, nor anything taken from it. God has done it, so that people fear before him."

The appropriate response to mystery is fear—not craven terror but reverent awe. God has made His ways inscrutable precisely so that we would fear Him, worship Him, bow before a wisdom that exceeds our own.

Later, the Preacher offers this counsel for living with what cannot be understood:

"When I applied my heart to know wisdom, and to see the business that is done on earth, how neither day nor night do one's eyes see sleep, then I saw all the work of God, that man cannot find out the work that is done under the sun. However much man may toil in seeking, he will not find it out. Even though a wise man claims to know, he cannot find it out."

This is bracing honesty. We cannot discover the full extent of God's work. No matter how diligently we seek, we will not reach the bottom of divine providence. Anyone who claims otherwise is deceived.

This limitation calls for humility, trust, and surrender of our need to understand in favor of a willingness to obey. "The end of the matter," the Preacher concludes, "Fear God and keep his commandments, for this is the whole duty of man."

V THE MYSTERY OF RELIGION

We may not understand God's ways, yet we can follow His commands. We may not comprehend His providence, yet we can trust His character. Mystery teaches us surrender instead of mastery, communion instead of full comprehension.

Job: The Silence That Speaks

No book in Scripture grapples more directly with the mystery of divine providence than Job.

For thirty-seven chapters, Job and his friends debate the meaning of his suffering. The friends offer explanations—Job must have sinned, suffering is always punishment, God's justice requires a rational accounting. Job protests his innocence and demands an audience with the Almighty. He wants answers. He wants God to explain Himself.

And then God speaks.

God's answer is unexpected. He does not explain why Job suffered. He does not vindicate the friends' theology or confirm Job's protests. Instead, He displays overwhelming wisdom and power—the foundations of the earth, the storehouses of snow, the wild donkey and the ostrich, the behemoth and the leviathan.

"Where were you when I laid the foundation of the earth? Tell me, if you have understanding."

The question is rhetorical but pointed. Job was nowhere when creation began. He does not understand how the sea was bounded or how the dawn was commanded. He cannot explain the instincts of animals or the movements of constellations. And if he cannot comprehend these lesser mysteries, how can he presume to comprehend the mystery of divine providence in human affairs?

Job's response is the model for how we are to treat mystery:

"I had heard of you by the hearing of the ear, but now my eye sees you; therefore I despise myself, and repent in dust and ashes."

Job does not say, "now I understand," but "now I *see* you." The encounter with God does not answer Job's intellectual questions; it surpasses them. In the presence of the living God, explanation gives way to worship. The need to understand is replaced by the reality of relationship.

This is Job's deepest teaching: we need God's presence, not answers. We come to God seeking explanations, and He gives us Himself. We insist on understanding, and He offers communion. In the end, communion is better than explanation.

Christ and the Mysteries of the Kingdom

Why Jesus Taught in Parables

When the disciples asked Jesus why He taught the crowds in parables, His answer was startling:

"To you it has been given to know the secrets of the kingdom of heaven, but to them it has not been given. For to the one who has, more will be given, and he will have an abundance, but from the one who has not, even what he has will be taken away. This is why I speak to them in parables, because seeing they do not see, and hearing they do not hear, nor do they understand."

The mysteries of the kingdom are given as gifts, not grasped, discovered, or earned. They are revealed by grace to those with hearts ready to receive. They remain hidden from those with hardened hearts, closed eyes, and who reject the light they have.

This principle shapes our approach to mystery. We cannot demand that God make Himself plain by force of intellect. We receive what He gives, wait for what He withholds, and trust that what remains hidden is hidden for good reason. What we need to know will be revealed at the right time.

Jesus continues, quoting Isaiah:

V THE MYSTERY OF RELIGION

"For this people's heart has grown dull, and with their ears they can barely hear, and their eyes they have closed, lest they should see with their eyes and hear with their ears and understand with their heart and turn, and I would heal them."

The closing of eyes and ears is self-inflicted. People choose a dull heart. Mysteries remain because the hearer is unwilling to receive, not because God is unwilling to reveal.

But to those who have received, who have responded to the light already given, more light is promised:

"But blessed are your eyes, for they see, and your ears, for they hear. For truly, I say to you, many prophets and righteous people longed to see what you see, and did not see it, and to hear what you hear, and did not hear it."

The disciples were living in the time of revelation. Mysteries hidden from prophets and kings were being disclosed before their eyes in the person of Jesus Himself. The secret of the ages was standing before them, teaching, healing, dying, rising.

The Mystery of the Incarnation

The greatest mystery of all is the one John announces in the prologue to his Gospel:

"And the Word became flesh and dwelt among us, and we have seen his glory, glory as of the only Son from the Father, full of grace and truth."

The eternal Word—through whom all things were made, who was with God and was God from the beginning—took on human nature. The infinite entered the finite. The Creator became creature. The one who fills heaven and earth was contained in a woman's womb, nursed at a woman's breast, grew in wisdom and stature in a backwater village of a conquered province.

Paul calls this the "mystery of godliness":

"Great indeed, we confess, is the mystery of godliness: He was manifested in the flesh, vindicated by the Spirit, seen by angels, proclaimed among the nations, believed on in the world, taken up in glory."

We confess this mystery rather than explain it. We proclaim it instead of dissecting it. The church's creeds protect the mystery from heresy—affirming Christ as truly God and truly man, two natures in one person, without confusion or division. The creeds do not explain how this is possible; they simply mark the boundaries of the mystery.

Jesus Himself pointed to this mystery when He asked the Pharisees:

"What do you think about Christ? Whose son is he?" They said to him, "The son of David." He said to them, "How is it then that David, in the Spirit, calls him Lord, saying, 'The Lord said to my Lord, sit at my right hand, until I put your enemies under your feet'? If then David calls him Lord, how is he his son?"

The question silenced the Pharisees. They had no answer. This demonstrates that the Messiah exceeds every category and expectation, containing a mystery beyond human wisdom.

Hidden and Revealed

Throughout His ministry, Jesus displayed a pattern of hiddenness and revelation that confounds our expectations.

He performed miracles but then commanded silence: "See that you say nothing to anyone." He revealed His glory on the mount of transfiguration but forbade the disciples to speak of it "until the Son of Man is raised from the dead." He taught openly in the temple courts but spoke of His death and resurrection in terms so veiled that even His closest followers did not understand.

"I have yet many things to say to you," Jesus told the disciples at in the upper room, "but you cannot bear them now. When the Spirit of truth comes, he will guide you into all the truth."

V THE MYSTERY OF RELIGION

There are things we cannot bear. Truths for which we are not ready. Mysteries that must remain sealed until the time of their opening. Jesus Himself practiced this principle with His disciples, revealing what they could receive, withholding what would overwhelm them, trusting the Spirit to complete in time what He had begun.

This pattern should shape our own approach to divine mystery. We are not entitled to know everything. We are not capable of bearing everything. We receive what is given, when it is given, as we are able to bear it. And we trust that what remains hidden is hidden in love, by a Savior who knows our frame and remembers that we are dust.

The Mystery of the Kingdom

Jesus spoke repeatedly of the "mystery" or "mysteries" of the kingdom of heaven—realities that are present but hidden, coming but not yet fully arrived, revealed to some but concealed from others.

The kingdom is like a mustard seed—the smallest of seeds that grows into the greatest of shrubs. It is like leaven hidden in flour, working invisibly until the whole lump is transformed. It is like a treasure hidden in a field, a pearl of great price, a net cast into the sea that gathers fish of every kind.

These parables do not explain the kingdom. They *evoke* it. They circle around a reality too large for direct description, approaching it from multiple angles, trusting that the accumulation of images will create understanding that no single statement could convey.

This is how mystery works. We cannot capture it in a formula or reduce it to a proposition. We must approach it indirectly and with humility, recognizing that we are touching something infinite.

When Peter confessed that Jesus was the Christ, the Son of the living God, Jesus responded: "Blessed are you, Simon Bar-Jonah! For flesh and blood has not revealed this to you, but my Father who is in heaven."

The deepest mysteries are revealed, not discovered. They come as gifts, not achievements. The proper response is gratitude for grace, not pride in our insight.

Paul and the Mystery Revealed

The Mystery Hidden for Ages

No New Testament writer uses the language of mystery more than Paul. For Paul, the entire gospel is a mystery—a divine secret now disclosed in Christ, not something unknowable.

"Now to him who is able to strengthen you according to my gospel and the preaching of Jesus Christ, according to the revelation of the mystery that was kept secret for long ages but has now been disclosed and through the prophetic writings has been made known to all nations, according to the command of the eternal God, to bring about the obedience of faith—to the only wise God be glory forevermore through Jesus Christ!"

The mystery was kept secret. Now it is disclosed. It was hidden in ages past. Now it is made known. This is the pattern: concealment followed by revelation, silence followed by proclamation, darkness giving way to light.

But notice that even the revealed mystery points beyond itself to "the only wise God." The disclosure is not total. The revelation is not exhaustive. We truly know, but we do not fully know. We see clearly enough to believe and obey, but not so clearly that faith is replaced by sight.

The Mystery of Christ

In Ephesians, Paul describes his particular role in relation to the mystery:
"When you read this, you can perceive my insight into the mystery of Christ, which was not made known to the sons of men in other generations as it has now been revealed to his holy apostles and prophets by the Spirit.

V THE MYSTERY OF RELIGION

This mystery is that the Gentiles are fellow heirs, members of the same body, and partakers of the promise in Christ Jesus through the gospel."

The specific content of the mystery, in this passage, is the inclusion of the Gentiles. What had been hinted in the prophets—that God's salvation would extend to all nations—is now revealed in its fullness. Jews and Gentiles together, one body in Christ, heirs of the same promise.

This was scandalous to first-century Jewish sensibilities. The mystery of Christ overturned ethnic and religious boundaries that had seemed permanent. It revealed that God's purposes had always been wider than Israel alone, that the particular election of one nation served the universal redemption of all nations.

Paul continues:

"To me, though I am the very least of all the saints, this grace was given, to preach to the Gentiles the unsearchable riches of Christ, and to bring to light for everyone what is the plan of the mystery hidden for ages in God, who created all things."

The riches of Christ are "unsearchable"—literally, untraceable, unable to be fully explored. Paul has been given grace to proclaim them, to bring the mystery to light. But even the apostle who received this revelation by direct commission cannot exhaust its depths. The mystery remains mysterious even as it is revealed.

Now We See in a Mirror Dimly

Paul's most famous statement about the limits of human knowledge comes in his hymn to love:

"For we know in part and we prophesy in part, but when the perfect comes, the partial will pass away... For now we see in a mirror dimly, but then face to face. Now I know in part; then I shall know fully, even as I have been fully known."

This passage establishes the eschatological frame for all Christian knowledge. We know—but in part. We see—but dimly, as in the polished bronze mirrors of the ancient world that gave only imperfect reflections. We prophesy—but incompletely.

The "perfect" is coming. The dim mirror will give way to face-to-face encounter. The partial knowledge will be replaced by full knowledge. But not yet. In this age, between the resurrection and the return, we walk by faith and not by sight.

This is not cause for despair but for hope. The limitation is temporary. The dimness will clear. And in the meantime, we have enough light to walk by—not enough to satisfy our curiosity, but enough to guide our steps.

Paul's counsel to the Corinthians is relevant here: "Do not pronounce judgment before the time, before the Lord comes, who will bring to light the things now hidden in darkness and will disclose the purposes of the heart."

There are things hidden in darkness that will be brought to light. There are purposes of the heart that will be disclosed. But not yet. Not by us. We are to refrain from premature judgment, from the presumption that we can see what only the Lord's coming will reveal.

Wisdom in a Mystery

In his first letter to the Corinthians, Paul contrasts the wisdom of God with the wisdom of the world:

"Yet among the mature we do impart wisdom, although it is not a wisdom of this age or of the rulers of this age, who are doomed to pass away. But we impart a secret and hidden wisdom of God, which God decreed before the ages for our glory. None of the rulers of this age understood this, for if they had, they would not have crucified the Lord of glory."

The wisdom of God is secret and hidden. It does not operate by the logic of worldly power. It appears foolish to those whose eyes have not been

V THE MYSTERY OF RELIGION

opened—so foolish that the rulers of this age crucified the Lord of glory, not recognizing who He was.

Paul continues with a quotation that captures the transcendence of divine mystery:

"What no eye has seen, nor ear heard, nor the heart of man imagined, what God has prepared for those who love him"—these things God has revealed to us through the Spirit. For the Spirit searches everything, even the depths of God."

The mystery exceeds the eye, ear, and imagination. It cannot be seen, heard, or conceived by natural human faculties. But it has been revealed—through the Spirit, who alone can search the depths of God.

This establishes both the reality of revelation and its limits. We know by the Spirit what we could never know by nature. But even Spirit-given knowledge does not exhaust the depths of God. The Spirit searches those depths; we receive what the Spirit discloses. The ocean is infinite; we drink from the cup we are given.

Holding Mystery Rightly

The Posture of Reverent Inquiry

What, then, does Scripture teach about how we are to approach divine mystery?

First, we are to approach with *humility*. The gap between Creator and creature is infinite. Our highest thoughts about God fall short of reality. The appropriate posture is not mastery but surrender, not comprehension but worship.

Moses removed his sandals before the burning bush. Isaiah cried, "Woe is me!" in the presence of the Holy One. John fell at the feet of the risen Christ "as though dead." The encounter with divine mystery produces not pride in our knowledge but awe at our finitude.

Second, we are to approach with *trust*. The hidden things belong to the Lord. What He has chosen not to reveal, He has hidden for good reason. We do not need to know everything to know Him. We can trust His character even when we cannot trace His providence.

Job learned this in the whirlwind. His questions were not answered, but his soul was satisfied. The presence of God was better than any explanation could have been. And so it is for all who learn to trust in the dark.

Third, we are to approach with *patience*. Some mysteries are sealed until their appointed time. Revelation is progressive—what was hidden from prophets and kings has been disclosed in Christ, but even now we see only in part. The full unveiling awaits the eschaton. Until then, we wait with the patience of faith.

"The secret things belong to the LORD our God, but the things revealed belong to us and to our children forever." We are to occupy ourselves with what has been revealed, living faithfully in the light we have been given, trusting that what remains dark will be illuminated in its time.

Fourth, we are to approach with *worship*. Mystery is not a problem to be solved but a reality to be adored. The inexhaustibility of God is not a frustration but a glory. We will spend eternity exploring depths that can never be fully plumbed—and this is not a defect in heaven but its endless delight.

Paul's great doxology in Romans captures this spirit:

"Oh, the depth of the riches and wisdom and knowledge of God! How unsearchable are his judgments and how inscrutable his ways! 'For who has known the mind of the Lord, or who has been his counselor?' 'Or who has given a gift to him that he might be repaid?' For from him and through him and to him are all things. To him be glory forever. Amen."

The proper response to mystery is not frustration but doxology. Not the demand for more information but the offering of praise. The inscrutable ways and unsearchable judgments are not obstacles to worship but occasions for it.

V THE MYSTERY OF RELIGION

Mystery and Marriage

We return now to the theme with which this chapter began: the mystery of marriage.

Paul, writing to the Ephesians about the relationship between husbands and wives, quotes Genesis—"Therefore a man shall leave his father and mother and hold fast to his wife, and the two shall become one flesh"—and then adds: "This mystery is profound, and I am saying that it refers to Christ and the church."

Marriage participates in the mystery of Christ and the church. It does not merely illustrate that relationship; it *embodies* it. The one-flesh union of husband and wife is a window into the eternal union between the Bridegroom and His bride.

This means that marriage, rightly understood, is itself a school of mystery. The daily encounter with another person—so familiar and yet so finally unknowable—teaches us something about our relationship with God. We never fully comprehend our spouses. We live with them for decades, and still they surprise us, still they exceed our categories, still they remain mysteriously *other* even in the closest intimacy.

And this is preparation for eternity. If we cannot exhaust the mystery of a finite human being, how much less the mystery of the infinite God? If decades of marriage still leave us learning, what will millennia of communion with Christ be like?

Omar and Michelle discovered this truth through the hard work of their healing. They had thought they knew each other. They had thought their relationship was transparent, comprehensible, and manageable. But the crisis revealed depths in each of them that neither had suspected—wounds and fears and longings that had been hidden even from themselves.

The process of rediscovery was painful. It required patience, trust, and the willingness to be surprised. But it also deepened their marriage in ways that the comfortable years had never done. They learned to hold each other as mysteries to be explored rather than problems to be solved. They learned that intimacy is not the elimination of mystery but its embrace.

And in learning this about each other, they learned something about God. The One who seemed to have abandoned them in their suffering had been present all along, hidden but not absent, working in the darkness, bringing forth beauty from ashes. They could not explain His ways. They could barely trace His hand. But they could trust His heart—and that trust, hard-won through tribulation, was worth more than any explanation could have been.

Living in the Mystery

We do not choose whether to live with mystery. We only choose how.

We can live with resentment, demanding answers God has not given, refusing to trust what we cannot understand. This path leads to bitterness, to the slow erosion of faith, to the spiritual exhaustion of those who fight against their own finitude.

Or we can live with surrender, accepting the limits of human knowledge, trusting the character of the God who has revealed Himself in Christ. This path leads to peace—not the peace of having all questions answered, but the deeper peace of resting in One whose wisdom exceeds our own.

The prophets and apostles, with one voice, call us to the second path. They testify that the hidden God is also the saving God, that the mystery conceals not indifference but love, that what we cannot see we can nevertheless trust.

"Truly, you are a God who hides himself, O God of Israel, the Savior."

Hidden and Savior. Both are true. Both must be held together. The God who exceeds our understanding is the same God who entered our world to redeem it. The mystery we cannot pierce is the same mystery that that became pierce-able, taking on flesh, dying on a cross, and rising from a tomb.

We live in that mystery. We are held by it. And one day, when faith gives way to sight, and the dim mirror clears, we will see face to face the One we have trusted in the dark. Every question will be answered or transcended. Every wound will be healed. Every tear will be wiped away.

Until then, we walk by faith. We hold the mystery with reverence. We worship the God who hides Himself, knowing that He hides not to abandon but to invite—inviting us deeper in, further up, closer to the heart of a love that passes understanding.

This is the mystery of religion. And it is enough.

The Sacramental Vision

The Catholic tradition has long held that marriage is one of the seven sacraments—an outward sign of an inward grace, a means by which God communicates Himself to His people. While Protestant traditions have generally been more cautious with sacramental language, the best of Protestant theology has recognized that marriage possesses a sacramental dimension that cannot be reduced to mere metaphor.

Cardinal Marc Ouellet, in his theological exploration of marriage and family, writes: "Marriage is not merely *like* the relationship between Christ and the church. It *participates* in that relationship. The grace of the sacrament is not an external addition to natural marriage but the elevation of natural marriage into the supernatural order, making it a real means of sanctification for the spouses."

This sacramental vision transforms how we understand marital difficulty. If marriage is merely a contract, then conflict is a sign of failure—an indication that perhaps this contract should be renegotiated or dissolved. But if marriage is a sacrament, then conflict becomes a crucible of transformation, a called to cruciform love. The friction between two sinful

239

people living in close proximity is not a bug but a feature—the very means by which God shapes us into the image of His Son.

Consider Omar and Michelle, whose story we have traced through these pages. Their marriage nearly collapsed under the weight of his depression and her trauma. They fell into destructive cycles—the demon dialogues, as their therapist called them—that seemed impossible to escape. By any reasonable measure, they were incompatible. Their needs clashed. Their wounds triggered each other. Their communication had broken down entirely.

And yet they stayed. Not because staying was easy, not because they felt like staying, but because they had glimpsed something that transcended their present suffering: the mystery that their marriage was meant to proclaim. Christ does not abandon His bride. The church, for all her failures, is not discarded. And so Omar and Michelle, stumbling and bleeding, continued to reach for each other in the darkness.

This is not romantic advice. It is sacramental theology. And it changes everything.

The Cloud of Unknowing

But here we must pause and acknowledge something that the modern church is often reluctant to admit: much of our relationship with God is shrouded in mystery. We do not see clearly. We walk by faith, not by sight. And the God we worship is not a God who can be fully grasped, contained, or comprehended.

The anonymous author of *The Cloud of Unknowing*, that strange and beautiful fourteenth-century mystical text, understood this better than most:

"For He may well be loved, but He may not be thought. By love, He may be grasped and held, but by thought, never. And therefore, though it may be good sometimes to think particularly about God's kindness and worth...

V THE MYSTERY OF RELIGION

yet in the work of contemplation, they must be cast down and covered with a cloud of forgetting. And you shall step above them with a devout and pleasing stirring of love, and try to pierce that darkness above you. You shall strike upon that thick cloud of unknowing with a sharp dart of longing love—and do not leave that place no matter what happens."

This is not the comfortable, domesticated God of much popular Christianity. This is the God who dwells in thick darkness, who spoke to Moses from a cloud, who hides Himself even as He reveals Himself. And our relationship with this God—including the relationship we enact through marriage—must make room for mystery, for not-knowing, for the humble acknowledgment that we are in the presence of One who exceeds our categories.

Hans Urs von Balthasar, the Swiss theologian, explored this theme in his profound meditation *Mysterium Paschale*:

"The mystery of God is not a problem to be solved but a reality to be inhabited. We do not approach the divine as detectives approach a crime scene, searching for clues that will dispel all confusion. We approach as lovers approach the beloved—knowing that what we encounter will always be greater than what we comprehend, and that this excess is not a defect but a glory."

Omar learned this in the months after Haiti. His old faith had been built on certainties—clear answers to clear questions, a God who made sense, a theology that explained everything. That faith could not survive Esther's death. It collapsed under the weight of a seven-year-old's last breath.

What emerged in its place was something else: a faith comfortable with shadows, a trust that did not require understanding, a love for a God who refused to be domesticated. Omar stopped demanding explanations. He started seeking presence. And in that shift, he discovered a different kind of intimacy—not the intimacy of full comprehension but the intimacy of full surrender.

Augustine and the Restless Heart

St. Augustine of Hippo, that towering figure of the early church, understood the mystery of divine love better than almost anyone. His *Confessions*—that remarkable combination of autobiography, philosophy, and prayer—begins with words that have echoed through the centuries:

"You have made us for Yourself, O Lord, and our hearts are restless until they rest in You."

This restlessness is the signature of the creature made for mystery. We are not built for small gods, manageable deities, or comfortable spiritualities that promise fulfillment without transformation. We are built for the infinite—and until we find our home in the infinite, we will be perpetually unsatisfied.

Augustine explored this theme in his reflections on marriage and sexuality, recognizing that our longing for union with another human being is itself a sign of a deeper longing:

"In the embrace of beloved and lover, there is a shadow of the divine embrace. The pleasure of the flesh, rightly ordered, points beyond itself to the pleasure of communion with God. All our earthly loves are training grounds for the only love that will fully satisfy—the love that is God Himself, poured out for us and received into us forever."

This insight transforms how we understand marital intimacy. The physical union of husband and wife is not merely biological, not merely pleasurable, but *sacramental*—a sign that participates in the reality it signifies. When Omar and Michelle learned to reach for each other again after months of distance and conflict, they were doing more than repairing a relationship. They were enacting the mystery of Christ and the church, the divine pursuit and the creaturely response, the love that will not let us go.

Knowing and Not Knowing

V THE MYSTERY OF RELIGION

J. I. Packer, in his classic work *Knowing God*, drew a crucial distinction between knowing *about* God and actually *knowing* God:

"One can know a great deal about God without much knowledge of Him. I am sure that many of us have never really grasped this. We find in ourselves a deep interest in theology. We read books of theological exposition and apologetics. We dip into Christian biography and history. We discuss religion and compare notes on Christian experience. We think this is fine, and I am not denying that it is fine. But none of this can be called knowing God."

True knowledge of God, Packer argued, comes through relationship—through the kind of intimate acquaintance that develops only over time, through difficulty and delight, through the thousand daily encounters that gradually form us into people who recognize the divine presence when it draws near.

This is why marriage, for all its difficulties, can be such a profound school of spiritual formation. In the daily encounter with another person—in the friction of differing personalities, the challenge of sustained commitment, the hard work of communication and repair—we learn lessons that cannot be taught in any other way.

Eusebius, the church historian, observed in the fourth century: "The married life, when entered with devotion to Christ, becomes a gymnasium of virtue. The spouses are each other's teachers, refining one another through love and conflict alike, until both are shaped more fully into the image of the Master they serve."

Omar and Michelle discovered this truth through painful experience. Their conflicts—the demon dialogues, the cycles of pursuit and withdrawal—were not interruptions to their spiritual growth. They were the curriculum. Every rupture that was followed by repair, every wound that was acknowledged and tended, every moment when they chose connection over self-protection: these were the exercises that built the muscles of faith.

The Presence of the Present

Brother Lawrence, the seventeenth-century Carmelite monk whose simple wisdom has influenced millions, taught that the spiritual life was not about special experiences but about the mundane moments:

"We need not cry out to God in great anguish or elaborate prayers. He is nearer than we think. The time of business does not differ from the time of prayer. In the noise and clatter of my kitchen, while several persons are calling for different things at the same time, I possess God in as great tranquility as if I were upon my knees at the blessed sacrament."

This practice of the presence of God applies with particular force to marriage. The mystery is not elsewhere, waiting to be accessed through extraordinary spiritual experiences. The mystery is here, now, in the person lying next to you in bed, in the dishes that need washing, in the child who won't stop crying, in the conversation that keeps going wrong.

Brother Lawrence continued: "The most holy practice, the nearest to daily life, and the most essential for the spiritual life, is the practice of the presence of God, that is to find joy in His divine company and to make it a habit of speaking with Him in all humility and loving Him in all things, without trying to find rules or special devotions."

For Omar and Michelle, learning this practice transformed their recovery. They began to recognize the Spirit's presence in the small things: the nudge to pray instead of fight, the unexpected tenderness that arose after conflict, the moments of grace that punctuated their ordinary days. God was not absent from their struggle. He was in the midst of it, working through it, using it for purposes they could only dimly perceive.

The Fathers on Mystery

V THE MYSTERY OF RELIGION

The great teachers of the early church were unanimous in their insistence that God exceeds our comprehension—and that this excess is good news rather than bad.

Athanasius of Alexandria, the fourth-century defender of Trinitarian orthodoxy, wrote: "God is not bound by our categories. When we speak of the Father and the Son and the Holy Spirit, we speak truly—but we do not speak completely. The mystery of the Trinity is not a puzzle we have solved but a truth we inhabit, living always at the edge of our understanding, sustained by faith."

Gregory of Nazianzus, went even further: "If you have understood, then what you have understood is not God. For God is above understanding, beyond speech, greater than thought. Only the person who confesses this limitation can begin to approach the truth."

And Basil the Great, ours and Gregory's friend, applied this understanding to the Christian life: "We are called to imitate a God we cannot fully know. This should humble us in our certainties and embolden us in our love. For if even the infinite God reaches out to us in mercy, how much more should we reach out to one another?"

This patristic wisdom offers a corrective to both theological arrogance and spiritual despair. We need not have all the answers. We need not understand everything that is happening in our marriages, our sufferings, our lives. The mystery is vast, and our comprehension is small. But we are invited into relationship with the One who holds all mysteries—and that relationship is enough.

Marriage as Icon

We return now to the central claim of this chapter: that marriage, in its fullness, is an icon of the divine love.

Ray Ortlund explains: "An icon is not a mere illustration. It is a window. It participates in the reality it represents. And Christian marriage, when lived faithfully, becomes just such a window—a place where the love of Christ for His church becomes visible, tangible, experiential. When a husband sacrifices for his wife, the world sees something of Christ's sacrifice. When a wife respects and supports her husband, the world sees something of the church's glad submission to her Lord."

This is not a burden but a gift. It means that the ordinary moments of married life—the morning coffee, the evening conversation, the making up after an argument—are freighted with eternal significance. We are not merely managing a household. We are participating in the mystery of salvation.

Angela McCarthy, reflecting on the theology of marriage, writes: "The sacrament of marriage draws the spouses into the paschal mystery of Christ's death and resurrection. Their love will be crucified—disappointments will come, dreams will die, conflicts will wound. But if they allow that crucified love to be raised by grace, they will discover something more precious than their romantic beginnings: a love tested by fire and found genuine."

This is precisely what Omar and Michelle discovered. Their romantic love had been crucified—by his depression, by her trauma, by the accumulated wounds of months of conflict. But in the resurrection power of the Spirit, something new emerged. Not a return to innocence, but an arrival at maturity. Not the giddy love of newlyweds, but the tempered love, a cruciform love, of veterans who had fought through the darkness and emerged still holding hands.

Beauty in the Shadows

The mystery of God includes not only His transcendence but also His hiddenness. Deus absconditus, the theologians call it: the hidden God, the

V THE MYSTERY OF RELIGION

God who conceals Himself even as He reveals, who speaks in silence and acts in apparent inaction.

Hans Urs von Balthasar reflected on this dimension of divine mystery:

"The beauty of God is not always obvious. It may be hidden in suffering, obscured by tragedy, veiled by the very ordinariness of daily life. And yet, for those with eyes to see, the beauty breaks through—in the faithfulness of a long marriage, in the patience of a parent with a difficult child, in the forgiveness offered when revenge would be so much easier. The hidden God is the beautiful God, and His beauty is most visible in precisely those places we would least expect to find it."

Michelle found this beauty in an unexpected place: in the very wound that Pastor David had inflicted. As her therapist helped her process the trauma, as she named what had been done to her and released the shame she had carried, something transformed. Her pain became a credential. Her wound became a window. She found herself able to sit with other women who had experienced similar abuse, offering a presence and a hope that could only come from one who had walked that road.

"My story is not just my pain," she wrote in her journal. "It is my ministry. What was meant for evil, God is using for good. I am not glad it happened—I never will be. But I am learning to see the beauty that God is bringing out of it. And that is a different kind of glad."

The Practice of Mystery

How then do we live in light of this mystery? How do we practice what we cannot fully comprehend?

First, we cultivate wonder. The posture appropriate to mystery is not analysis but awe. We approach our marriages, our sufferings, our lives not as problems to be solved but as gifts to be received with gratitude and humility.

Second, we embrace not-knowing. The Cloud of Unknowing reminds us that God cannot be grasped by thought alone, but only by love. We must become comfortable with shadows, with questions that have no answers, with the vast spaces beyond the reach of our understanding.

Third, we look for Christ. The mystery hidden for ages is now revealed: Christ in you, the hope of glory. We look for His presence in our spouses, in our conflicts, in the ordinary moments of our ordinary days. And when we look, we find Him—hidden but present, working in ways we cannot trace, bringing beauty from ashes.

Fourth, we practice the presence. Like Brother Lawrence in his kitchen, we learn to remain aware of God amid daily life. Not straining for extraordinary experiences, but attending to the extraordinary presence in ordinary things.

Fifth, we trust the process. The mystery is unfolding according to a divine timetable, not ours. We cannot rush it. We can only surrender to it, trusting that the One who began a good work will be faithful to complete it.

A Marriage Transfigured

Two years after their crisis, Omar and Michelle found themselves in a very different place.

The wounds had not disappeared. The scars remained. But something had transformed. Where there had been suspicion, there was now growing trust. Where there had been withdrawal, there was now cautious intimacy. Where there had been the performance of love, there was now—slowly, imperfectly, but genuinely—the reality.

"Our marriage is different now," Michelle told a friend. "Not perfect. Still messy. But there's something *real* about it that wasn't there before. I think we were both pretending before—pretending to be whole, pretending to have it together, pretending to be something we weren't.

Now we've seen each other at our worst. And somehow, that's made the love more honest."

Omar, preaching to his congregation on a Sunday in late autumn, tried to articulate what they had learned:

"I used to think a good marriage meant having no serious conflict. Getting it right from the start. Being compatible in all the important ways. But I've learned something different. A good marriage—a *faithful* marriage—is one that walks through fire and comes out refined. It's not about the absence of difficulty but the presence of commitment. Staying when leaving would be easier. Reaching when withdrawal would be safer. Telling the truth when pretense would be more comfortable."

He paused.

"This is the mystery. Marriage is not meant to make us happy—at least, not primarily. Marriage is meant to make us *holy*. To sanctify us. To shape us into the image of Christ. And that shaping happens through the friction, the failure, the forgiveness, the ten thousand small choices to love when love doesn't feel like anything at all."

He looked at Michelle in the third row.

"Christ in you. Christ in us. The hope of glory. This is the secret hidden for ages and now revealed. And it's lived out—stumblingly, imperfectly, but really—in the mystery of a man and a woman choosing each other, over and over again, until death do them part."

The Mystery and the Morning

We end where we began: with mystery.

The mystery of suffering, and how God meets us in it. The mystery of marriage, and how two become one. The mystery of the Trinity, and how the Father and the Son and the Spirit invite us into their eternal dance. The mystery of Christ and the church, and how our small human loves are caught up into something infinite.

We do not fully understand these mysteries. We will not—cannot—in this age. But we are invited to participate in them, to live inside them, to allow them to shape us into people of depth and beauty.

J. I. Packer, reflecting on the limits of human understanding, wrote: "We cannot know God completely—we are too small, and He is too great. But we can know Him truly. Not exhaustively, but authentically. Not as scholars dissecting an object of study, but as children knowing their Father, as lovers knowing their Beloved. This is the knowledge that matters. This is the knowledge that saves."

And so we press on. Not because we understand everything, but because we trust the One who does. Not because the road is easy, but because we do not walk it alone. Not because we have arrived, but because we know who waits at the journey's end.

The groaning and the glory. The darkness and the dawn. The mystery that exceeds us and the love that holds us.

Christ in us.

The hope of all glorious things to come.

"I myself have been made a minister of this same Gospel, and though it is true at this moment that I am suffering on behalf of you who have heard the Gospel, yet I am far from sorry about it. Indeed, I am glad, because it gives me a chance to complete in my own sufferings something of the untold pains for which Christ suffers on behalf of his body, the Church. For I am a minister of the Church by divine commission, a commission granted to me for your benefit and for a special purpose: that I might fully declare God's word—that sacred mystery which up to now has been hidden in every age and every generation, but which is now as clear as daylight to those who love God. They are those to whom God has planned to give a vision of the full wonder and splendour of his secret plan for the sons of men. And the secret is simply this: Christ in you! Yes, Christ in you bringing with him the hope of all glorious things to come."

— Colossians 1:24-27 (Phillips)

Endnotes

1. Ephesians 5:32: "This mystery is profound, and I am saying that it refers to Christ and the church" (ESV). The Greek word *mystērion* appears 27 times in the New Testament, with Paul using it predominantly to describe the hidden purposes of God now revealed in Christ.
2. The Greek *mystērion* in the New Testament does not carry the modern connotation of a puzzle to be solved. Rather, it refers to divine secrets previously hidden but now disclosed through revelation. The term has roots in Hellenistic mystery religions but is significantly transformed in Paul's usage to describe God's redemptive purposes in Christ.
3. Ray Ortlund Jr., *Marriage and the Mystery of the Gospel*, Short Studies in Biblical Theology (Wheaton, IL: Crossway, 2016), 23. Ortlund's work explores the typological relationship between human marriage and the Christ-church union throughout the biblical narrative.
4. Isaiah 45:15: "Truly, you are a God who hides himself, O God of Israel, the Savior" (ESV). The phrase *Deus absconditus* (hidden God) became an important concept in later theology, particularly in Luther's thought, distinguishing between what God reveals and what He conceals.
5. Isaiah 55:8-9: "For my thoughts are not your thoughts, neither are your ways my ways, declares the LORD. For as the heavens are higher than the earth, so are my ways higher than your ways and my thoughts than your thoughts" (ESV).
6. Deuteronomy 29:29: "The secret things belong to the LORD our God, but the things that are revealed belong to us and to our

children forever, that we may do all the words of this law" (ESV). This verse establishes a fundamental distinction between revealed and hidden truth that shaped later Jewish and Christian approaches to divine mystery.
7. Daniel 2:22: "He reveals deep and hidden things; he knows what is in the darkness, and the light dwells with him" (ESV).
8. Daniel 2:20-22 (ESV). Daniel's doxology establishes the proper posture toward mystery: praise for the God who reveals, not frustration at what remains hidden.
9. Daniel 12:4: "But you, Daniel, shut up the words and seal the book, until the time of the end. Many shall run to and fro, and knowledge shall increase" (ESV).
10. 1 Peter 1:10-12: "Concerning this salvation, the prophets who prophesied about the grace that was to be yours searched and inquired carefully, inquiring what person or time the Spirit of Christ in them was indicating when he predicted the sufferings of Christ and the subsequent glories. It was revealed to them that they were serving not themselves but you, in the things that have now been announced to you through those who preached the good news to you by the Holy Spirit sent from heaven, things into which angels long to look" (ESV).
11. Ecclesiastes 3:11: "He has made everything beautiful in its time. Also, he has put eternity into man's heart, yet so that he cannot find out what God has done from the beginning to the end" (ESV).
12. Ecclesiastes 3:14: "I perceived that whatever God does endures forever; nothing can be added to it, nor anything taken from it. God has done it, so that people fear before him" (ESV).
13. Ecclesiastes 8:16-17: "When I applied my heart to know wisdom, and to see the business that is done on earth, how neither day nor night do one's eyes see sleep, then I saw all the work of God, that

man cannot find out the work that is done under the sun. However much man may toil in seeking, he will not find it out. Even though a wise man claims to know, he cannot find it out" (ESV).

14. Ecclesiastes 12:13: "The end of the matter; all has been heard. Fear God and keep his commandments, for this is the whole duty of man" (ESV).
15. Job 38:4: "Where were you when I laid the foundation of the earth? Tell me, if you have understanding" (ESV). God's response to Job (chapters 38-41) is notable for what it does not say—no explanation of Job's suffering, no vindication of either Job's or his friends' theological frameworks.
16. Job 42:5-6: "I had heard of you by the hearing of the ear, but now my eye sees you; therefore I despise myself, and repent in dust and ashes" (ESV). Job's response moves from hearsay knowledge to direct encounter, from theological proposition to personal relationship.
17. Matthew 13:11-13: "To you it has been given to know the secrets of the kingdom of heaven, but to them it has not been given. For to the one who has, more will be given, and he will have an abundance, but from the one who has not, even what he has will be taken away. This is why I speak to them in parables, because seeing they do not see, and hearing they do not hear, nor do they understand" (ESV).
18. Matthew 13:14-15, quoting Isaiah 6:9-10 (ESV).
19. Matthew 13:16-17: "But blessed are your eyes, for they see, and your ears, for they hear. For truly, I say to you, many prophets and righteous people longed to see what you see, and did not see it, and to hear what you hear, and did not hear it" (ESV).
20. John 1:14: "And the Word became flesh and dwelt among us, and we have seen his glory, glory as of the only Son from the Father, full of grace and truth" (ESV). The Greek *eskēnōsen* ("dwelt" or

"tabernacled") evokes the Old Testament tabernacle, suggesting that in Jesus, God's presence has taken up residence among His people in a new and permanent way.

21. 1 Timothy 3:16: "Great indeed, we confess, is the mystery of godliness: He was manifested in the flesh, vindicated by the Spirit, seen by angels, proclaimed among the nations, believed on in the world, taken up in glory" (ESV). This verse may preserve an early Christian hymn or creedal formula.

22. Matthew 22:42-46 (ESV). Jesus's question about Psalm 110:1 demonstrates that the Messiah transcends the categories of Davidic expectation.

23. Mark 1:44: "See that you say nothing to anyone" (ESV). The "messianic secret" in Mark's Gospel has been extensively studied; Jesus's commands to silence suggest that His identity could only be properly understood after the crucifixion and resurrection.

24. Mark 9:9: "And as they were coming down the mountain, he charged them to tell no one what they had seen, until the Son of Man had risen from the dead" (ESV).

25. John 16:12-13: "I still have many things to say to you, but you cannot bear them now. When the Spirit of truth comes, he will guide you into all the truth" (ESV).

26. Romans 16:25-27: "Now to him who is able to strengthen you according to my gospel and the preaching of Jesus Christ, according to the revelation of the mystery that was kept secret for long ages but has now been disclosed and through the prophetic writings has been made known to all nations, according to the command of the eternal God, to bring about the obedience of faith—to the only wise God be glory forevermore through Jesus Christ! Amen" (ESV).

27. Ephesians 3:4-6: "When you read this, you can perceive my insight into the mystery of Christ, which was not made known to the sons

of men in other generations as it has now been revealed to his holy apostles and prophets by the Spirit. This mystery is that the Gentiles are fellow heirs, members of the same body, and partakers of the promise in Christ Jesus through the gospel" (ESV).

28. Ephesians 3:8-9: "To me, though I am the very least of all the saints, this grace was given, to preach to the Gentiles the unsearchable riches of Christ, and to bring to light for everyone what is the plan of the mystery hidden for ages in God, who created all things" (ESV). The Greek *anexichniastos* ("unsearchable") literally means "untraceable" or "beyond exploration."

29. 1 Corinthians 13:9-12: "For we know in part and we prophesy in part, but when the perfect comes, the partial will pass away... For now we see in a mirror dimly, but then face to face. Now I know in part; then I shall know fully, even as I have been fully known" (ESV). Ancient mirrors were polished bronze, providing only imperfect reflections.

30. 1 Corinthians 4:5: "Therefore do not pronounce judgment before the time, before the Lord comes, who will bring to light the things now hidden in darkness and will disclose the purposes of the heart" (ESV).

31. 1 Corinthians 2:6-8: "Yet among the mature we do impart wisdom, although it is not a wisdom of this age or of the rulers of this age, who are doomed to pass away. But we impart a secret and hidden wisdom of God, which God decreed before the ages for our glory. None of the rulers of this age understood this, for if they had, they would not have crucified the Lord of glory" (ESV).

32. 1 Corinthians 2:9-10: "'What no eye has seen, nor ear heard, nor the heart of man imagined, what God has prepared for those who love him'—these things God has revealed to us through the Spirit. For

the Spirit searches everything, even the depths of God" (ESV). The quotation is a free rendering of Isaiah 64:4.

33. Exodus 3:5: Moses removing his sandals before the burning bush; Isaiah 6:5: "Woe is me! For I am lost; for I am a man of unclean lips"; Revelation 1:17: John falling at Christ's feet "as though dead."

34. Romans 11:33-36: "Oh, the depth of the riches and wisdom and knowledge of God! How unsearchable are his judgments and how inscrutable his ways! 'For who has known the mind of the Lord, or who has been his counselor?' 'Or who has given a gift to him that he might be repaid?' For from him and through him and to him are all things. To him be glory forever. Amen" (ESV).

35. Ephesians 5:31-32: Paul quotes Genesis 2:24 and then adds his interpretive comment about the mystery of Christ and the church.

36. Ortlund, *Marriage and the Mystery of the Gospel*, 45.

37. Marc Cardinal Ouellet, *Mystery and Sacrament of Love: A Theology of Marriage and the Family for the New Evangelization*, trans. Michelle K. Borras and Adrian J. Walker (Grand Rapids: Eerdmans, 2015), 67.

38. *The Cloud of Unknowing*, anonymous fourteenth-century English mystical text. The quotation is from Chapter 6. The work teaches a form of contemplative prayer that emphasizes love over intellect and embraces the "unknowing" that characterizes our encounter with the infinite God.

39. Hans Urs von Balthasar, *Mysterium Paschale: The Mystery of Easter*, trans. Aidan Nichols (San Francisco: Ignatius Press, 1990), 23. Balthasar (1905-1988) was one of the most influential Catholic theologians of the twentieth century, known for his theological aesthetics and dramatic approach to doctrine.

40. Augustine of Hippo, *Confessions*, Book I, Chapter 1: "You have made us for yourself, O Lord, and our hearts are restless until they

V THE MYSTERY OF RELIGION

rest in you." This famous opening has shaped Christian spirituality for sixteen centuries.

41. Augustine's understanding of sexuality and marriage, developed in works like *On the Good of Marriage* and *On Holy Virginity*, recognized both the goodness of marital union and its sacramental significance as a sign of Christ and the church.

42. J.I. Packer, *Knowing God* (Downers Grove, IL: InterVarsity Press, 1973), 32. Packer's distinction between knowing about God and knowing God has been foundational for evangelical spirituality.

43. Eusebius of Caesarea (c. 260-339) was a church historian and theologian whose *Ecclesiastical History* remains a primary source for early church history. His theological writings also addressed practical matters of Christian living.

44. Brother Lawrence (c. 1614-1691), *The Practice of the Presence of God* (various editions). Lawrence was a Carmelite lay brother whose simple wisdom about maintaining awareness of God amid daily tasks has influenced millions of readers across traditions.

45. Brother Lawrence, *The Practice of the Presence of God*, Second Conversation.

46. Athanasius of Alexandria (c. 296-373) was the principal defender of Nicene orthodoxy against Arianism. His theological works, including *On the Incarnation*, emphasized both the reality of the Incarnation and the limits of human comprehension of divine mystery.

47. Gregory of Nazianzus (329-390), one of the Cappadocian Fathers, was known for his eloquent theological orations. His apophatic emphasis—stressing what cannot be said about God—balanced the cataphatic affirmations of Nicene theology.

48. Basil of Caesarea (330-379), another Cappadocian Father, was known for his ascetical writings, his defense of the divinity of the Holy Spirit, and his practical wisdom about Christian community.
49. Ortlund, *Marriage and the Mystery of the Gospel*, 89.
50. Angela McCarthy, *The Shape of Marriage: Living the Mystery* (San Francisco: Ignatius Press, 2018), 112. McCarthy explores the sacramental dimensions of marriage from a Catholic perspective.
51. von Balthasar, *Mysterium Paschale*, 45.
52. Packer, *Knowing God*, 37.
53. Colossians 1:24-27 (J.B. Phillips translation). This passage, which serves as the epigraph for the chapter, encapsulates the theme of mystery revealed in Christ and lived out through participation in His sufferings.

VI

WHEN THE HEAVENS ROLLED BACK

A Narrative of the Last Days in the Garden State

Part One: The Weight of the Age

The billboards along the Turnpike never went dark anymore. They pulsed through the night with images that would have been unthinkable a generation ago—bodies intertwined in configurations that defied not just decency but anatomy, advertisements for pleasure houses and chemical euphoria, invitations to "liberate yourself from the prison of monogamy." One sign, towering over Exit 14, displayed a naked figure emerging from a chrysalis of religious symbols—crosses, crescents, stars—with the slogan: *"You are your own god now."*

Sister Magdalena Okonkwo turned her face from the window of the basement on Bergen Street, Newark. As she did, she felt it again—that gentle pressure behind her sternum, that wordless knowing that had guided her for forty years. The Spirit was grieved. She could feel His grief as clearly as she felt her own heartbeat.

Do not be conformed to this world, the inner voice reminded her—not audibly, but with a clarity that was more than memory. *But be transformed by the renewing of your mind.*

She was sixty-three years old. She had been born in Lagos, baptized in London, and had come to America in 1994 believing it was a Christian nation. Perhaps it had been, in some nominal way. Perhaps it had only ever been Laodicea—neither hot nor cold, rich and increased with goods, not knowing it was wretched and blind and naked.

But Laodicea had been offered eye salve. Laodicea had been offered a chance to repent.

What America had become was Babylon herself.

The collapse had not come suddenly. It had come through a thousand small surrenders.

First, the redefinition of love as mere desire. Then the celebration of desire as identity. Then the protection of identity as sacred right. Then the criminalization of any voice that questioned whether desire alone could bear the weight of meaning.

Sister Magdalena remembered the warnings. Not just from Scripture—though those had been clear enough—but from the Spirit Himself, speaking through prophets and teachers, through dreams and promptings, through that still small voice that cut through the noise of the age.

The Spirit expressly says that in latter times some will depart from the faith, Paul had written to Timothy, *giving heed to deceiving spirits and doctrines of demons.*

She had heard that warning in her bones long before the seminaries closed. She had felt the Spirit's urgency when the churches began to soften, to accommodate, to explain away the hard words of Jesus. *Something is coming*, the inner witness had testified. *Be ready. Be watchful. Do not sleep as others do.*

Many had not listened. Many had called it alarmism, fundamentalism, fear-mongering. But the Spirit had been faithful, even when the shepherds were not.

The man they called the Architect had emerged seven years ago—though "emerged" was too gentle a word. He had *manifested*, as if from the

VI WHEN THE HEAVENS ROLLED BACK

sea itself, a man of such preternatural beauty that the networks could not look away. His face was on every screen. His voice was in every ear. He spoke of humanity's next phase, of consciousness unshackled, of pleasure as the highest good and shame as the only sin.

"You have been told that your desires are fallen," he proclaimed in his first global address. "But I tell you: your desires are divine. Every appetite is holy. Every hunger is sacred. The only corruption is denial. The only evil is restraint."

The world had received him as a savior.

But the Spirit had testified otherwise.

Brother Thomas Chen remembered the night the Architect first appeared on the global broadcast. He had been watching with his seminary colleagues, and while they debated politics and psychology, something had risen in his chest—a fire, an alarm, a knowing that bypassed his intellect entirely.

This is the one, the Spirit had witnessed. *The man of sin. The son of perdition. Watch. Pray. Do not be deceived.*

Thomas had spoken the warning aloud, and his colleagues had laughed. "You sound like a dispensationalist street preacher," one had said. "Let's not be sensationalist."

But Thomas had learned, over decades of walking with the Spirit, to trust that inner witness even when it seemed foolish. Especially when it seemed foolish. For God had chosen the foolish things of the world to shame the wise.

He had begun to prepare that very night.

Now, seven years later, Thomas sat in the corner of the basement reviewing his worn Bible by candlelight. He had traced the pattern a thousand times: Daniel's fourth beast, dreadful and terrible, with iron teeth and ten horns. The little horn that rose among them, speaking great things, before whom three of the first horns were plucked up by the roots.

"He shall speak words against the Most High," Thomas whispered, his finger tracing Daniel 7:25, "and shall wear out the saints of the Most High."

As he read, the Spirit illuminated the text—not with new revelation, but with deeper understanding. The wearing out was not merely persecution. It was the slow erosion of hope through prolonged suffering. It was the temptation to doubt, to compromise, to wonder if God had forgotten His promises.

I have not forgotten, the Spirit assured him. *I am the deposit guaranteeing your inheritance. I am the seal marking you for the day of redemption. What the Father promised, I am working to complete.*

Thomas closed his eyes and let the Comforter comfort him.

Part Two: Babylon Ascendant

The city had transformed into something unrecognizable.

What had once been churches were now temples of the body—the Cathedral of Saint Patrick in Manhattan converted into what they called an "Experience Center," where congregants gathered not for worship but for orchestrated rituals of flesh. The stained glass windows remained, but they now depicted not saints but idealized human forms in states of ecstasy, backlit by programmed LEDs that pulsed in rhythm with the synthesized music within.

Every Friday night—they still called it Friday, though the old week had been abolished in favor of the "Pleasure Cycle"—millions gathered for what the Unified Network called "Communion." Not bread and wine but designer pharmaceuticals and partners selected by algorithm, matched for maximum stimulation, discarded by morning.

"Do what thou wilt shall be the whole of the Law," the Architect had declared. But he had refined it: "Do what thou wilt, and the System shall provide."

And the System did provide.

VI WHEN THE HEAVENS ROLLED BACK

For those who bore the mark.

The Spirit had given the believers wisdom to understand what was happening.

Sister Consolata, who had been a marine biologist before the universities were closed, had prayed for discernment when the Architect first announced his "Liberation Protocols." That night, she had dreamed of a woman sitting on a scarlet beast, holding a golden cup filled with abominations. When she woke, the interpretation was already in her mind, placed there by the One who searches all things, even the deep things of God.

"It is the great harlot," she had told the congregation. "Babylon. The spirit of false religion merged with worldly power. The cup she holds is the wine of her fornication—the intoxicating promise of pleasure without consequence, freedom without truth."

Pastor Elijah had tested the word, as Scripture commanded. He had searched the Scriptures. He had prayed. And the Spirit had borne witness: *This word is true. Receive it. Act on it.*

They had begun preparing that very week—stockpiling food, establishing safe houses, creating networks of communication that did not depend on the Architect's infrastructure. The Spirit had given them wisdom, and they had obeyed.

Many had not. Many had called them paranoid, extreme, lacking in faith. "God will provide," they had said, as if provision required no cooperation, as if wisdom were unnecessary when one had grace.

But the Spirit had provided through wisdom. That was His way—not magic, but guidance; not shortcuts, but paths through the wilderness.

The mark had been introduced as liberation.

"Why should commerce be complicated?" the Architect had asked. "Why carry cards, remember passwords, prove identity? Your body is your credential. Your consciousness is your currency."

The neural implant—installed at the base of the skull, interfacing directly with the brain's pleasure centers—did more than enable buying and selling. It connected the bearer to the Unified Consciousness, a network of shared sensation. When one member experienced pleasure, all could share it. The dopamine of millions, aggregated and distributed. Ecstasy on demand.

But the Spirit had warned them.

Young Marcus, only fifteen at the time, had been taken to a "Youth Liberation Center" where children were prepared to receive the mark. The night before the procedure, he had dreamed of a lamb with seven horns and seven eyes—the sevenfold Spirit of God. In the dream, the Lamb had spoken: *Do not take it. Whatever they threaten, whatever they promise—do not take it. I am with you.*

Marcus had fled that night. He had wandered for three weeks, starving, hunted, until the believers found him. When he told them of his dream, old Mr. Castellanos had wept.

"The Spirit is still speaking," he said. "Even to the children. Especially to the children. Joel prophesied it: 'Your sons and daughters shall prophesy, your young men shall see visions.'"

The Spirit was faithful. Even in the darkness, He was faithful.

Part Three: The Market of Souls

The control was total.

Without the mark, one could not access currency. But it went beyond that. The smart homes would not open for the unmarked. The autonomous vehicles would not transport them. The medical systems would not treat them. The food distribution centers—there were no more

VI WHEN THE HEAVENS ROLLED BACK

grocery stores, only algorithmic allocation based on Social Harmony Scores—would not feed them.

But the Spirit provided wisdom for survival.

He taught them which abandoned buildings were safe. He prompted believers to share resources across networks they did not know existed. He stirred the consciences of the marked who had not fully surrendered—moved them to smuggle food and medicine at great personal risk.

I will never leave you nor forsake you, the Spirit reminded them. *Even in the valley of the shadow of death, you need not fear. The rod and staff of the Shepherd are still with you.*

Brother Thomas had mapped the system carefully, guided by insights he knew came from beyond his own intellect. The Architect controlled not merely commerce but *desire itself*. The mark connected its bearer to an artificial reward system. Compliance generated pleasure. Resistance generated pain.

"This is why they cannot repent," Thomas explained to the congregation. "The mark does not merely identify them—it transforms them. It makes repentance neurologically impossible."

"Then there is no hope for them?" asked Marcus.

The Spirit stirred in Thomas's heart, and he answered with more wisdom than he possessed: "With man, it is impossible. But with God, all things are possible. The Spirit who raised Christ from the dead can regenerate even the most hardened heart. I do not know what mercy the Lord may show at the end. I only know that we must not take the mark. Whatever the cost."

The cost was high.

But the Spirit sustained them.

The sexual revolution had not stopped at consent. It had not stopped at adults. It had not stopped at humanity itself.

The "Liberated Zones" in every major city offered experiences that Magdalena could not bring herself to name. Children were taught in mandatory "Body Autonomy" classes that any boundary was oppression, that any reluctance was repression, that their bodies belonged to the Collective Consciousness.

But the Spirit groaned within the believers—the groaning Paul had described, too deep for words.

When Magdalena prayed for the city, she felt that groaning. It was not her sorrow alone but the Spirit's sorrow, the grief of the Holy One who had brooded over the waters at creation and now brooded over the ruins of what humanity had become.

The whole creation groans, Paul had written. *And not only the creation, but we ourselves, who have the firstfruits of the Spirit, groan inwardly as we wait eagerly for adoption as sons, the redemption of our bodies.*

The Spirit was groaning. And He was teaching them to groan with Him—not in despair but in longing, not in hopelessness but in anticipation.

The night is far spent, He whispered. *The day is at hand.*

Part Four: The Tribulation of the Saints

The persecution had begun as mockery. Then marginalization. Then criminalization.

The Architect had declared all exclusive truth claims to be "cognitive terrorism." Only Christianity refused synthesis. Only Christianity insisted on the scandal of particularity: that there was one name under heaven by which men could be saved, and that name was Jesus. Only Christianity insisted that the body was a temple, not a playground.

For this, they were hunted.

But the Spirit gave them words.

VI WHEN THE HEAVENS ROLLED BACK

Sister Imani remembered the day they took her husband Jerome.

The officers had burst into their apartment at three in the morning. Jerome had been dragged from bed, accused of "propagating exclusivist ideologies" because he had been caught reading the Bible to their sons.

In that moment, Imani had felt the Spirit surge within her—not fear, but a strange, supernatural calm. Words came to her mouth that she had not planned:

"You may take his body, but you cannot take his soul. You may silence his voice, but the Word of God is not chained. What you do tonight will be remembered in eternity, and the Judge of all the earth will do right."

The officers had hesitated. One of them—young, his eyes flickering with something that might have been conscience—had looked away.

Jerome had caught her eyes as they dragged him out. "The Spirit is with you," he said. "He will be Father to our boys. Do not be afraid."

She never saw him again. But the Spirit had fulfilled the promise. He had been Father to her sons, guiding them, teaching them, preparing them for the day they too would be taken. And when that day came, they had not recanted. They had not taken the mark. They had endured to the end.

When they deliver you up, Jesus had promised, *do not worry about how or what you should speak. For it will be given to you in that hour what you should speak; for it is not you who speak, but the Spirit of your Father who speaks in you.*

The Spirit had spoken. The Spirit always spoke when His children needed Him most.

The little congregation gathered each evening at sunset—the eighteen souls who remained. They called themselves simply *the Remnant* now, for the old denominational names had become meaningless. There were former Catholics among them, and Pentecostals, and Orthodox, and Baptists. The fire had burned away everything but the essential confession: *Jesus is Lord. And my body is not my own.*

Pastor Elijah opened the worn Bible to Matthew 24.

"Remember what our Lord told us," he said, his voice barely above a whisper, for the surveillance drones could detect sound through walls. "He told us that these things must come to pass."

As he read, the Spirit moved among them, making the ancient words alive. This was His ministry—to take the things of Christ and declare them to the believers, to remind them of everything Jesus had said, to guide them into all truth.

"Then they will deliver you up to tribulation and kill you, and you will be hated by all nations for My name's sake. And then many will be offended, will betray one another, and will hate one another."

"We have seen this," Imani said quietly. "We have lived this."

"Yes," Elijah replied. "And what else did He say?"

"And because lawlessness will abound, the love of many will grow cold. But he who endures to the end shall be saved."

The Spirit stirred within them—not just memory, but *presence*. He was the Helper Jesus had promised, the One who would be with them forever, the One who would not leave them as orphans.

I am here, He testified within each heart. *I have always been here. I will be here until the end, and beyond the end, forever.*

Young Sarah spoke up, her voice trembling but firm. "They brought me before the magistrate last month. Before you rescued me. They said if I would just... participate... in their ritual, they would clear my debt."

She looked at her hands.

"I didn't know what to say. I was so afraid. But then—" She paused, tears falling. "Then the Spirit reminded me. He brought the words to my mind: *'Do you not know that your body is the temple of the Holy Spirit who is in you, whom you have from God, and you are not your own? For you were bought with a price; therefore glorify God in your body.'*"

She lifted her eyes to the group.

VI WHEN THE HEAVENS ROLLED BACK

"I told them that my body was a temple. That I was bought with a price. That I would not glorify the beast with my body."

Pastor Elijah crossed the room and placed his hand on her shoulder. "The Spirit gave you those words," he said. "And He gave you strength to speak them. That is His ministry—to remind us of truth when we most need to hear it, to give us power when our own strength fails."

She wept. They wept with her.

And the Spirit, present among them, wept too—not in sorrow alone, but in the deep solidarity of One who had been with them through every dark night and would be with them still.

Part Five: The Economy of Babylon

The control was total.

But the Spirit gave them what they needed.

He provided through unexpected channels—a marked woman who had been convicted by a dream, leaving food at a designated spot; a former police officer whose conscience would not let him rest, warning them of raids before they came; even the ravens of the field, as it were, bringing sustenance to prophets in hiding.

Brother Thomas had learned to follow the Spirit's promptings even when they seemed irrational. One night, he felt an urgent pressure to move the congregation from their basement to a warehouse three miles away. He had no logical reason—the basement seemed secure enough. But he had learned not to argue with that inner witness.

They moved that night. By morning, the basement had been raided. Every person inside—a family of believers they did not know, who had taken refuge there after the congregation left—was taken.

"How did you know?" Marcus asked him.

Thomas shook his head. "I didn't know. The Spirit knew. He searches all things—even the plans of the enemy. And He warns His children when danger comes."

The Spirit of truth will guide you into all truth, Jesus had promised. *He will tell you things to come.*

Not every prompting was dramatic. Most were quiet—a sense that someone needed encouragement, a Scripture rising unbidden to mind, a gentle conviction about an attitude or action that needed correction. The Spirit was forming them, shaping them, preparing them for what was ahead.

He was also stirring their longing.

Part Six: The Stirring of Anticipation

In those dark days, the Spirit did something strange and wonderful among them.

He kindled anticipation.

It began with dreams. Sister Consolata dreamed of a wedding feast—tables stretching beyond sight, laden with food that shone with inner light, and at the head of the table, a figure of such radiance that she could not look directly at Him. She woke with joy burning in her chest, a joy that had no earthly explanation.

Mr. Castellanos dreamed of his wife, dead thirty years, standing in a garden more vivid than any earthly garden. She had smiled at him and said, "Soon, my love. Very soon. He is preparing a place."

Little Dinah, who had known only trauma in her twelve years, dreamed of a city with gates of pearl and streets of gold—images from Revelation that she had never read, placed in her mind by the Spirit who teaches all things. She woke laughing for the first time since they had rescued her.

VI WHEN THE HEAVENS ROLLED BACK

"The Spirit is stirring us," Pastor Elijah said when they shared their dreams. "He is the *arrabon*—the down payment, the deposit, the guarantee of our inheritance. He is giving us foretastes of what is to come."

Paul had written of this: *Eye has not seen, nor ear heard, nor have entered into the heart of man the things which God has prepared for those who love Him. But God has revealed them to us through His Spirit.*

The Spirit was revealing. Not everything—they still saw through a glass darkly—but enough. Enough to kindle hope. Enough to strengthen faith. Enough to transform endurance from grim determination into eager expectation.

The anticipation grew as the signs multiplied.

The sun had begun to dim—not metaphorically but literally, a third of its light failing as Revelation had foretold. The stars fell. The powers of the heavens shook.

And the Spirit whispered: *Look up. Your redemption draws near.*

Sister Magdalena felt it most acutely. The Spirit within her had begun to strain toward something—like a compass needle trembling toward true north, like a river rushing toward the sea. Her whole being ached with longing she could barely articulate.

Come, Lord Jesus, her spirit cried, and she knew it was not her own prayer alone but the Spirit praying through her. *Come quickly.*

Paul had written of this too: *The Spirit Himself bears witness with our spirit that we are children of God, and if children, then heirs—heirs of God and joint heirs with Christ, if indeed we suffer with Him, that we may also be glorified together.*

The Spirit was bearing witness. He was testifying to their adoption, reminding them of their inheritance, assuring them that the sufferings of this present time were not worthy to be compared with the glory that would be revealed.

And He was groaning with them—groaning for the redemption that was coming, groaning with longings too deep for words, interceding for them with the Father according to the will of God.

Part Seven: The Maranatha Cry

They had stopped counting the days. Time had become strange in the darkness. Winter seemed permanent.

But they gathered still. They broke bread still—what little bread remained. They shared the cup—wine they had hidden in the walls for three years. And they sang.

Not loudly. Never loudly. But they sang.

"O come, O come, Emmanuel, And ransom captive Israel, That mourns in lonely exile here, Until the Son of God appear..."

And as they sang, the Spirit joined their singing—not with audible voice, but with that inner resonance that turned their thin, hungry voices into something more. The communion of saints, spanning centuries. The great cloud of witnesses, adding their voices from beyond the veil. The angels, hovering at the edges of the visible, their harmonies undergirding the melody.

At the end of the hymn, they whispered the word that the earliest church had whispered, the word that Paul had written to the Corinthians, the word that was at once a prayer and a creed and a defiant hope:

"Maranatha."

Our Lord, come.

And the Spirit whispered back, as He had whispered to the church at the end of Revelation: *The Spirit and the Bride say, "Come!" And let him who hears say, "Come!" And let him who thirsts come. Whoever desires, let him take the water of life freely.*

The Spirit was saying *Come*. The Bride was saying *Come*. And the One who sat on the throne was answering: *Surely I am coming quickly.*

VI WHEN THE HEAVENS ROLLED BACK

Sister Magdalena could no longer walk. The hunger had taken her strength. Brother Thomas carried her to the gatherings, his own bones visible through his skin.

"I am tired," she confessed to him one evening. "I am tired in my soul. I have kept my body pure. I have refused their mark. But I am so tired. How much longer must we endure?"

Thomas opened his Bible, but before he could find the passage, the Spirit brought words to his mind—words of comfort, words precisely fitted to Magdalena's need:

"Sister, the Spirit has not forgotten you. He who began a good work in you will complete it. You have the firstfruits of the Spirit, and you groan inwardly, waiting for the adoption. But the adoption is coming. The redemption of your body is coming. This light affliction, which is but for a moment—"

"Is working for us a far more exceeding and eternal weight of glory," Magdalena finished, the Spirit bringing the words to her own memory.

She closed her eyes. "The Spirit and the Bride say, 'Come,'" she whispered.

"Maranatha," Thomas answered.

And within them both, the Spirit stirred with anticipation that was almost unbearable—the longing of a bride for her bridegroom, the yearning of the whole creation for the revealing of the sons of God.

Soon, the Spirit testified. *Very soon.*

Part Eight: Signs That Could Not Be Mistaken

In the final weeks, the world had reached a crescendo of corruption.

The Architect declared himself the fulfillment of all religions, the final avatar, the culmination of human consciousness. He installed his image in the rebuilt temple in Jerusalem—a holographic presence that demanded worship, that spoke with his voice, that promised eternal pleasure through the Unified Consciousness.

"When you see the abomination of desolation spoken of by Daniel the prophet standing in the holy place," Jesus had warned, *"then let those who are in Judea flee to the mountains."*

The Spirit had prepared them for this moment. For years, He had been teaching them, warning them, giving them wisdom to understand the times. Now, when the sign appeared, they knew what it meant.

The end of the age, the Spirit testified. *The consummation. The time is at hand.*

The sexual depravity reached depths that made Sodom seem innocent. The blood of the martyrs flowed like rivers. And still the world celebrated, still they drank the wine of her fornication.

But the sky had begun to change.

Pastor Elijah gathered them for what he sensed would be the last time.

As he opened his Bible, he felt the Spirit's presence with unusual intensity—not just the quiet companionship he had known for decades, but something more. Something expectant. Something that vibrated with barely contained anticipation.

"Brothers and sisters," he said, "I do not know the day. I do not know the hour. Our Lord told us that not even the angels in heaven know, nor the Son, but only the Father. But the Spirit—"

He paused. The words were coming to him, but they were not his own.

"The Spirit is testifying. Can you feel it? He is the guarantee of our inheritance, and He is telling us that the inheritance is about to be claimed. He is the seal marking us for the day of redemption, and He is telling us that the day of redemption is at hand."

He opened to Matthew 24:29-31:

"Immediately after the tribulation of those days the sun will be darkened, and the moon will not give its light; the stars will fall from heaven, and the

powers of the heavens will be shaken. Then the sign of the Son of Man will appear in heaven, and then all the tribes of the earth will mourn, and they will see the Son of Man coming on the clouds of heaven with power and great glory. And He will send His angels with a great sound of a trumpet, and they will gather together His elect from the four winds, from one end of heaven to the other."

"Immediately after the tribulation," he repeated. "We are in the tribulation. We have been refined in the tribulation. And the Lord—"

He looked at each face. Gaunt. Scarred. Shining.

"The Lord keeps His promises. And the Spirit is saying *Come*."

Part Nine: The Night Before

None of them could sleep that night. There was an electricity in the air—not metaphorical, but actual, a tingling that made their skin prickle and their hearts race. Outside, the sky was darker than it had ever been. The stars were falling—great streaks of light plummeting toward the horizon, the powers of the heavens being shaken.

But inside them, the Spirit was *blazing*.

Sister Imani felt it first—a joy rising in her chest that had no earthly source, a laughter bubbling up that made no logical sense given their circumstances. The Spirit of God, the Spirit of joy unspeakable and full of glory, was filling her.

She began to pray aloud. Not the hesitant whispers they had learned in hiding, but a full voice, a free voice.

"Father, You promised that You would never leave us nor forsake us. You promised that the gates of hell would not prevail against Your church. You promised that our light affliction, which is but for a moment, is working for us a far more exceeding and eternal weight of glory."

Others joined her, and as they prayed, the Spirit prayed through them—interceding with groanings that could not be uttered, aligning their hearts with the will of the Father, preparing them for what was about to happen.

"You promised that You would come again. You promised that where You are, we would be also. You promised that You would wipe away every tear from our eyes, and there would be no more death, nor sorrow, nor crying, nor pain."

Mr. Castellanos lifted his hands toward the shaking sky:

"You promised, Lord. You promised."

Young Sarah, her voice stronger than it had ever been, spoke the words of the martyrs:

"They overcame him by the blood of the Lamb and by the word of their testimony, and they did not love their lives to the death."

And then the Spirit moved upon Sister Magdalena—the Spirit who gives strength to the weary, who raises up those who are bowed down, who fills the hungry with good things. Her voice, thin and frail from starvation, suddenly rang out with supernatural clarity:

"The Spirit and the Bride say, 'Come!' And let him who hears say, 'Come!' Let him who thirsts come. Whoever desires, let him take the water of life freely."

The whole congregation took up the cry:

"Come, Lord Jesus! Come!"

And from within them, the Spirit Himself joined the cry—the longing of God for His people meeting the longing of His people for God, two rivers rushing together toward their confluence.

Then Magdalena began to sing the oldest hymn they knew:

"Christ is risen from the dead, Trampling down death by death, And upon those in the tombs, Bestowing life..."

They sang it together. Eighteen voices. The last church in Newark.

VI WHEN THE HEAVENS ROLLED BACK

And as they sang, the Spirit *surged* within them—not quiet now, not gentle, but rushing like a mighty wind, burning like tongues of fire, crying out *Abba, Father!* through their spirits.

And the eastern sky began to split.

Part Ten: The Shout, the Voice, the Trumpet

It did not begin with light.

It began with sound.

A *crack*—like reality itself tearing at the seams. Then a silence so absolute that Sister Imani felt her heart might stop from the weight of it. Then, building from that silence like a wave rising from an impossibly deep ocean, a *voice*.

Not a human voice. Not even an angelic voice, as they had imagined angels. This was older. This was the voice that had spoken creation into being. This was the voice that had called light from darkness, life from dust, Lazarus from the tomb.

"ARISE!"

And within them, the Spirit *leaped*—not in fear but in recognition, in homecoming, in the joy of a child seeing its Father after long absence. *This is what I have been preparing you for*, the Spirit testified. *This is the moment. This is the day. This is the consummation of all My work in you.*

Brother Thomas recognized what was happening. He had read the words a thousand times:

"For the Lord Himself will descend from heaven with a shout, with the voice of an archangel, and with the trumpet of God."

The archangel's voice shook the foundations of reality itself. Michael—it must be Michael, the great prince who stands for the children of God—was calling the dead to rise.

And they appeared.

Not crawling from graves. Not emerging from earth. They simply *materialized*—as if they had always been there, just beyond the veil of the visible, waiting for the word that would make them manifest.

In the basement, in the space between one heartbeat and the next, Reverend Williams stood among them—*the real Reverend Williams*—his face radiant with a light that seemed to come from within, his body not the broken thing they had secretly buried but something new, something whole, something that was still recognizably *him* and yet utterly transformed.

Imani gasped. Beside her, shimmering into existence like dawn breaking, stood her husband Jerome. And beside him, her sons—David and Emmanuel—their forms luminous, their smiles the same smiles she remembered from before the darkness took them.

Thomas wept. His wife—dead twenty years—was simply *there*, as if she had stepped through a door from another room, a room that had been there all along, a room they could not see until this moment.

The Spirit within the living witnesses bore testimony: *These are the dead in Christ. These are those who sleep in Jesus. They have been with the Lord all this time, and now they are revealed. Now the veil is torn. Now you see what has always been true—that death is not the end, that those who die in Christ are alive in Christ, that the communion of saints is not metaphor but reality.*

"The dead in Christ shall rise first," Paul had written.

And they were rising. They were appearing. They were *becoming visible*.

Across the world, in every place where the martyrs had fallen, the same thing was happening. Not corpses clawing from soil, but *presences* manifesting—stepping through the membrane between eternity and time as easily as one might step through a curtain.

The Spirit bore witness to all of it. He was the One who had sustained these saints through their dying. He was the One who had carried them into the presence of Christ. He was the One who now revealed them to the living, completing the work He had begun in them, bringing them forth in glory.

"We shall not all sleep," Paul had written, *"but we shall all be changed."*

The change was beginning.

Part Eleven: The Gathering

And then the trumpet sounded.

Not a sound that could be produced by metal or breath. A sound that reached into the marrow of their bones, that rewrote their very being, that transformed them in the twinkling of an eye.

Sister Magdalena felt it first. The weariness that had pressed on her for years—gone. The hunger—irrelevant. The frailty of her starved limbs—transformed.

But it was not just her body that changed. The Spirit within her—the Spirit who had indwelt her since her baptism in London forty years ago—was doing something new. He was not leaving her; He was *completing* her. He was not departing; He was *filling* her fully, without the limitations that mortal flesh had imposed.

This is what I have always been working toward, the Spirit testified. *This is the goal of My indwelling—not just to comfort you in your mortality, but to raise you to immortality. Not just to seal you for redemption, but to accomplish the redemption. This corruptible is putting on incorruption. This mortal is putting on immortality.*

She looked at her hands. Still her hands—she recognized the shape, the lines she had known for sixty-three years. But they were *different* now. They glowed faintly, as if lit from within. The Spirit who had always been *in* her was now shining *through* her.

All around her, the living saints were changing. Thomas's aged frame straightening, the years falling away like discarded garments. Imani's scars fading like mist before sunrise. Little Dinah, who had known only fear and violation in her twelve years, now radiant with a wholeness she had never experienced, her body no longer a thing to be used but a temple fully glorified.

The Spirit was completing His temple-building work. Every body He had indwelt was now being raised to the glory that had always been intended.

And then they rose.

Not by effort. Not by will. The earth simply... released them.

Their feet left the ground. The laws of physics acknowledged their true Master and let them go.

"Then we who are alive and remain shall be caught up together with them in the clouds to meet the Lord in the air."

They rose through the ceiling—through it, not around it, because matter could not hold them anymore. They rose past the burning streets, past the drones, past the soldiers who stared in wonder at figures of light ascending from basements and catacombs across the world.

And as they rose, the Spirit rose with them—not departing from them but carrying them, bearing them up as an eagle bears its young on its wings.

The Spirit and the Bride say, "Come!" The words echoed through Magdalena's transformed mind. She was part of the Bride now—fully, completely, visibly. And the Spirit was still with her, would always be with her, was bearing her toward the One she had longed for.

From every direction, from every hidden church and secret gathering, believers were rising. A multitude that no one could number.

Sarah rose, her body no longer a thing that had been violated but a vessel of light. Marcus rose, the boy who had fled the "Liberation Center," now liberated indeed. Mr. Castellanos rose, weeping tears of joy that evaporated into light.

Revelation 7 was coming true:

VI WHEN THE HEAVENS ROLLED BACK

"After these things I looked, and behold, a great multitude which no one could number, of all nations, tribes, peoples, and tongues, standing before the throne and before the Lamb, clothed with white robes."

Part Twelve: The Meeting

And in the clouds, He was waiting.
Not a picture. Not a symbol. Not an idea.
Him.
Jesus of Nazareth. The Son of Man. The Son of God. The Alpha and the Omega. The Lamb who was slain. The Lion of Judah. The Bright and Morning Star.
He was there.
And the Spirit within them *rejoiced*—rejoiced with a joy that Magdalena now understood had always been straining toward this moment. The Spirit had been given to them as a deposit, a guarantee, a down payment. But this was the full inheritance. This was the consummation. This was the moment when the Spirit's work in them was complete, when the sealing was vindicated, when the guarantee was fulfilled.
"It is finished," the Spirit seemed to say. *"I have brought you home."*

Jesus looked at His Bride—not as a collective, but as individuals. He saw each face. He knew each name. He had walked with each of them through every moment of their lives, by His Spirit.
He looked at Magdalena.
His eyes were like a flame of fire—not destroying but *seeing*, seeing through every pretense, every shame, every secret, and loving still. And in those eyes, she saw the truth the Spirit had been testifying to all along: she was beloved. She was His. She had always been His.
"Well done," He said, and His voice was a universe of love compressed into two words. "Well done, good and faithful servant."

She had kept her body pure. She had refused the mark. She had endured to the end. But even as the words of commendation washed over her, she knew it had never been her own strength. It had been the Spirit—comforting, guiding, warning, strengthening, filling her with power beyond her own.

"Enter into the joy of your Lord."

The joy. The *joy*. Not just relief that the suffering was over. Not just happiness that she had survived. But *His* joy—the joy set before Him for which He had endured the cross. The joy of bringing many sons and daughters to glory. The joy of presenting His Bride to Himself, holy and blameless and without wrinkle or spot.

The Spirit had prepared her for this joy. Now she entered it fully.

The martyrs were there—not as memories but as persons. Polycarp and Perpetua. Bonhoeffer and countless nameless faithful from every age. And they were all *one*—united in love while remaining themselves.

This was the communion of saints. This was the fellowship of the Spirit made visible. This was what the Spirit had been creating all along, in every believer, in every age—a temple, a body, a bride.

"And so we shall always be with the Lord," Paul had promised.

Always.

Forever.

Without end.

Epilogue: The World Below

Below them, the world had stopped.

The Architect stood in his tower, surrounded by screens showing the impossible—a sky filled with ascending forms of light, a throne of glory descending, the Lamb who was also the Lion.

For the first time in seven years, he was afraid.

VI WHEN THE HEAVENS ROLLED BACK

His pleasure networks were in chaos. The marks he had placed on billions were burning. On every screen, the same message appeared:

"BEHOLD, HE IS COMING WITH CLOUDS, AND EVERY EYE WILL SEE HIM."

He had worn out the saints of the Most High.
But the Ancient of Days had taken His seat.
And the Son of Man had come.
And the books were opened.

Above the clouds, beyond the reach of sorrow, the great multitude joined their voices with the angels:
"Worthy is the Lamb who was slain To receive power and riches and wisdom, And strength and honor and glory and blessing!"
And every creature in heaven and earth added their voice:
"Blessing and honor and glory and power Be to Him who sits on the throne, And to the Lamb, forever and ever!"
And from the throne came a voice:
"Behold, I make all things new."

Sister Magdalena stood in the light that had no need of sun or moon, for the Lamb Himself was the light. The Spirit who had indwelt her was now her atmosphere, her environment, her eternal communion with the Triune God.

She looked at the world below—the world that had chosen Babylon, that had drunk the wine of her fornication, that had traded the eternal for the immediate.

And she felt no hatred. Only the sorrow of Christ Himself.

But the sorrow did not diminish the joy. Nothing could diminish the joy. For the Spirit's work was complete. The Bride was home. The wedding feast was about to begin.

She whispered one last time the word that had sustained her:

"Maranatha."

And the Lord, descending to make war before her in all His glory, answered:

"Yes, beloved. I have come."

THE END OF THE AGE.

THE BEGINNING OF EVERYTHING.

"He who testifies to these things says, 'Surely I am coming quickly.'"
"Amen. Even so, come, Lord Jesus!"
"The grace of our Lord Jesus Christ be with you all. Amen."
—Revelation 22:20-21

Endnotes

1. The setting of Newark, New Jersey, places this apocalyptic narrative in a specific American urban context. Newark's history as both an industrial center and a city marked by economic decline and renewal

provides symbolic resonance for a story about civilizational collapse and divine redemption.

2. Romans 12:2: "Do not be conformed to this world, but be transformed by the renewal of your mind, that by testing you may discern what is the will of God, what is good and acceptable and perfect" (ESV). This Pauline injunction serves as the moral framework for the believers' resistance to the dystopian culture.

3. Revelation 3:14-22 contains Christ's letter to the church at Laodicea, characterized by lukewarm faith and material self-satisfaction: "For you say, I am rich, I have prospered, and I need nothing, not realizing that you are wretched, pitiable, poor, blind, and naked" (v. 17, ESV). The offer of "eye salve" (v. 18) represents the opportunity for repentance.

4. The identification of the corrupt culture as "Babylon" draws on Revelation 17-18, where Babylon the Great represents the world system opposed to God—characterized by economic exploitation (18:3), sexual immorality (17:2), and persecution of the saints (17:6).

5. 1 Timothy 4:1: "Now the Spirit expressly says that in later times some will depart from the faith by devoting themselves to deceitful spirits and teachings of demons" (ESV). Paul's warning to Timothy about apostasy in the latter times provides scriptural grounding for the narrative's depiction of widespread spiritual defection.

6. The phrase "still small voice" alludes to 1 Kings 19:12, where God speaks to Elijah not in wind, earthquake, or fire, but in "a still small voice" (KJV) or "a low whisper" (ESV). This has become a standard description of the Spirit's inner witness.

7. The figure of "the Architect" represents the Antichrist, drawing on multiple biblical descriptions: "the man of sin" and "the son of

perdition" (2 Thessalonians 2:3, KJV), the beast from the sea (Revelation 13:1-10), and the little horn of Daniel 7:8, 24-25.

8. 2 Thessalonians 2:3-4 describes the "man of lawlessness" who "opposes and exalts himself against every so-called god or object of worship, so that he takes his seat in the temple of God, proclaiming himself to be God" (ESV).

9. 1 Corinthians 1:27: "But God chose what is foolish in the world to shame the wise; God chose what is weak in the world to shame the strong" (ESV). The narrative emphasizes that the Spirit's warnings often seem foolish by worldly standards.

10. Daniel 7:7-8, 19-25 describes the fourth beast with iron teeth and ten horns, and the little horn that rises among them, "speaking great things" and making "war with the saints" (v. 21, ESV).

11. Daniel 7:25: "He shall speak words against the Most High, and shall wear out the saints of the Most High, and shall think to change the times and the law; and they shall be given into his hand for a time, times, and half a time" (ESV). The phrase "wear out" (*bela* in Aramaic) suggests gradual exhaustion through prolonged oppression.

12. Ephesians 1:13-14: "In him you also, when you heard the word of truth, the gospel of your salvation, and believed in him, were sealed with the promised Holy Spirit, who is the guarantee of our inheritance until we acquire possession of it, to the praise of his glory" (ESV). The Greek *arrabōn* (guarantee, deposit, down payment) indicates that the Spirit is the first installment of the full inheritance to come.

13. The phrase "the Comforter" translates the Greek *paraklētos* (John 14:16, 26; 15:26; 16:7), variously rendered as Comforter, Helper, Advocate, or Counselor—one who comes alongside to aid.

VI WHEN THE HEAVENS ROLLED BACK

14. The conversion of Saint Patrick's Cathedral into an "Experience Center" represents the narrative's vision of sacred spaces being repurposed for hedonistic ends—a symbolic desecration parallel to the "abomination of desolation" (Matthew 24:15; Daniel 9:27, 11:31, 12:11).

15. "Do what thou wilt shall be the whole of the Law" is the central maxim of Thelema, the religious philosophy developed by occultist Aleister Crowley (1875-1947). Its appearance in the narrative represents the triumph of radical autonomy over divine law.

16. The mark of the beast is described in Revelation 13:16-17: "Also it causes all, both small and great, both rich and poor, both free and slave, to be marked on the right hand or the forehead, so that no one can buy or sell unless he has the mark, that is, the name of the beast or the number of its name" (ESV).

17. 1 Corinthians 2:10: "these things God has revealed to us through the Spirit. For the Spirit searches everything, even the depths of God" (ESV). The Spirit's comprehensive knowledge enables Him to guide believers with perfect wisdom.

18. Revelation 17:3-4: "And I saw a woman sitting on a scarlet beast that was full of blasphemous names, and it had seven heads and ten horns. The woman was arrayed in purple and scarlet, and adorned with gold and jewels and pearls, holding in her hand a golden cup full of abominations and the impurities of her sexual immorality" (ESV).

19. The "wine of her fornication" (Revelation 17:2, KJV; "wine of her sexual immorality," ESV) represents the intoxicating allure of the Babylonian system—promising pleasure while delivering spiritual death.

20. Joel 2:28-29: "And it shall come to pass afterward, that I will pour out my Spirit on all flesh; your sons and your daughters shall

prophesy, your old men shall dream dreams, and your young men shall see visions. Even on the male and female servants in those days I will pour out my Spirit" (ESV). Peter quotes this passage at Pentecost (Acts 2:17-18) to explain the Spirit's outpouring.

21. The neural implant connecting to pleasure centers represents a technological realization of the beast's control over both commerce and consciousness—making disobedience not just economically costly but neurologically painful.

22. Hebrews 13:5: "I will never leave you nor forsake you" (ESV), quoting Deuteronomy 31:6. Psalm 23:4: "Even though I walk through the valley of the shadow of death, I will fear no evil, for you are with me; your rod and your staff, they comfort me" (ESV).

23. Matthew 19:26: "With man this is impossible, but with God all things are possible" (ESV). The narrative applies this principle to the seemingly impossible regeneration of those who have received the mark.

24. Romans 8:26-27: "Likewise the Spirit helps us in our weakness. For we do not know what to pray for as we ought, but the Spirit himself intercedes for us with groanings too deep for words. And he who searches hearts knows what is the mind of the Spirit, because the Spirit intercedes for the saints according to the will of God" (ESV).

25. Romans 8:22-23: "For we know that the whole creation has been groaning together in the pains of childbirth until now. And not only the creation, but we ourselves, who have the firstfruits of the Spirit, groan inwardly as we wait eagerly for adoption as sons, the redemption of our bodies" (ESV).

26. Romans 13:12: "The night is far gone; the day is at hand. So then let us cast off the works of darkness and put on the armor of light" (ESV).

27. The criminalization of "exclusive truth claims" as "cognitive terrorism" represents an extrapolation of contemporary trends toward viewing religious particularity as inherently harmful—the logical endpoint of a therapeutic culture that values affirmation over truth.

28. Matthew 10:19-20: "When they deliver you over, do not be anxious how you are to speak or what you are to say, for what you are to say will be given to you in that hour. For it is not you who speak, but the Spirit of your Father speaking through you" (ESV). This promise of Spirit-given speech in persecution has sustained martyrs throughout church history.

29. 1 Corinthians 6:19-20: "Or do you not know that your body is a temple of the Holy Spirit within you, whom you have from God? You are not your own, for you were bought with a price. So glorify God in your body" (ESV). This passage provides the theological foundation for the believers' refusal to participate in the system's sexual rituals.

30. Matthew 24:9-13: "Then they will deliver you up to tribulation and put you to death, and you will be hated by all nations for my name's sake. And then many will fall away and betray one another and hate one another. And many false prophets will arise and lead many astray. And because lawlessness will be increased, the love of many will grow cold. But the one who endures to the end will be saved" (ESV).

31. John 14:16-18: "And I will ask the Father, and he will give you another Helper, to be with you forever, even the Spirit of truth... I will not leave you as orphans; I will come to you" (ESV).

32. The Spirit's ministry of guidance is described in John 16:13: "When the Spirit of truth comes, he will guide you into all truth, for he will

not speak on his own authority, but whatever he hears he will speak, and he will declare to you the things that are to come" (ESV).

33. The Greek *arrabōn* (deposit, guarantee) appears three times in the New Testament: Ephesians 1:14, 2 Corinthians 1:22, and 2 Corinthians 5:5. In each case, the Spirit is identified as the down payment guaranteeing the believer's full inheritance.

34. 1 Corinthians 2:9-10: "What no eye has seen, nor ear heard, nor the heart of man imagined, what God has prepared for those who love him—these things God has revealed to us through the Spirit" (ESV), quoting Isaiah 64:4.

35. 1 Corinthians 13:12: "For now we see in a mirror dimly, but then face to face. Now I know in part; then I shall know fully, even as I have been fully known" (ESV).

36. Romans 8:16-17: "The Spirit himself bears witness with our spirit that we are children of God, and if children, then heirs—heirs of God and fellow heirs with Christ, provided we suffer with him in order that we may also be glorified with him" (ESV).

37. The ancient Advent hymn "O Come, O Come, Emmanuel" dates to at least the eighth century in its Latin form (*Veni, Veni, Emmanuel*). Its use in the narrative connects the believers' longing with centuries of Christian anticipation.

38. "Maranatha" is an Aramaic phrase appearing in 1 Corinthians 16:22, meaning either "Our Lord, come!" (*marana tha*) or "Our Lord has come" (*maran atha*). The first interpretation expresses eschatological longing; the second, confessional affirmation. Both meanings resonate in the narrative.

39. Revelation 22:17: "The Spirit and the Bride say, 'Come.' And let the one who hears say, 'Come.' And let the one who is thirsty come; let the one who desires take the water of life without price" (ESV). This

verse depicts the Spirit and the Church united in longing for Christ's return.

40. Philippians 1:6: "And I am sure of this, that he who began a good work in you will bring it to completion at the day of Jesus Christ" (ESV).

41. 3 Corinthians 4:17: "For this light momentary affliction is preparing for us an eternal weight of glory beyond all comparison" (ESV).

42. The dimming of the sun and falling of stars alludes to Matthew 24:29: "Immediately after the tribulation of those days the sun will be darkened, and the moon will not give its light, and the stars will fall from heaven, and the powers of the heavens will be shaken" (ESV). Similar imagery appears in Revelation 6:12-14 and 8:12.

43. Luke 21:28: "Now when these things begin to take place, straighten up and raise your heads, because your redemption is drawing near" (ESV).

44. The "abomination of desolation" (Matthew 24:15; Mark 13:14) references Daniel 9:27, 11:31, and 12:11. The phrase describes an act of sacrilege that desecrates the holy place—historically associated with Antiochus IV Epiphanes's desecration of the temple in 167 BC, and prophetically with end-times events.

45. Matthew 24:29-31 (ESV). This passage, part of the Olivet Discourse, describes the visible return of Christ following the tribulation.

46. 1 Thessalonians 4:16: "For the Lord himself will descend from heaven with a cry of command, with the voice of an archangel, and with the sound of the trumpet of God" (ESV).

47. Michael the archangel appears in Daniel 10:13, 21; 12:1; Jude 9; and Revelation 12:7. Daniel 12:1 describes him as "the great prince who has charge of your people" who will arise at the time of unprecedented tribulation.

48. 1 Thessalonians 4:16: "And the dead in Christ will rise first" (ESV). The resurrection of deceased believers precedes the transformation of living believers in Paul's eschatological sequence.
49. The description of resurrection bodies as "transformed" rather than merely resuscitated reflects Paul's teaching in 1 Corinthians 15:42-44: "So is it with the resurrection of the dead. What is sown is perishable; what is raised is imperishable. It is sown in dishonor; it is raised in glory. It is sown in weakness; it is raised in power. It is sown a natural body; it is raised a spiritual body" (ESV).
50. 1 Corinthians 15:51-52: "Behold! I tell you a mystery. We shall not all sleep, but we shall all be changed, in a moment, in the twinkling of an eye, at the last trumpet. For the trumpet will sound, and the dead will be raised imperishable, and we shall be changed" (ESV).
51. 1 Corinthians 15:53-54: "For this perishable body must put on the imperishable, and this mortal body must put on immortality. When the perishable puts on the imperishable, and the mortal puts on immortality, then shall come to pass the saying that is written: 'Death is swallowed up in victory'" (ESV).
52. 1 Thessalonians 4:17: "Then we who are alive, who are left, will be caught up together with them in the clouds to meet the Lord in the air, and so we will always be with the Lord" (ESV). The Latin *rapio* (to seize, snatch away) in the Vulgate translation of this verse gives rise to the term "rapture."
53. Deuteronomy 32:11: "Like an eagle that stirs up its nest, that flutters over its young, spreading out its wings, catching them, bearing them on its pinions" (ESV). The image of God as an eagle bearing His people on wings appears also in Exodus 19:4.
54. Revelation 7:9: "After this I looked, and behold, a great multitude that no one could number, from every nation, from all tribes and peoples and languages, standing before the throne and before the

VI WHEN THE HEAVENS ROLLED BACK

Lamb, clothed in white robes, with palm branches in their hands" (ESV).

55. The titles applied to Christ—"Jesus of Nazareth," "Son of Man," "Son of God," "Alpha and Omega," "Lamb who was slain," "Lion of Judah," "Bright and Morning Star"—are drawn from throughout the New Testament: the Gospels, Daniel 7:13-14, Revelation 1:8, 5:5-6, and 22:16.

56. Revelation 1:14: "his eyes were like a flame of fire" (ESV). This description of the risen Christ emphasizes His penetrating vision that sees all things clearly.

57. Matthew 25:21: "His master said to him, 'Well done, good and faithful servant. You have been faithful over a little; I will set you over much. Enter into the joy of your master'" (ESV).

58. Hebrews 12:2: "looking to Jesus, the founder and perfecter of our faith, who for the joy that was set before him endured the cross, despising the shame, and is seated at the right hand of the throne of God" (ESV).

59. Ephesians 5:27: Christ's purpose is "so that he might present the church to himself in splendor, without spot or wrinkle or any such thing, that she might be holy and without blemish" (ESV).

60. 1 Thessalonians 4:17: "and so we will always be with the Lord" (ESV). The promise of eternal presence with Christ is the ultimate hope of Christian eschatology.

61. Polycarp of Smyrna (c. 69-155 AD), bishop and martyr, was burned at the stake for refusing to curse Christ. Perpetua (c. 181-203 AD) was a young noblewoman martyred in Carthage, whose prison diary survives as one of the earliest Christian texts written by a woman. Dietrich Bonhoeffer (1906-1945), German theologian and pastor, was executed by the Nazis for his participation in the resistance.

62. The phrase "communion of saints" (*communio sanctorum*) appears in the Apostles' Creed and refers to the spiritual unity of all believers—living and dead—in Christ. The narrative portrays this communion as a present reality made visible at the eschaton.
63. Revelation 1:7: "Behold, he is coming with the clouds, and every eye will see him, even those who pierced him, and all tribes of the earth will wail on account of him. Even so. Amen" (ESV).
64. Daniel 7:25: "he shall wear out the saints of the Most High" (ESV). Daniel 7:9: "the Ancient of Days took his seat" (ESV). Daniel 7:13-14 describes the Son of Man coming with the clouds of heaven to receive dominion from the Ancient of Days.
65. Revelation 5:12: "Worthy is the Lamb who was slain, to receive power and wealth and wisdom and might and honor and glory and blessing!" (ESV).
66. Revelation 5:13: "And I heard every creature in heaven and on earth and under the earth and in the sea, and all that is in them, saying, 'To him who sits on the throne and to the Lamb be blessing and honor and glory and might forever and ever!'" (ESV).
67. Revelation 21:5: "And he who was seated on the throne said, 'Behold, I am making all things new'" (ESV).
68. Revelation 21:23: "And the city has no need of sun or moon to shine on it, for the glory of God gives it light, and its lamp is the Lamb" (ESV).
69. The Paschal Troparion, "Christ is risen from the dead, trampling down death by death, and upon those in the tombs bestowing life," is the central hymn of Eastern Orthodox Easter celebration, dating to at least the eighth century. Its use in the narrative connects the believers' hope to the ancient liturgical tradition.
70. Revelation 22:20-21: "He who testifies to these things says, 'Surely I am coming soon.' Amen. Come, Lord Jesus! The grace of the Lord

Jesus be with all. Amen" (ESV). These final verses of Scripture express the church's eschatological longing and confidence.

VII
THE RELIGION OF THE GREAT HARLOT

A Warning Against Counterfeit Faith in the Last Days

The Woman on the Beast

In the seventeenth chapter of Revelation, the apostle John is carried away in the Spirit to witness a vision that has haunted the church for two millennia:

"Then one of the seven angels who had the seven bowls came and talked with me, saying to me, 'Come, I will show you the judgment of the great harlot who sits on many waters, with whom the kings of the earth committed fornication, and the inhabitants of the earth were made drunk with the wine of her fornication.' So he carried me away in the Spirit into the wilderness. And I saw a woman sitting on a scarlet beast which was full of names of blasphemy, having seven heads and ten horns. The woman was arrayed in purple and scarlet, and adorned with gold and precious stones and pearls, having in her hand a golden cup full of abominations and the filthiness of her fornication. And on her forehead a name was written: MYSTERY, BABYLON THE GREAT, THE MOTHER OF HARLOTS AND OF THE ABOMINATIONS OF THE EARTH."

—Revelation 17:1-5

John marveled with great amazement—the Greek suggests horror, not admiration. For what he saw was not merely a political entity or an economic system, but a *religious* reality. The harlot holds a golden cup—the vessel of worship, of communion, of sacrament. She is dressed in the colors of royalty and priesthood. She sits upon waters, which the angel interprets as "peoples, multitudes, nations, and tongues."

This is counterfeit religion. This is the devil's masterwork—not atheism, which is too obvious, but a spirituality that satisfies the religious impulse while directing worship away from the living God. She is called "mother of harlots," which means she has daughters. She has offspring. Her religion reproduces.

And she is drunk on the blood of the saints.

The Testimony of the Early Church

What the Fathers Saw

We do not read Revelation in a vacuum. For two millennia, the church has wrestled with its imagery, and the earliest interpreters—those closest to the apostolic age, many of whom faced the very persecutions John's vision addressed—left us their understanding. Their witness is not infallible, but it is instructive. They saw things we may miss, and they faced pressures that clarify the text's original meaning.

The early church fathers were nearly unanimous in identifying Babylon with Rome—the imperial power that dominated their world, that demanded worship of Caesar, that shed the blood of the martyrs. But they also understood that Rome was not merely a political entity. Rome was a *spiritual* reality, a manifestation of the world-system opposed to God, a carrier of the harlot's religion.

Irenaeus of Lyon, writing in the second century as a disciple of Polycarp (who himself had known the apostle John), understood Babylon as the embodiment of worldly power aligned against Christ. In his work *Against*

Heresies, he traced the lineage of false religion from the earliest corruptions through to the coming Antichrist:

"By means of the events which shall occur in the time of Antichrist it is shown that he, being an apostate and a robber, is anxious to be adored as God; and that, although a mere slave, he wishes himself to be proclaimed as a king. For he being endued with all the power of the devil, shall come, not as a righteous king, nor as a legitimate king in subjection to God, but an impious, unjust, and lawless one... setting aside idols to persuade men that he himself is God."

Irenaeus understood that the harlot's religion would culminate in a figure who demanded worship—not alongside the true God, but in place of Him. This was the pattern of Babylon from Nebuchadnezzar's golden image to Caesar's divine claims: the exaltation of the creature demanding the worship owed only to the Creator.

Hippolytus of Rome, writing in the early third century, composed both a *Commentary on Daniel* and a treatise *On Christ and Antichrist* that developed these themes further. He saw the four kingdoms of Daniel's vision culminating in Rome, and he understood that Rome's fall would give way to something worse—a final manifestation of the beast that would deceive the nations:

"The golden head of the image and the lioness denoted the Babylonians; the shoulders and arms of silver, and the bear, represented the Persians and Medes; the belly and thighs of brass, and the leopard, meant the Greeks, who held the sovereignty from Alexander's time; the legs of iron, and the beast dreadful and terrible, expressed the Romans, who hold the sovereignty at present; the toes of the feet which were part clay and part iron, and the ten horns, were emblems of the kingdoms that are yet to rise; the other little horn that grows up among them meant the Antichrist in their midst."

Hippolytus understood that the harlot rode upon the beast—that false religion and worldly power were intertwined, mutually supporting, feeding off each other. The state provided the power; the harlot provided the spiritual justification. Together they formed a system of control that demanded total allegiance.

Victorinus of Pettau, martyred around 304 AD, wrote the earliest surviving Latin commentary on Revelation. He identified Babylon explicitly with Rome but saw in Rome a pattern that would recur:

"Babylon, that is, the Roman city, which has ruled over the kings of the earth, sitting upon seven hills, drunk with the blood of the saints."

Yet Victorinus also understood that the imagery transcended any single empire. Babylon was a *type*—a recurring pattern of worldly power opposed to God, seductive in its appeal, murderous in its methods. Every generation would face its own Babylon, its own manifestation of the harlot's religion.

The City of Man Against the City of God

Augustine of Hippo, writing in the early fifth century as Rome itself was falling to barbarian invasions, developed the most comprehensive framework for understanding Babylon in his monumental *City of God*. For Augustine, human history was the story of two cities—the city of God and the city of man—intermingled in time but destined for separation in eternity.

"Two cities have been formed by two loves: the earthly by the love of self, even to the contempt of God; the heavenly by the love of God, even to the contempt of self. The former, in a word, glories in itself, the latter in the Lord."

Babylon, for Augustine, was not merely Rome or any single empire. It was the *civitas terrena*—the earthly city—in all its manifestations throughout history. Wherever human beings organized themselves around self-love, self-glorification, and self-worship, there Babylon stood. Wherever the creature was exalted above the Creator, there the harlot held court.

This framework is essential for understanding the harlot's religion in our own time. We are not looking merely for a future city or a specific political entity. We are discerning a *spirit*—the spirit of the world, the spirit of self-worship, the spirit that pervades human culture whenever it turns from God.

Augustine recognized that this spirit could infiltrate even the visible church:

"In this wicked world, in these evil days, when the Church measures her future loftiness by her present humility... in these days, I say, many reprobate are mingled in the Church with the good."

The wheat and the tares grow together. The city of God and the city of man are intermingled even within the church's visible boundaries. Not everyone who claims the name of Christ belongs to Him. Not every religion that uses Christian vocabulary is genuine Christianity.

The Pattern Across the Ages

Tertullian of Carthage, writing around 200 AD, understood that Rome's persecution of Christians was fundamentally religious, not merely political:

"We are worshippers of one God, of whose existence and character Nature teaches all men... We have rejected your gods, we refuse to acknowledge the emperor's divinity... we offer prayer for the safety of our princes to the eternal, the true, the living God."

The conflict was over worship. Rome could tolerate many religions—indeed, the empire was remarkably pluralistic—but it could not tolerate a religion that refused to acknowledge Caesar as lord. The harlot's religion always demands synthesis. It always requires that the true God be placed alongside other gods, that His exclusive claims be softened, that His worship be blended with the world's worship.

Christians died because they would not add a pinch of incense to Caesar's altar. Not because Rome demanded they abandon Christ entirely—at least not initially—but because Rome demanded they *add*

Caesar to their devotion. The harlot is not satisfied with total rejection of God; she is satisfied with His demotion. She is content if He becomes one god among many, one option among options, one path among paths.

Cyprian of Carthage, martyred in 258 AD, faced a church that had been compromised by persecution. Many Christians had offered sacrifice to Roman gods to save their lives—the *lapsi*, the "fallen ones." Cyprian wrestled with how to restore them while maintaining the church's integrity:

"The Lord's breast alone was not wounded by the javelin of the enemy, because it was protected by the breastplate of faith. He who had not armed himself for the battle was prostrated: he who had not watched and kept the Lord's precepts was overpowered."

Cyprian understood that compromise with the harlot's religion was spiritual death, even when undertaken to preserve physical life. The church could not accommodate itself to Babylon's demands and remain the church. Those who had fallen needed genuine repentance, not easy restoration.

This is the testimony of the early church: Babylon is real. The harlot's religion is present in every age. She demands compromise, synthesis, the softening of exclusive claims. She offers acceptance in exchange for apostasy, survival in exchange for surrender. And the church that yields to her seduction ceases to be the church of Jesus Christ.

Jerome and the Coming Deception

Jerome, the great translator of the Latin Vulgate, writing in the late fourth and early fifth centuries, saw in Babylon both present and future significance. Commenting on Daniel's visions, he wrote:

"Let us not follow the opinion of some commentators and suppose him to be either the Devil or some demon, but rather one of the human race, in whom Satan will wholly take up his residence in bodily form."

Jerome understood that the final manifestation of Babylon's religion would be personal—embodied in an individual who would demand worship while claiming to fulfill human aspirations. This was not merely institutional corruption but incarnate evil, a human vessel filled with satanic deception.

He also warned that this deception would be persuasive precisely because it would appeal to legitimate desires:

"He will be born of the Jewish people... and will reign in Jerusalem, and will rebuild the temple... so that he may deceive even the elect, if it were possible."

The deception would look *religious*. It would use sacred language, sacred spaces, sacred expectations. It would present itself as the fulfillment of prophecy, the answer to prayer, the culmination of hope. This is why only the elect would escape—and even they only by divine protection, not by their own discernment.

The Witness Applied

What shall we draw from this patristic testimony?

First, the harlot's religion is not merely future but present. Every generation faces its own Babylon, its own pressure to compromise, its own temptation to blend true worship with false. The early church faced Caesar; we face other powers. But the pattern is identical.

Second, the danger comes not primarily from obvious paganism but from *synthesis*. The harlot does not always demand the total rejection of Christ; she is satisfied if He is merely demoted, relativized, made one option among many. This is her subtlety. This is why she deceives even those who think they worship the true God.

Third, the compromise that Babylon demands often seems small. A pinch of incense. A momentary acknowledgment. A slight softening of exclusive claims. But small compromises lead to total apostasy. The early

VII THE RELIGION OF THE GREAT HARLOT

martyrs died over what seemed like trifles because they understood that there are no trifles when it comes to the lordship of Christ.

Fourth, the church itself can become Babylonized. When the church pursues power, wealth, cultural acceptance, and influence at the cost of faithfulness, she becomes indistinguishable from the harlot. When she silences the prophetic voice to maintain comfortable relations with the state, she drinks from the golden cup. When she revises her message to avoid persecution, she has already fallen.

The fathers call us to vigilance. They call us to recognize the patterns. They call us to resist compromise, even unto death.

For the harlot is always recruiting. And her cup is always full.

The Leaven of Herod

The Warning Jesus Gave

In the Gospel of Mark, sandwiched between two miracles of provision, Jesus issued a cryptic warning that His disciples failed to understand:

"Then He charged them, saying, 'Take heed, beware of the leaven of the Pharisees and the leaven of Herod.'" (Mark 8:15)

The disciples, preoccupied with their lack of bread, missed the point entirely. Jesus rebuked them: "Do you not yet perceive nor understand? Is your heart still hardened?" (Mark 8:17).

We have spent much time in this book examining the leaven of the Pharisees—the corruption of religion through hypocrisy, external conformity without internal transformation, the substitution of human tradition for divine command. But the leaven of Herod has received less attention, and in our present moment, it may be the more pressing danger.

What was the leaven of Herod?

Herod represented political power accommodated to religious language. The Herodian dynasty maintained a facade of Jewish identity while serving

Roman interests. Herod the Great rebuilt the temple in magnificent splendor—and murdered innocents in Bethlehem. His descendants kept the Jewish feasts—and collaborated with the empire that occupied the holy land. The Herodians were pragmatists who believed that political power, properly wielded, could secure the future of God's people.

They were wrong.

The leaven of Herod is the corruption that occurs when the people of God place their trust in political power, when they believe that the kingdom of God can be advanced through the kingdoms of this world, when they conflate national identity with covenant identity, when they compromise their prophetic witness for a seat at the table of earthly authority.

This leaven works slowly, invisibly, pervasively—just as yeast works through dough. It does not announce itself as idolatry. It presents itself as wisdom, as stewardship, as the responsible exercise of citizenship. But left unchecked, it transforms the entire loaf. It converts the church from an outpost of heaven into a chaplaincy for empire.

The Temptation in the Wilderness

Before Jesus began His public ministry, He faced three temptations in the wilderness. The third—or the second, in Luke's ordering—was explicitly political:

"Then the devil, taking Him up on a high mountain, showed Him all the kingdoms of the world in a moment of time. And the devil said to Him, 'All this authority I will give You, and their glory; for this has been delivered to me, and I give it to whomever I wish. Therefore, if You will worship before me, all will be Yours.'" (Luke 4:5-7)

Notice what Satan offered: all the kingdoms of the world, all their authority, all their glory. And notice his claim: "This has been delivered to me, and I give it to whomever I wish." Jesus did not dispute this claim. The

VII THE RELIGION OF THE GREAT HARLOT

prince of this world does exercise a kind of dominion over earthly political systems. They are not neutral territory.

Satan's offer was a shortcut to dominion—a way to establish the kingdom without the cross, to reign without first suffering, to achieve through political means what could only be legitimately accomplished through sacrificial love.

Jesus refused. "Get behind Me, Satan! For it is written, 'You shall worship the LORD your God, and Him only you shall serve.'" (Luke 4:8)

But the temptation did not end in the wilderness. It followed Jesus throughout His ministry. After the feeding of the five thousand, the crowds attempted to "take Him by force to make Him king" (John 6:15). Jesus withdrew. His disciples repeatedly misunderstood His mission in political terms, arguing about who would sit at His right and left hand in the coming kingdom. Even after the resurrection, they asked, "Lord, will You at this time restore the kingdom to Israel?" (Acts 1:6).

The political temptation is persistent. It appeals to legitimate desires—for justice, for righteousness, for the vindication of God's people. But it offers these goods through illegitimate means: the exercise of worldly power rather than the way of the cross.

And Satan still offers this bargain to the church.

Israel's Demand for a King

The pattern is as old as the people of God.

In the days of Samuel, when Israel was governed by judges who ruled under God's direct authority, the elders came to the aging prophet with a demand:

"Look, you are old, and your sons do not walk in your ways. Now make us a king to judge us like all the nations." (1 Samuel 8:5)

The request displeased Samuel, but God's response revealed the deeper issue:

REDEEMING RELIGION

"And the LORD said to Samuel, 'Heed the voice of the people in all that they say to you; for they have not rejected you, but they have rejected Me, that I should not reign over them. According to all the works which they have done since the day that I brought them up out of Egypt, even to this day—with which they have forsaken Me and served other gods—so they are doing to you also.'" (1 Samuel 8:7-8)

"They have rejected Me, that I should not reign over them."

The desire for a human king—a political savior, a strong leader who would fight their battles and secure their future—was, at its root, a rejection of divine kingship. It was a failure of faith. It was the belief that God's invisible reign was insufficient, that what they needed was visible power "like all the nations."

God granted their request, but He also warned them what it would cost. The king would take their sons for his armies and their daughters for his service. He would take the best of their fields and vineyards and give them to his servants. He would take a tenth of their grain and flocks. "And you will cry out in that day because of your king whom you have chosen for yourselves, and the LORD will not hear you in that day" (1 Samuel 8:18).

They would get their king. And they would discover that human kings, even the best of them, cannot deliver what God alone provides. They would learn that political power is a jealous master that demands ever-increasing sacrifice. They would find that trusting in princes leads ultimately to disappointment, exile, and judgment.

The warning echoes through the centuries: "Do not put your trust in princes, in human beings, who cannot save. When their spirit departs, they return to the ground; on that very day their plans come to nothing. Blessed are those whose help is the God of Jacob, whose hope is in the LORD their God." (Psalm 146:3-5)

The Prophets Against Political Alliance

VII THE RELIGION OF THE GREAT HARLOT

The Old Testament prophets thundered against Israel's tendency to seek security through political alliance rather than trust in God.

When Assyria threatened from the north, Israel looked to Egypt for help. Isaiah confronted this with devastating clarity:

"Woe to those who go down to Egypt for help, and rely on horses, who trust in chariots because they are many, and in horsemen because they are very strong, but who do not look to the Holy One of Israel, nor seek the LORD!" (Isaiah 31:1)

Egypt had horses and chariots. Egypt had military might. Egypt seemed like a reasonable ally against the Assyrian threat. But Isaiah saw through the political calculus to the spiritual reality: trusting in Egypt was a failure to trust in God.

"Now the Egyptians are men, and not God; and their horses are flesh, and not spirit. When the LORD stretches out His hand, both he who helps will fall, and he who is helped will fall down; they all will perish together." (Isaiah 31:3)

The Egyptians are men, not God. Their horses are flesh, not spirit. Political power, however impressive, is merely human. It cannot save. It cannot deliver. It cannot accomplish what only God can accomplish.

Jeremiah delivered the same message a century later, as Judah vacillated between Babylon and Egypt:

"Thus says the LORD: 'Cursed is the man who trusts in man and makes flesh his strength, whose heart departs from the LORD. For he shall be like a shrub in the desert, and shall not see when good comes, but shall inhabit the parched places in the wilderness, in a salt land which is not inhabited. Blessed is the man who trusts in the LORD, and whose hope is the LORD. For he shall be like a tree planted by the waters, which spreads out its roots by the river, and will not fear when heat comes; but its leaf will be green, and will not be anxious in the year of drought, nor will cease from yielding fruit.'" (Jeremiah 17:5-8)

Cursed is the man who trusts in man. Cursed is the one who makes flesh his strength. Cursed is the heart that departs from the LORD to find security in political alliance.

This is the prophetic witness, consistent across the centuries: political power cannot do what God alone can do. To trust in it is to be cursed. To hope in it is to be disappointed. To make it the object of faith is to commit idolatry.

The American Temptation

We must now speak plainly about a particular manifestation of the leaven of Herod that afflicts the American church.

The United States of America is not the kingdom of God. The United States of America is not a covenant nation in the sense that ancient Israel was. The United States of America, for all its genuine blessings and historical contributions, is a temporal political entity that will one day pass away, as all earthly kingdoms pass away.

This seems obvious when stated plainly. But the practice of many American Christians suggests they believe otherwise.

Christian nationalism is the leaven of Herod in American form. It is the conflation of Christian identity with American identity, the merger of cross and flag, the belief that God's purposes in history are specially and uniquely bound up with the success of one political nation. It transforms the church from a pilgrim people whose citizenship is in heaven into a political constituency whose primary concern is earthly power. It converts prophetic witness into partisan advocacy. It makes the gospel a means to political ends rather than an end in itself.

This leaven works on both the left and the right of the political spectrum, though its forms differ.

On the right, it manifests as the belief that America is or was a "Christian nation" in a covenantal sense, that recovering America's greatness is essentially a religious duty, that certain political leaders are divinely appointed instruments of national salvation, that opposing certain political movements is tantamount to opposing God Himself. It wraps the gospel in the flag and cannot distinguish between patriotism and piety. It treats political defeats as spiritual catastrophes and political victories as revivals.

On the left, it manifests as the belief that progressive political causes *are* the gospel, that social justice as defined by secular ideologies is equivalent to the justice Scripture demands, that the kingdom of God will be realized through legislative achievement, that Christians who do not support certain political agendas are unfaithful to Jesus. It wraps the gospel in a different flag—the flag of secular progressivism—and cannot distinguish between political activism and Christian discipleship.

Both are forms of the leaven of Herod. Both subordinate the eternal to the temporal. Both reduce the church to a political faction. Both are betrayals of Christ.

The Marks of Political Idolatry

How do we recognize when political engagement has become political idolatry? Here are the marks:

When political identity determines fellowship more than Christ does. When you feel more kinship with an unbeliever who shares your politics than with a believer who does not, the leaven has spread. When you cannot worship alongside Christians who vote differently, when political disagreement becomes grounds for breaking communion, when you would sooner have a politically aligned pagan as a neighbor than a politically different saint—you have made politics your functional religion.

When political figures are treated as messianic. When any human leader is spoken of in terms that should be reserved for Christ alone—as the one who will save the nation, restore what was lost, defeat the forces of evil—idolatry is present. No president, no prime minister, no party leader can bear the weight of messianic expectation. To place such expectations on them is to court inevitable disappointment and to commit the sin of Israel in demanding a king.

When political opponents are demonized rather than evangelized. The Christian recognizes that our battle is not against flesh and blood but against principalities and powers. Our political opponents are not our ultimate enemies; they are lost sheep for whom Christ died. When we hate them, slander them, wish evil upon them, rejoice in their suffering—we have ceased to follow the One who commanded us to love our enemies and pray for those who persecute us.

When political victory is conflated with spiritual victory. The kingdom of God does not advance through electoral success. The church has thrived under hostile governments and languished under friendly ones. Our hope is not in who occupies the seat of power but in the One who is seated at the right hand of the Father. When we despair at political losses as if the gospel itself had been defeated, or exult in political wins as if the kingdom had finally come, we have confused the kingdoms.

When we compromise moral witness for political access. The prophets of Israel did not trim their message to maintain favor with kings. John the Baptist lost his head rather than stay silent about Herod's adultery. When the church softens its witness on matters of clear biblical teaching in order to maintain political alliance—when we overlook in our allies what we would condemn in our opponents—we have sold our birthright for a mess of political pottage.

When fear drives us more than faith. Political idolatry feeds on fear—fear of what "they" will do if they gain power, fear of cultural decline, fear of persecution, fear of irrelevance. But "God has not given us a spirit of fear, but of power and of love and of a sound mind" (2 Timothy 1:7). When our political engagement is driven by anxiety about outcomes rather than faithfulness to calling, we have forgotten who is actually in control.

The Idol Factory of the Heart

John Calvin, for all his strangeness, rightly described the human heart as a "perpetual factory of idols." We do not need to go looking for idolatry; we manufacture it constantly. And political idolatry is among the most seductive forms because it disguises itself as virtue.

The Christian who worships power thinks he is being responsible.

The Christian who trusts in princes thinks she is being strategic.

The Christian who conflates nation with kingdom thinks he is being faithful.

The Christian who demonizes opponents thinks she is being discerning.

But the heart is deceitful above all things, and desperately wicked—who can know it? (Jeremiah 17:9). We are capable of baptizing our idolatries with religious language, of convincing ourselves that our will to power is actually zeal for God's kingdom, of believing that our political tribe is the righteous remnant and our opponents are the servants of darkness.

This is why we must be ruthless in self-examination. This is why we must hold our political commitments loosely while holding our commitment to Christ absolutely. This is why we must allow the Word of God to judge our politics rather than using our politics to judge the Word of God.

A Prelude to Greater Deception

Here is the gravest danger of political idolatry: it prepares the heart for greater deception.

Those who have learned to trust in political saviors are primed to receive the ultimate political savior—the one who will come with solutions to every crisis, answers to every fear, promises of security and prosperity. Those who have conflated kingdom with nation will struggle to discern when national loyalty demands the betrayal of Christ. Those who have made political identity more fundamental than Christian identity will find it easy to add the mark of the beast to their political affiliation.

Remember Daniel's vision: the beast is a *political* entity. It exercises *political* power. It demands *political* allegiance. And the harlot rides upon it—false religion using political power for her purposes.

The end-time deception will not be merely spiritual; it will be political. The Antichrist will not only demand worship; he will exercise governmental authority. The mark of the beast will not only be a religious symbol; it will be an economic and political necessity. Those who have spent their lives investing ultimate hope in political systems will find it nearly impossible to resist when the ultimate political system offers them everything they have sought.

This is why Jesus warned about the leaven of Herod in the same breath as the leaven of the Pharisees. Religious corruption and political corruption work together. The Pharisees provided theological justification for the status quo; the Herodians provided political enforcement. Together they crucified Christ.

And together, their spiritual descendants will persecute His church.

The Christian who has already learned to bow to political pressure, to trim the gospel for political access, to invest hope in earthly power—this Christian has been practicing for apostasy. When the pressure intensifies, when the cost of faithfulness becomes total, they will discover that their faith was never in Christ alone. They will fall away because they were never truly grounded in the first place.

But the Christian who has learned to hold all political loyalties loosely, who has practiced saying "Jesus is Lord" when it cost them culturally, who has refused to make the flag an idol even when accused of being unpatriotic—this Christian will have the spiritual muscle memory to resist when the final test comes.

We must develop that muscle memory now.

The Prophetic Posture

What then is the proper posture of the church toward political power?

Prophetic, not partisan. The church must speak truth to power, whoever holds it. We must be equally willing to confront wickedness in leaders we voted for as in leaders we opposed. We must refuse to become the court chaplains of any regime, blessing its every action. When Nathan confronted David's adultery, he did not first calculate the political implications. When Elijah opposed Ahab, he did not worry about maintaining access. The prophet speaks God's word regardless of political consequence.

Engaged, not entangled. Christians may and should participate in the political process. We are citizens of earthly nations as well as the heavenly city. We may vote, hold office, advocate for justice, work for the common good. But we must do so as ambassadors of another kingdom, not as ultimate loyalists to this one. We are passing through. Our citizenship is elsewhere. We must not become so entangled in earthly politics that we lose sight of our primary mission: to proclaim Christ and Him crucified.

Hopeful, not anxious. We do not need to be driven by fear of political outcomes because we know how the story ends. Christ wins. Every knee will bow. The kingdoms of this world will become the kingdoms of our Lord and of His Christ. This knowledge should make us the least anxious political actors on the scene—not passive or disengaged, but fundamentally untroubled by electoral results. Our hope does not rise or fall with any party's fortunes.

Loving, not tribal. We must refuse to treat political opponents as enemies to be destroyed. We must see in them image-bearers of God for whom Christ died. We must pray for their salvation, not merely their defeat. We must maintain relationships across political divides, demonstrating that the unity we have in Christ transcends the divisions that fragment the world.

Come Out of Her

The call of this book is to come out of Babylon. And Babylon is not only religious corruption; it is political idolatry. It is the merger of throne and altar in opposition to God. It is the beast that demands worship and the harlot that provides theological justification for the demand.

To come out of Babylon is to renounce the leaven of Herod as thoroughly as the leaven of the Pharisees.

It is to say: "My hope is not in elephants or donkeys but in the Lion of the tribe of Judah."

It is to say: "My identity is not first American or British or any other nationality but Christian—citizen of a kingdom that cannot be shaken."

It is to say: "I will not bow to any political power that demands what belongs to God alone, even if that power wraps itself in religious language and claims divine sanction."

It is to say: "I will hold my political opinions loosely and my commitment to Christ absolutely, and when they conflict, I will choose Christ."

The hour is late. The leaven has spread further than we know. The foundations of political idolatry have been laid over generations, and many who think they are building the kingdom of God are actually building the kingdom of the beast.

The Architect of our story did not emerge from a vacuum. He emerged from a world that had been prepared—by entertainment that glorified pleasure, by education that relativized truth, and by *churches that had conflated political power with spiritual faithfulness*. When he arose, promising to solve every problem and fulfill every fear-driven desire, millions who called themselves Christians were ready to receive him. They had been practicing for years.

Let us not practice for apostasy.

Let us purge the leaven of Herod.

Let us remember that Christ refused the devil's offer of political power—and calls us to do the same.

"For here we have no continuing city, but we seek the one to come." (Hebrews 13:14)

Our city is coming. Its builder and maker is God. And no election, no regime, no political revolution can hasten or delay its arrival.

Until then, we are pilgrims. We are ambassadors. We are prophets.

Let us live accordingly.

The Ancient Pattern of False Worship

The religion of the great harlot did not emerge suddenly at the end of history. Her foundations were laid in Eden, when the serpent offered Eve a different kind of worship—a religion of self-deification, of knowledge without obedience, of desire as its own justification.

"You will be like God," the serpent promised. And this has been the harlot's message ever since: *You are your own god. Your desires are divine. Your appetites are sacraments.*

We see her in the golden calf at Sinai, when the people grew impatient with Moses and demanded gods they could see and control. Aaron fashioned the idol and declared, "This is your god, O Israel, who brought you out of Egypt!" (Exodus 32:4). Notice the theological sleight of hand: he attributed the true God's works to a false god. The harlot always mingles truth with lie, always co-opts the language of salvation for her own purposes.

We see her in the Baals of Canaan, the fertility cults that promised prosperity through ritual prostitution, that merged worship with sensuality, that made religion the servant of appetite. The prophet Hosea understood this pattern intimately. God commanded him to marry a prostitute precisely to illustrate Israel's spiritual adultery:

"For their mother has played the harlot; she who conceived them has behaved shamefully. For she said, 'I will go after my lovers, who give me my bread and my water, my wool and my linen, my oil and my drink.'"

—Hosea 2:5

The harlot's religion promises material provision. It offers tangible benefits. It delivers immediate satisfaction. And it does so while using the vocabulary of faith.

The Prophetic Witness Against Counterfeit Religion

The Old Testament prophets thundered against this false worship with a consistency that should alarm us. Their warnings were not primarily against paganism—against the worship of obviously foreign gods—but against the corruption of Yahweh worship itself. Against religion that maintained the forms while abandoning the substance. Against faith that honored God with lips while hearts remained far from Him.

Isaiah delivered this indictment:

"To what purpose is the multitude of your sacrifices to Me?" says the LORD. "I have had enough of burnt offerings of rams and the fat of fed cattle. I do not delight in the blood of bulls, or of lambs or goats. When you come to appear before Me, who has required this from your hand, to trample My courts? Bring no more futile sacrifices; incense is an abomination to Me. The New Moons, the Sabbaths, and the calling of assemblies—I cannot endure iniquity and the sacred meeting. Your New Moons and your appointed feasts My soul hates; they are a trouble to Me, I am weary of bearing them." (Isaiah 1:11-14)

God hated their *religious* gatherings. Not because religion itself was wrong, but because it had become a cover for wickedness. Isaiah continues:

"When you spread out your hands, I will hide My eyes from you; even though you make many prayers, I will not hear. Your hands are full of blood." (Isaiah 1:15)

The people were praying. They were assembling. They were sacrificing. They were keeping the calendar of sacred feasts. And God called it abomination.

VII THE RELIGION OF THE GREAT HARLOT

This is the harlot's religion—external compliance without internal transformation. Religious activity that masks unchanged hearts. Worship that coexists comfortably with injustice.

Jeremiah confronted the same pattern:

"Do not trust in these lying words, saying, 'The temple of the LORD, the temple of the LORD, the temple of the LORD are these.' For if you thoroughly amend your ways and your doings, if you thoroughly execute judgment between a man and his neighbor, if you do not oppress the stranger, the fatherless, and the widow, and do not shed innocent blood in this place, or walk after other gods to your hurt, then I will cause you to dwell in this place, in the land that I gave to your fathers forever and ever. Behold, you trust in lying words that cannot profit. Will you steal, murder, commit adultery, swear falsely, burn incense to Baal, and walk after other gods whom you do not know, and then come and stand before Me in this house which is called by My name, and say, 'We are delivered to do all these abominations'? Has this house, which is called by My name, become a den of thieves in your eyes?" (Jeremiah 7:4-11)

"The temple of the LORD!" was their mantra. They believed that religious observance would protect them regardless of how they lived. They had turned God's house into a "den of thieves"—a hiding place for those who committed wickedness and then retreated to sacred space expecting immunity.

Jesus quoted this very passage when He cleansed the temple. The pattern persists.

The Abominations in the Temple

Ezekiel's Vision of Horror

In the eighth chapter of Ezekiel, the prophet receives a vision that should haunt every believer who takes the holiness of God seriously.

The Lord seizes Ezekiel by a lock of his hair and transports him in visions to Jerusalem—to the temple itself, the dwelling place of God's presence, the holiest site on earth. But what Ezekiel sees there is not worship. It is abomination.

"And He said to me, 'Go in, and see the wicked abominations which they are doing there.' So I went in and saw, and there—every sort of creeping thing, abominable beasts, and all the idols of the house of Israel, portrayed all around on the walls. And there stood before them seventy men of the elders of the house of Israel, and in their midst stood Jaazaniah the son of Shaphan. Each man had a censer in his hand, and a thick cloud of incense went up. Then He said to me, 'Son of man, have you seen what the elders of the house of Israel do in the dark, every man in the room of his idols? For they say, "The LORD does not see us, the LORD has forsaken the land."'" (Ezekiel 8:9-12)

The elders of Israel—the spiritual leaders, the guardians of the covenant, the men responsible for preserving true worship—were conducting secret idol worship *within the temple precincts*. They had not abandoned the temple. They had not stopped coming to the public services. They maintained their positions of authority in the official religion.

But in the dark, in hidden chambers, they worshipped other gods.

And their theological justification was this: "The LORD does not see us, the LORD has forsaken the land."

This is the essence of practical atheism wearing religious clothes. This is the agnosticism that denies, not with the lips but with the life, that God truly sees, truly knows, truly cares. They did not announce their unbelief; they practiced it in secret while maintaining public piety.

The Multiple Altars

But God was not finished revealing the horror. He showed Ezekiel more:

VII THE RELIGION OF THE GREAT HARLOT

"And He brought me to the door of the north gate of the LORD's house; and to my dismay, women were sitting there weeping for Tammuz." (Ezekiel 8:14)

Tammuz was a Babylonian deity—a dying-and-rising god associated with fertility, whose worshippers mourned his annual "death" in elaborate rituals. The women of Israel had imported this pagan worship and were practicing it *at the entrance of God's house.*

This was not happening in some distant high place. It was happening at the temple gate. The two religions coexisted in the same space.

And then, the final abomination:

"So He brought me into the inner court of the LORD's house; and there, at the door of the temple of the LORD, between the porch and the altar, were about twenty-five men with their backs toward the temple of the LORD and their faces toward the east, and they were worshiping the sun toward the east." (Ezekiel 8:16)

Twenty-five men—likely the chief priests, those responsible for the most sacred services—stood *between the porch and the altar*, the holiest accessible space, with their backs to God's temple, worshipping the sun.

They had not left the temple. They were standing in the temple. But they were facing the wrong direction. They were offering worship to a created thing while standing in the presence of the Creator.

This is the image of syncretism in its most developed form. The external forms of true religion are maintained. The sacred spaces are occupied. The religious calendar continues. But the heart has turned elsewhere. Other gods have been installed alongside the LORD—or in His place—while the religious structure remains intact.

The Modern Temples and Their Hidden Chambers

We must ask ourselves: Are there hidden chambers in our churches where other gods are worshipped?

The question is not whether we have literally erected statues to Baal. The question is whether we have functionally installed other objects of ultimate devotion while maintaining the outward forms of Christian worship.

The altar of self-fulfillment: In how many churches has the message been subtly shifted from "Deny yourself, take up your cross, and follow Me" to "Discover yourself, fulfill your potential, and let Jesus help you become your best self"? The vocabulary remains Christian, but the functional deity has become the autonomous self. We worship in the temple of the LORD with our faces toward the mirror.

The altar of cultural acceptance: How many churches have revised their message—not in peripheral matters but in central confessions—in order to remain respectable in the eyes of the watching world? When the fear of being thought bigoted outweighs the fear of being thought unfaithful, a new god has been installed. We worship in the temple of the LORD with our faces toward the opinion polls.

The altar of political power: When churches align themselves so thoroughly with political movements that the gospel becomes a means to partisan ends, an exchange has occurred. The kingdom of God has been conflated with the kingdoms of this world. We worship in the temple of the LORD with our faces toward Washington, or London, or wherever earthly power resides.

The altar of therapeutic comfort: When the church's primary function becomes helping people feel better about themselves rather than confronting them with the claims of Christ, when sin is renamed as dysfunction and repentance is replaced by self-acceptance, a substitution has been made. We worship in the temple of the LORD with our faces toward the therapist's couch.

These altars are often hidden. They do not announce themselves. The elders who worship before them would be shocked to hear their practices described as idolatry. "The LORD does not see," they assume. "Who will know?"

But God sees. God knows. And God will not share His glory with another.

The Rise of Christian Agnosticism

One of the most subtle forms of temple corruption in our age is what we've defined in volume one as "Christian agnosticism"—not the formal denial of God's existence, but the practical denial that we can know truth about Him.

It sounds like humility. It presents itself as intellectual sophistication. It says things like:

"Who can really know what God thinks about these matters?"

"We must hold our convictions loosely—none of us has the full truth."

"It's arrogant to claim that our interpretation is the right one."

"We see through a glass darkly, so we shouldn't be too certain about anything."

This posture *sounds* pious. It *feels* humble. But examine it closely and you will find the elders of Ezekiel's vision: "The LORD does not see. The LORD has forsaken the land."

If God has not spoken clearly—if Scripture is so ambiguous that we cannot know what He requires—then effectively He is absent. If every interpretation is equally valid, then no interpretation is binding. If we cannot know the truth, then we are free to construct our own.

Christian agnosticism uses the language of epistemological humility to achieve the same end as practical atheism: freedom from divine accountability. If we cannot know what God demands, we cannot be held responsible for failing to obey. If truth is inaccessible, then we are masters of our own morality.

But God *has* spoken. He has spoken through prophets and apostles, through Scripture and through His Son. "Long ago, at many times and in many ways, God spoke to our fathers by the prophets, but in these last days he has spoken to us by his Son" (Hebrews 1:1-2). The Word became flesh and dwelt among us. The truth is not inaccessible—it is incarnate.

Yes, we see through a glass darkly. Yes, we know in part. But partial knowledge is still knowledge. Limited understanding is still understanding. The things that have been revealed belong to us and to our children forever (Deuteronomy 29:29).

The appropriate response to limited knowledge is not agnosticism but trust—trust in the One who knows fully, who has revealed what we need to know, who calls us to obey what has been made clear while waiting for the full revelation yet to come.

The Second Agnosticism - Type Two Christian Agnosticism

The Creed Without the Cross

There is the second form of Christian agnosticism that is, also mentioned volume one, and I believe it is more dangerous than the first because it is harder to detect.

The first agnosticism doubts that we can know truth about God. It questions doctrine, revises creeds, softens exclusive claims. It is recognizable because it changes what is *believed*.

The second agnosticism affirms every article of the creed while living as though none of it were true. It does not doubt doctrine; it simply ignores its implications. It professes traditional faith while practicing functional atheism. It attends gatherings, reads Scripture, sings hymns, and returns home to live unholy, unconsecrated lives indistinguishable from the world around them.

This is the agnosticism of the will rather than the intellect. It says with the mouth, "Jesus is Lord," while the life declares, "I am my own master." It affirms the resurrection on Sunday and lives for this world alone on

VII THE RELIGION OF THE GREAT HARLOT

Monday. It believes in heaven and hell in theory while making every practical decision as though this life were all there is.

James diagnosed this condition with surgical precision:

"But be doers of the word, and not hearers only, deceiving yourselves. For if anyone is a hearer of the word and not a doer, he is like a man observing his natural face in a mirror; for he observes himself, goes away, and immediately forgets what kind of man he was." (James 1:22-24)

Hearers only. They listen to the Word. They nod along with the sermon. They underline verses in their Bibles. But they do not *do*. And in not doing, they deceive themselves—they believe they are Christians because they hold Christian beliefs, attend Christian gatherings, consume Christian content. But their lives bear no evidence of transformation.

The Practical Denial

Consider what this second agnosticism looks like in practice:

They believe that God sees all things—and indulge in secret sin as though invisible.

They believe that Christ will return—and make no preparation for His coming.

They believe in the judgment seat—and live without fear of giving account.

They believe the body is a temple of the Holy Spirit—and defile it without hesitation.

They believe that covetousness is idolatry—and pursue wealth as eagerly as any pagan.

They believe that the love of money is the root of all evil—and structure their lives around its acquisition.

They believe that friendship with the world is enmity with God—and carefully cultivate the world's approval.

They believe that those who practice the works of the flesh will not inherit the kingdom—and practice them anyway, presuming on grace.

This is not struggling against sin while clinging to Christ. Every genuine believer struggles. This is *practicing* sin—habitually, comfortably, without conviction or repentance—while maintaining religious observance. It is the unholy life wrapped in the garments of profession.

Paul warned Titus about such people:

"They profess to know God, but in works they deny Him, being abominable, disobedient, and disqualified for every good work." (Titus 1:16)

They *profess* to know God. The profession is real. The doctrinal statement is signed. The creed is recited. But in *works*—in the actual conduct of life—they deny Him. Their practice preaches a different sermon than their lips. Their lives announce what their words contradict: "There is no God who sees. There is no judgment to fear. There is no holiness required."

This is agnosticism. Not the agnosticism of the philosophy classroom but the agnosticism of the lived life. Functional denial of everything formally affirmed.

The Self-Deceived

The terrifying feature of this second agnosticism is its capacity for self-deception.

The person who openly doubts Christian truth at least knows where they stand. They have questions. They acknowledge uncertainty. There is something to work with, something to address.

But the person who holds all the right beliefs while living all the wrong ways is convinced they are in good standing. They have checked all the boxes. They attend church—box checked. They read the Bible—box checked. They give money—box checked. They believe the doctrines—box checked. What more could be required?

Repentance. Transformation. Actual holiness. A life that corresponds to profession.

Jesus addressed this self-deception in the Sermon on the Mount:

"Not everyone who says to Me, 'Lord, Lord,' shall enter the kingdom of heaven, but he who does the will of My Father in heaven." (Matthew 7:21)

And He followed with the most frightening words in all of Scripture:

"Many will say to Me in that day, 'Lord, Lord, have we not prophesied in Your name, cast out demons in Your name, and done many wonders in Your name?' And then I will declare to them, 'I never knew you; depart from Me, you who practice lawlessness!'" (Matthew 7:22-23)

They called Him Lord. They did religious works in His name. They had every expectation of acceptance. And He declared: "I never knew you."

Not "I knew you once and you fell away." Not "I knew you but you disappointed Me." But "I *never* knew you." The relationship they assumed existed had never been real. The faith they professed had never been genuine. The Christianity they practiced had been empty from the start.

"You who practice lawlessness." Despite all the religious activity, the actual pattern of life was lawless—not submitted to Christ's lordship, not conformed to God's commands, not transformed by the Spirit's power. Orthodoxy without obedience. Creed without cross. Faith without fruit.

The Lordship Test

The antidote to this second agnosticism is the lordship of Christ applied to every area of life.

It is not enough to believe that Jesus is Lord. The demons believe that—and tremble (James 2:19). It is not enough to call Him Lord with our lips. The self-deceived do that. What is required is *actual submission*—the bending of the will, the reordering of priorities, the transformation of habits, the consecration of the whole self to His authority.

Jesus made this explicit:

"But why do you call Me 'Lord, Lord,' and not do the things which I say?" (Luke 6:46)

The question hangs over every Christian who professes faith while resisting obedience. Why do you call Him Lord if you do not do what He says? What does "Lord" mean if not "the One whose commands I obey"? What content does the title carry if it produces no corresponding submission?

To call Jesus "Lord" while living by our own will is to take His name in vain. It is to empty the word of meaning. It is to profess with the lips what the life denies.

The second agnosticism must be confronted with the same call to examination as the first:

Do you believe God sees you? Then why do you sin as though you were invisible?

Do you believe Christ is returning? Then why do you live as though He were never coming?

Do you believe in judgment? Then why do you live without fear?

Do you believe in heaven? Then why do you invest everything in earth?

Do you believe the gospel transforms? Then where is the transformation?

The Call to Consistency

We do not earn salvation by works. Let that be clear. Salvation is by grace alone through faith alone in Christ alone. No amount of obedience can merit what only the cross provides.

But saving faith produces obedience. Grace transforms. The Spirit who regenerates also sanctifies. Where there is no fruit, there is reason to doubt whether there is genuine root.

VII THE RELIGION OF THE GREAT HARLOT

"What does it profit, my brethren, if someone says he has faith but does not have works? Can faith save him?... Thus also faith by itself, if it does not have works, is dead." (James 2:14, 17)

Dead faith. Not weak faith struggling toward strength. Not imperfect faith growing toward maturity. But *dead* faith—faith that has no vital connection to Christ, no animating power of the Spirit, no evidence of life. The corpse of religion without its soul.

The call of this book is not merely to believe rightly but to *live* rightly—to bring every area of life under the lordship of Christ, to practice what we profess, to embody what we believe.

Let us not be among those who honor Him with lips while hearts remain far from Him. Let us not hold the form of godliness while denying its power. Let us not deceive ourselves with religious activity that masks unchanged hearts.

Let us repent of our practical atheism.

Let us close the gap between profession and practice.

Let us become, by the Spirit's power, doers of the Word and not hearers only.

For the One who knows the secrets of hearts will not be fooled by the recitation of creeds. And on that Day, the question will not be "What did you believe?" but "Did you know Me? And did your life reflect that knowledge?"

"Examine yourselves as to whether you are in the faith. Test yourselves. Do you not know yourselves, that Jesus Christ is in you?—unless indeed you are disqualified." (2 Corinthians 13:5)

Let the examination begin.

The Universalist Betrayal

Closely related to Christian agnosticism is the increasingly common embrace of functional universalism—the belief, sometimes explicit but more often implicit, that all religious paths ultimately lead to God, that all sincere seekers will be saved regardless of their explicit faith in Christ, that the particularity of the gospel is merely cultural packaging for a universal truth accessible through many routes.

This too masquerades as love. It presents itself as generous and inclusive. It asks: "How could a loving God condemn sincere seekers just because they were born in the wrong culture, raised in the wrong religion, never heard the gospel in a form they could understand?"

The question seems compassionate. But notice what it assumes: that human sincerity is the measure of salvation, that cultural context excuses rejection of God's revelation, that the work of Christ was perhaps helpful but not necessary.

This is the altar of human autonomy installed in the holy place. It begins with God's love but ends with human merit. It starts with divine compassion but finishes with the exaltation of human religiosity. It transforms the gospel from good news about what God has done into general religious truth about what humans can achieve.

Peter declared: "There is salvation in no one else, for there is no other name under heaven given among men by which we must be saved" (Acts 4:12). Jesus Himself said: "I am the way, the truth, and the life. No one comes to the Father except through Me" (John 14:6). These are not culturally conditioned opinions. They are revealed truth.

The narrowness of the gospel is not a defect to be apologized for. It is the nature of salvation itself. Just as there is only one cure for a disease, regardless of what other remedies people sincerely believe in, so there is only one salvation from sin, regardless of what other paths people sincerely pursue. The exclusivity of Christ is not arrogance—it is reality.

Universalism, in its Christian form, stands in the temple and preaches that the temple is unnecessary. It uses the language of Christ to deny the necessity of Christ. It affirms religious sincerity while emptying religious content of significance. It is the ultimate syncretism—the merging of all religions into a contentless whole where every path leads up the same mountain.

But the mountain has a name. And the path has a gate. And the gate is narrow. And few find it.

The Weeping for Tammuz

Ezekiel saw women weeping for Tammuz at the temple gate—mourning a dying god, participating in fertility rituals, importing Babylonian religious practice into Israelite worship.

What are our versions of Tammuz worship?

The incorporation of New Age spirituality: In how many churches have practices derived from Eastern religions and New Age movements been baptized with Christian vocabulary and incorporated into worship? Contemplative practices emptied of Christian content, visualization techniques borrowed from the occult, energy healing disguised as prayer ministry—these are the rituals of Tammuz performed at the temple gate.

The embrace of expressive individualism as spiritual authenticity: The Tammuz cult was about *feeling*—about entering emotionally into the death and resurrection of the god, about experiencing the divine through affect rather than truth. How much contemporary worship has become Tammuz worship—experiences manufactured, emotions manipulated, authenticity measured by intensity of feeling rather than conformity to truth?

The sacralization of sexuality: Tammuz worship included ritual prostitution—the merging of religious devotion with sexual expression. When churches bless what God has forbidden, when they celebrate as good what Scripture calls sin, when they redefine love to mean the affirmation of desire rather than the pursuit of holiness, they weep for Tammuz at the temple gate.

The women weeping for Tammuz had not abandoned Israel's God—at least not in their own minds. They simply added another devotion. They simply made room for another experience. They simply expanded their spirituality to include other sources.

But God does not share His temple with Tammuz.

The Sun Worship of the Priests

The final abomination Ezekiel witnessed was the most shocking: priests standing in the holiest place, facing away from God's temple, worshipping the sun.

These were not laypeople confused about proper worship. These were the religious professionals—the men trained in Torah, ordained to offer sacrifices, responsible for maintaining the pure worship of YHWH. And they had turned their backs on Him.

The sun was worshipped throughout the ancient Near East as the source of life, light, and power. To worship the sun was to worship the creation rather than the Creator. It was to look at the natural order and find ultimate meaning there rather than in the One who made it.

What are our forms of sun worship?

The worship of science and reason as ultimate arbiters of truth: When Christians functionally grant to scientific consensus the authority that belongs to Scripture—when they revise their understanding of creation, of humanity, of morality, of miracle, based not on biblical exegesis but on the reigning scientific paradigm—they face the sun. Science is a good gift, a useful tool for understanding God's creation. But when it becomes the measure by which revelation is judged rather than a discipline that operates under revelation's authority, it has become an idol.

The worship of progress and human achievement: The Enlightenment promised that human reason and effort would solve all problems, end all suffering, create utopia on earth. This faith in progress—

this confidence that humanity is ascending toward perfection through its own devices—is sun worship. It looks at human capability and finds there the source of hope. It turns its back on the God who alone can save and faces instead the rising sun of human potential.

The worship of nature itself: Environmental concern is appropriate stewardship. But when creation is treated as sacred in itself, when the earth becomes "Mother" and humanity the problem, when ecological activism takes on religious fervor while traditional religion is dismissed as irrelevant, the sun is being worshipped. The creature has been elevated to the place of the Creator.

The priests who worshipped the sun had not left the temple. They stood in the most sacred space. But their hearts had departed. Their worship had been redirected. Their faces were turned away from the One who dwelt in the holy of holies.

How many pastors, priests, and teachers stand in sacred spaces today with their backs toward the living God, facing instead the rising sun of cultural relevance, academic respectability, or political influence?

The Lord's Verdict

God's response to what Ezekiel saw was unambiguous:

"Then He said to me, 'Have you seen this, O son of man? Is it a trivial thing to the house of Judah to commit the abominations which they commit here?... Therefore I also will act in fury. My eye will not spare nor will I have pity; and though they cry in My ears with a loud voice, I will not hear them.'" (Ezekiel 8:17-18)

"Is it a trivial thing?"

The question echoes across the centuries. We who have grown comfortable with syncretism, who have made peace with practical agnosticism, who have learned to smile at universalist sentiment, who have incorporated the worship of self and culture and progress into our religion—do we think these are trivial things?

God did not think so. He brought judgment on Jerusalem. He allowed the temple to be destroyed. He sent His people into exile.

And He will judge again.

The harlot's cup is full of abominations. But many of those abominations were first practiced in secret chambers of the temple itself—by elders who maintained their public positions while worshipping idols in the dark, by women who added Tammuz to their devotion, by priests who turned their backs on the Holy One to worship the sun.

The reformation that is needed is not merely against the obvious corruptions of the world. It is against the subtle corruptions within the church—the syncretism we have tolerated, the agnosticism we have dignified, the universalism we have celebrated, the hidden altars we have built while maintaining the facade of orthodoxy.

God sees the secret chambers.

God knows who weeps for Tammuz at His gates.

God observes whose back is turned to Him, even in the holy place.

And God calls His people to tear down the altars, to cleanse the temple, to face once again toward the One who alone is worthy of worship.

The reformation must begin in the house of God.

"Thus says the LORD: 'Stand in the ways and see, and ask for the old paths, where the good way is, and walk in it; then you will find rest for your souls.' But they said, 'We will not walk in it.'" (Jeremiah 6:16)

Let us not say, "We will not walk in it."

Let us return to the old paths.

Let us tear down the hidden altars.

Let us turn our faces toward the Lord.

The Bitterness of the Elder Brother

VII THE RELIGION OF THE GREAT HARLOT

The Brother Who Stayed Home

In the parable of the prodigal son, we rightly celebrate the father's lavish welcome of the returning wastrel—the robe, the ring, the fattened calf, the feast. But Jesus did not end the story there. He introduced another character whose response reveals a different kind of lostness:

"Now his older son was in the field. And as he came and drew near to the house, he heard music and dancing. So he called one of the servants and asked what these things meant. And he said to him, 'Your brother has come, and because he has received him safe and sound, your father has killed the fatted calf.' But he was angry and would not go in." (Luke 15:25-28)

The elder brother had never left. He had served faithfully in the fields. He had kept the rules, maintained the boundaries, fulfilled his obligations. By every external measure, he was the righteous one.

And he was furious that grace had come to his brother.

"Lo, these many years I have been serving you; I never transgressed your commandment at any time; and yet you never gave me a young goat, that I might make merry with my friends. But as soon as this son of yours came, who has devoured your livelihood with harlots, you killed the fatted calf for him." (Luke 15:29-30)

Listen to the accounting language. "These many years I have been serving you." He had kept careful records. He knew exactly how much he was owed. His service was not love—it was investment, and he expected returns.

"I never transgressed your commandment at any time." The boast of the Pharisee. The claim of the self-righteous. And perhaps it was even true in external terms. But the heart that could not rejoice in a brother's restoration was a heart that had never understood the father at all.

"This son of yours." Not "my brother." He could not bring himself to acknowledge the relationship. The prodigal's sin had, in the elder brother's mind, severed familial bonds that grace had no right to restore.

333

This is Pharisaical religion. This is the bitterness that poisons the soul of those who have made faith a transaction rather than a relationship. They serve God not because they love Him but because they expect payment. And when they see grace lavished on those who have not earned it, rage rises in their hearts.

The Woman Passed Over

She has been faithful since her youth. She kept herself pure when her peers were experimenting. She attended every service, tithed every dollar, served on every committee. She prayed for a husband, believed God for a family, trusted that her faithfulness would be rewarded.

And then she watched.

She watched the woman who had lived promiscuously come to faith, be restored, and within two years marry a godly man. She watched the children come—one, then two, then three—while her own womb remained empty and her left hand remained bare. She watched the former prodigal receive what she had spent decades pursuing through obedience.

And bitterness took root.

"I did everything right," she whispers to herself in the dark hours. "I followed the rules. I kept myself for marriage. And *she*—she who broke every commandment—she gets the husband? She gets the family? Where is the justice in that?"

The bitterness is understandable. The pain is real. But the theology beneath it is poison.

For she has revealed what her obedience was really about. It was not about loving God. It was not about holiness for holiness' sake. It was about *earning*—earning blessing, earning reward, earning what she believed her faithfulness deserved. Her righteousness was a transaction, and God had failed to pay.

VII THE RELIGION OF THE GREAT HARLOT

But God does not owe us. He never has. The most faithful life imaginable does not put God in our debt. "When you have done all those things which you are commanded, say, 'We are unprofitable servants. We have done what was our duty to do.'" (Luke 17:10)

The woman who was restored received grace—unmerited, unearned, undeserved. That is what grace means. And the woman who has been faithful since her youth? She too has received grace—unmerited, unearned, undeserved. Her faithfulness was not the cause of God's favor but the fruit of it. Her purity was not payment for blessing but response to blessing already given.

When she cannot rejoice in her sister's restoration, she reveals that she never understood grace at all. She wanted payment for services rendered. She got something infinitely better—God Himself—but she was too busy calculating her wages to notice.

Men Looking Down on Men

The same sickness infects the brothers.

The man who has walked uprightly looks at the man who stumbled and sees not a fellow sinner saved by grace but an inferior. The pastor with the pristine reputation looks at the pastor who fell and was restored and thinks, "I would never." The elder who has served for decades looks at the new convert given responsibility and seethes at the injustice.

"The Pharisee stood and prayed thus with himself, 'God, I thank You that I am not like other men—extortioners, unjust, adulterers, or even as this tax collector.'" (Luke 18:11)

"I thank You that I am not like other men." This is the prayer of Pharisaical religion. It does not approach God in humility but in comparison. It does not see itself as a sinner in need of mercy but as a righteous man deserving reward. It looks horizontally at others rather than vertically at God—and in looking horizontally, it always finds someone to look down upon.

But Jesus' verdict was devastating:

"I tell you, this man went down to his house justified rather than the other; for everyone who exalts himself will be humbled, and he who humbles himself will be exalted." (Luke 18:14)

The tax collector—the one who could not even lift his eyes to heaven, who beat his breast and cried, "God, be merciful to me a sinner!"—went home justified. The Pharisee, with all his tithing and fasting and visible righteousness, went home condemned.

Because he had missed the point entirely.

The Religion That Meets Fire

This Pharisaical religion will face judgment. Make no mistake.

Paul warned the Corinthians about building on the foundation of Christ with worthless materials:

"Now if anyone builds on this foundation with gold, silver, precious stones, wood, hay, straw, each one's work will become clear; for the Day will declare it, because it will be revealed by fire; and the fire will test each one's work, of what sort it is. If anyone's work which he has built on it endures, he will receive a reward. If anyone's work is burned, he will suffer loss; but he himself will be saved, yet so as through fire." (1 Corinthians 3:12-15)

The elder brother's years of service, performed in bitterness and self-righteousness, are wood, hay, and stubble. They will not survive the fire. He may be saved—"yet so as through fire"—but he will suffer loss. The reward he calculated so carefully will evaporate. The wages he demanded will be revealed as worthless.

But there is a worse possibility still.

What if the Pharisaical religion was never genuine faith at all? What if the service was never rendered to Christ but only to self? What if the obedience was merely moral self-improvement dressed in religious vocabulary, with no actual relationship to the living God?

"Many will say to Me in that day, 'Lord, Lord, have we not prophesied in Your name, cast out demons in Your name, and done many wonders in Your name?' And then I will declare to them, 'I never knew you; depart from Me, you who practice lawlessness!'" (Matthew 7:22-23)

They expected reward for services rendered. They received dismissal. The transaction they thought they had made with God was revealed as fiction. He never knew them because they never knew Him. They used His name, performed religious works, accumulated spiritual credentials—but they never received Him. They never loved Him. They never wanted *Him*—only what they thought He would give them in exchange for their righteousness.

This is the final bankruptcy of Pharisaical religion. It seeks to earn from God rather than receive Him. It wants the gifts but not the Giver. It accumulates religious merit while missing the whole point of religion: union with God Himself.

The Antidote

The cure for the elder brother's bitterness is not to try harder at being generous. It is to recognize that he, too, is a prodigal.

He never left the father's house geographically, but his heart was far away. He never wasted the father's substance on riotous living, but he wasted his years in the father's house without enjoying the father's presence. He never transgressed the commandments externally, but his heart harbored resentment, pride, and self-righteousness that violated their deepest intent.

He, too, needed grace.

The father's words to him were an invitation:

"Son, you are always with me, and all that I have is yours. It was right that we should make merry and be glad, for your brother was dead and is alive again, and was lost and is found." (Luke 15:31-32)

"You are always with me." The father was not distant. The father was not withholding. The father was right there, available, accessible—but the elder brother had been too busy serving to notice. He had been so focused on earning that he had failed to receive.

"All that I have is yours." There was no need to calculate wages. There was no ledger to balance. Everything the father had belonged to the son—not as payment but as inheritance, not as transaction but as relationship.

The elder brother could have lived in joy all those years. He could have feasted on the father's abundance daily. He could have known the pleasure of the father's company rather than the drudgery of servitude. But he chose the far country of self-righteousness while remaining physically in the father's house.

Let us not make his mistake.

Let us rejoice when prodigals come home—even if their restoration seems faster and more dramatic than our own slow sanctification.

Let us refuse to keep accounts of what we are owed—for we are owed nothing but judgment, and we have received everything in Christ.

Let us look at other sinners not with contempt but with recognition—"there but for the grace of God go I."

And let us pursue God Himself, not His gifts—for He is the treasure, He is the reward, He is the inheritance. Everything else is wood, hay, and stubble.

"Whom have I in heaven but You? And there is none upon earth that I desire besides You. My flesh and my heart fail; but God is the strength of my heart and my portion forever." (Psalm 73:25-26)

He is our portion. Not marriage. Not family. Not vindication over those who sinned more visibly than we did. Not reward for services rendered.

Him.

When we have Him, we have everything.

When we want anything more than Him, we reveal that we never understood the gospel at all.

The Devil's Two Weapons: Passion and the Fear of Death

The writer of Hebrews reveals the mechanism by which Satan maintains his counterfeit kingdom:

"Inasmuch then as the children have partaken of flesh and blood, He Himself likewise shared in the same, that through death He might destroy him who had the power of death, that is, the devil, and release those who through fear of death were all their lifetime subject to bondage."

—Hebrews 2:14-15

The devil holds humanity in bondage through *the fear of death*. This is his primary lever of control. And this fear expresses itself in two seemingly opposite directions: the desperate pursuit of pleasure (to numb the fear) and the desperate pursuit of security (to delay the inevitable). Both are manifestations of the same bondage.

The harlot's religion exploits both impulses.

To those driven by the pursuit of pleasure, she offers a spirituality of appetite—a theology that baptizes desire, that calls indulgence "authenticity," that reframes self-gratification as self-actualization. She whispers, "If it feels good, it must be from God. If you want it, you deserve it. Your pleasure is sacred."

To those driven by the pursuit of security, she offers a spirituality of control—a religion of correct behavior and accumulated merit, of systems and certainties, of walls and boundaries that keep the chaos at bay. She whispers, "If you perform the right rituals, observe the right rules, maintain the right boundaries, you will be safe. God is predictable. Follow the formula."

Both are bondage. Both are counterfeits. The first produces hedonism; the second produces Pharisaism. And often, they coexist in the same person—libertinism in private, legalism in public.

Paul identifies this bondage when writing to the Galatians:

"Now the works of the flesh are evident, which are: adultery, fornication, uncleanness, lewdness, idolatry, sorcery, hatred, contentions, jealousies, outbursts of wrath, selfish ambitions, dissensions, heresies, envy, murders, drunkenness, revelries, and the like; of which I tell you beforehand, just as I also told you in time past, that those who practice such things will not inherit the kingdom of God."

—Galatians 5:19-21

Notice the breadth of this list. It includes the obvious—sexual immorality, drunkenness, revelry—but also the subtle: "contentions, jealousies, outbursts of wrath, selfish ambitions, dissensions, heresies, envy." The works of the flesh are not limited to bodily sins. They include the sins of the religious—the competitive spirit, the party factions, the ambition that masquerades as zeal.

The harlot's cup contains all of these. Her religion accommodates both the libertine and the legalist because both are operating in the flesh.

The Gross and the Subtle

The great deception of the last days will include both gross hedonism and subtle corruption. We must be warned against both.

The gross form is easier to recognize. It is the open celebration of what God calls sin. It is the revision of Scripture to accommodate sexual immorality. It is the pastor who preaches prosperity while living in luxury. It is the church that blesses what God has cursed. It is the theology that makes self-fulfillment the highest good and personal authenticity the supreme virtue.

Paul warned Timothy:

VII THE RELIGION OF THE GREAT HARLOT

"But know this, that in the last days perilous times will come: For men will be lovers of themselves, lovers of money, boasters, proud, blasphemers, disobedient to parents, unthankful, unholy, unloving, unforgiving, slanderers, without self-control, brutal, despisers of good, traitors, headstrong, haughty, lovers of pleasure rather than lovers of God, having a form of godliness but denying its power. And from such people turn away!"
—2 Timothy 3:1-5

"Lovers of pleasure rather than lovers of God, *having a form of godliness.*" This is religious hedonism. This is the harlot dressed in church clothes. She maintains the vocabulary of faith while gutting its substance. She speaks of love but means only affirmation. She speaks of grace but means only permission. She speaks of freedom but means only license.

The subtle form is harder to detect, and therefore more dangerous.

It is the religion that appears orthodox—that affirms the right doctrines, observes the right practices, maintains the right boundaries—while harboring hearts unchanged by the Spirit. It is Pharisaism in evangelical dress. It is the elder brother in the parable, faithfully serving in the field but seething with resentment, unable to celebrate the Father's lavish grace toward the prodigal.

Jesus reserved His harshest words not for prostitutes and tax collectors but for the religious leaders of His day:

"Woe to you, scribes and Pharisees, hypocrites! For you are like whitewashed tombs which indeed appear beautiful outwardly, but inside are full of dead men's bones and all uncleanness. Even so you also outwardly appear righteous to men, but inside you are full of hypocrisy and lawlessness."
—Matthew 23:27-28

Whitewashed tombs. Beautiful on the outside. Dead on the inside. This is the subtle counterfeit—the religion that looks right but lacks life, that maintains appearance while harboring corruption.

The Deception of the Elect

Jesus warned that the end-time deception would be severe enough to deceive, "if possible, even the elect" (Matthew 24:24). This suggests a counterfeit so convincing that only those kept by divine power will escape it.

What makes this deception so effective?

First, it will appeal to legitimate desires. The harlot does not offer what is obviously evil; she offers a counterfeit of what is genuinely good. She offers community, but without accountability. She offers acceptance, but without transformation. She offers spiritual experience, but without the cross. She offers the benefits of religion without its demands.

Second, it will use the language of Scripture. Satan quoted Scripture to Jesus in the wilderness. The harlot will quote it too—selectively, out of context, twisted to serve her purposes. She will speak of love and grace and freedom and blessing. She will sound biblical. She will feel spiritual.

Third, it will be supported by signs and wonders. Jesus warned of "false christs and false prophets" who would "show great signs and wonders" (Matthew 24:24). Paul wrote of the lawless one whose coming would be "according to the working of Satan, with all power, signs, and lying wonders" (2 Thessalonians 2:9). Miracles are not self-authenticating. Even genuine supernatural power can serve counterfeit religion.

Fourth, it will be embraced by the majority. The way that leads to destruction is broad, and many travel it. The way that leads to life is narrow, and few find it (Matthew 7:13-14). If your faith is popular, comfortable, and widely affirmed, that alone should prompt examination.

The Call of John the Baptist

Into this landscape of counterfeit religion, we need again the voice crying in the wilderness.

VII THE RELIGION OF THE GREAT HARLOT

John the Baptist emerged from the desert with a message that cut through the religious pretense of his day. He did not offer a more sophisticated theology or a more culturally relevant methodology. He called for *repentance*:

"In those days John the Baptist came preaching in the wilderness of Judea, and saying, 'Repent, for the kingdom of heaven is at hand!'"

—Matthew 3:1-2

When the Pharisees and Sadducees came to his baptism, John did not welcome them as spiritual seekers. He confronted them:

"Brood of vipers! Who warned you to flee from the wrath to come? Therefore bear fruits worthy of repentance, and do not think to say to yourselves, 'We have Abraham as our father.' For I say to you that God is able to raise up children to Abraham from these stones. And even now the ax is laid to the root of the trees. Therefore every tree which does not bear good fruit is cut down and thrown into the fire."

—Matthew 3:7-10

"Bear fruits worthy of repentance." Not words. Not membership. Not heritage. *Fruit*. Evidence. Changed lives.

John was not impressed by religious credentials. "We have Abraham as our father"—that is, "We have the right pedigree, the right tradition, the right tribe." John dismissed it. God could make children of Abraham from rocks. What He required was transformation. Your mothers religion, her true and tried faith, will not be applied to your account. You stand alone before God.

The ax was laid to the root. Not to the branches—not merely trimming behavior—but to the root. The fundamental orientation of the heart.

This is the examination we need. Not "Do I hold correct doctrines?" but "Has my heart been changed?" Not "Do I perform religious duties?" but "Is there fruit that proves the Spirit's presence?" Not "Am I part of the right church?" but "Am I known by God and knowing Him?"

343

A Word to Leaders

The harlot's religion finds its most dangerous expression in corrupt leadership. The shepherds who fleece the flock. The pastors who build empires rather than disciples. The teachers who tickle ears rather than transform hearts.

Ezekiel's prophecy against the shepherds of Israel speaks directly to our moment:

"Son of man, prophesy against the shepherds of Israel, prophesy and say to them, 'Thus says the Lord GOD to the shepherds: "Woe to the shepherds of Israel who feed themselves! Should not the shepherds feed the flocks? You eat the fat and clothe yourselves with the wool; you slaughter the fatlings, but you do not feed the flock. The weak you have not strengthened, nor have you healed those who were sick, nor bound up the broken, nor brought back what was driven away, nor sought what was lost; but with force and cruelty you have ruled them."'"

—Ezekiel 34:2-4

Leaders who feed themselves. Who use the flock for their own benefit. Who neglect the weak, the sick, the broken, the lost. Who rule with force rather than serve with gentleness.

The narcissism that pervades contemporary leadership culture has invaded the church. The celebrity pastor. The brand-building ministry. The platform-seeking preacher. All of it drinks from the harlot's cup—the golden cup of ambition disguised as ministry, of self-promotion packaged as kingdom work.

James warned:

"My brethren, let not many of you become teachers, knowing that we shall receive a stricter judgment." (James 3:1)

Stricter judgment. Leadership is not privilege; it is liability. Those who presume to speak for God will answer for every word. Those who guide others will account for where they led them.

VII THE RELIGION OF THE GREAT HARLOT

The leader who harbors hidden sin while preaching holiness to others drinks judgment upon himself. The pastor who covers abuse to protect reputation has become a son of the harlot. The teacher who twists Scripture for personal gain has exchanged the truth of God for a lie.

Repent. While there is time, repent. The ax is laid to the root.

The Way of Sanctification

How then shall we escape the harlot's religion? How do we discern the counterfeit from the genuine? How do we pursue the holiness without which no one will see the Lord (Hebrews 12:14)?

We must return to the measuring rod that Christ Himself provided.

The Sermon on the Mount is not a new law to be fulfilled by human effort. It is the description of a new kind of person—a person formed by the Spirit, shaped by the Beatitudes, living from a transformed heart. It is the portrait of what redeemed humanity looks like when God's kingdom has taken root within.

Consider the Beatitudes as the foundation of genuine spirituality:

"Blessed are the poor in spirit, for theirs is the kingdom of heaven" (Matthew 5:3). The religion of the harlot promises spiritual wealth, self-confidence, the power of positive confession. Jesus says the kingdom belongs to those who know their bankruptcy. True faith begins with the recognition that we have nothing to offer God, nothing to commend ourselves, no righteousness of our own. Have you come to the end of yourself? Do you approach God as a beggar or as a customer?

"Blessed are those who mourn, for they shall be comforted" (Matthew 5:4). The harlot's religion promises happiness without sorrow, blessing without brokenness. Jesus says those who mourn—over sin, over the state of the world, over their own failures—will be comforted. Is there godly sorrow in your spiritual life? Or have you settled for a faith that bypasses grief?

"Blessed are the meek, for they shall inherit the earth" (Matthew 5:5). The harlot's religion celebrates assertiveness, self-promotion, the will to power. Jesus says the meek—those who have surrendered their rights, who do not grasp for position, who entrust themselves to God—will inherit everything. Are you grasping or receiving? Demanding or trusting?

"Blessed are those who hunger and thirst for righteousness, for they shall be filled" (Matthew 5:6). The harlot's religion offers immediate satisfaction—spiritual fast food that fills without nourishing. Jesus says those who *hunger and thirst*—who feel the painful absence of righteousness, who ache for holiness—will be satisfied. Do you hunger for righteousness? Or are you content with religious mediocrity?

"Blessed are the merciful, for they shall obtain mercy" (Matthew 5:7). The harlot's religion is harsh toward outsiders while lenient toward insiders. Jesus says mercy given is mercy received. Are you quick to condemn or quick to forgive? Do you extend to others the grace you have received?

"Blessed are the pure in heart, for they shall see God" (Matthew 5:8). The harlot's religion is satisfied with external compliance—the whitewashed tomb. Jesus requires purity of heart, the deepest motives aligned with God's character. Is your heart pure? Not perfect—that awaits glory—but oriented toward purity, desiring it, pursuing it?

"Blessed are the peacemakers, for they shall be called sons of God" (Matthew 5:9). The harlot's religion thrives on conflict, on us-versus-them, on the tribal satisfaction of defeating enemies. Jesus says peacemakers bear the family resemblance of God. Do you sow peace or discord? Build bridges or burn them?

"Blessed are those who are persecuted for righteousness' sake, for theirs is the kingdom of heaven" (Matthew 5:10). The harlot's religion promises comfort, acceptance, cultural relevance. Jesus says persecution is a badge of authenticity—not because suffering is inherently good, but because genuine faith will inevitably clash with a world that has rejected God. Are

you willing to be persecuted? Or have you so accommodated your faith to the culture that no friction remains?

The Evidence of Transformation

Jesus concluded the Sermon on the Mount with a warning against self-deception:

"Not everyone who says to Me, 'Lord, Lord,' shall enter the kingdom of heaven, but he who does the will of My Father in heaven. Many will say to Me in that day, 'Lord, Lord, have we not prophesied in Your name, cast out demons in Your name, and done many wonders in Your name?' And then I will declare to them, 'I never knew you; depart from Me, you who practice lawlessness!'"

—Matthew 7:21-23

"Many will say." Not few. *Many*. Many who prophesied. Many who performed miracles. Many who engaged in spectacular religious activity. And Jesus will say, "I never knew you."

This is not a word against assurance; it is a word for examination. Not to create perpetual doubt, but to provoke honest self-assessment. The one who builds on rock is the one who *hears* these words and *does* them. The one who builds on sand hears but does not do.

What is the evidence of genuine transformation? Not religious activity alone, but fruit:

"But the fruit of the Spirit is love, joy, peace, longsuffering, kindness, goodness, faithfulness, gentleness, self-control. Against such there is no law. And those who are Christ's have crucified the flesh with its passions and desires."

—Galatians 5:22-24

Where the harlot's religion produces the works of the flesh, the Spirit produces fruit. Not merely external conformity, but inward transformation that naturally expresses itself in character.

Love—not mere sentiment, but self-giving action toward others' good.

Joy—not circumstantial happiness, but deep gladness rooted in God's faithfulness.

Peace—not avoidance of conflict, but settled confidence in God's sovereignty.

Patience—not mere tolerance, but willingness to suffer long without retaliation.

Kindness—not niceness, but active goodwill toward others.

Goodness—not perfectionism, but moral excellence flowing from a changed heart.

Faithfulness—not mere reliability, but covenant loyalty that endures.

Gentleness—not weakness, but strength under control.

Self-control—not repression, but the Spirit's mastery over the flesh.

This is the measuring rod. This is how we discern genuine faith from counterfeit. Not by the spectacular gifts, but by the steady fruit.

The Call to Consecration

Consecration means being set apart for God's purposes. It is not merely avoiding evil; it is being devoted to good. It is not merely clean hands; it is a pure heart.

Paul's appeal to the Romans sets forth the positive vision:

"I beseech you therefore, brethren, by the mercies of God, that you present your bodies a living sacrifice, holy, acceptable to God, which is your reasonable service. And do not be conformed to this world, but be transformed by the renewing of your mind, that you may prove what is that good and acceptable and perfect will of God."

—Romans 12:1-2

Present your bodies. Not merely your souls, your intentions, your beliefs—your *bodies*. The physical, material, everyday reality of your life.

VII THE RELIGION OF THE GREAT HARLOT

Your hands, your eyes, your tongue, your sexuality, your appetites. All of it placed on the altar.

A *living* sacrifice. The old sacrifices died. We are called to live—but to live as those who have already died. Dead to sin. Dead to self. Dead to the world's agenda. Alive to God.

Do not be conformed to this world. The world has a mold, a pattern, a shape it wants to press you into. Resist it. Do not let the culture's assumptions, values, priorities, and pleasures shape you.

But be transformed. This is not merely resistance—it is renewal. The mind is changed. The thought patterns are rewired. The imagination is purified. And from this renewed mind comes the ability to discern God's will—not as external command reluctantly obeyed, but as internal desire joyfully pursued.

This is consecration. This is sanctification. This is the narrow way that leads to life.

The Urgency of the Hour

Why does this matter now? Why this urgency?

Because the foundations of Babylon have been laid. Her pillars are being erected. The religion of the great harlot is not merely a future threat; it is a present reality.

The entertainment industry has discipled a generation to believe that pleasure is the highest good. The educational system has taught that truth is subjective and morality is personal preference. The therapeutic culture has made self-fulfillment the measure of all things. The church, in too many places, has accommodated rather than confronted, blended rather than distinguished, conformed rather than transformed.

The stage is being set.

And when the man of sin is revealed—when the lawless one comes with all power, signs, and lying wonders—those who have not loved the truth will believe the lie. Those who have not been grounded in Christ will be swept away. Those who have not learned to discern the Spirit from counterfeits will be deceived.

Paul warned the Thessalonians:

"The coming of the lawless one is according to the working of Satan, with all power, signs, and lying wonders, and with all unrighteous deception among those who perish, because they did not receive the love of the truth, that they might be saved. And for this reason God will send them strong delusion, that they should believe the lie, that they all may be condemned who did not believe the truth but had pleasure in unrighteousness."

—2 Thessalonians 2:9-12

"They did not receive the love of the truth." Not merely intellectual assent to truth, but *love* for it. Not merely doctrinal correctness, but passionate devotion to what is real, what is right, what is from God.

"God will send them strong delusion." This is sobering beyond words. There comes a point when persistent rejection of truth results in God's judicial hardening. When He gives people over to the lie they have chosen. When the ability to discern is removed because it was so long neglected.

The time to cultivate love for truth is now. The time to build on the rock is before the storm comes. The time to examine yourself is while examination is still possible.

Again I Say, Come Out of Her, My People

Near the end of Revelation, after the long description of Babylon's corruption and coming judgment, a voice from heaven issues this command:

"Come out of her, my people, lest you share in her sins, and lest you receive of her plagues. For her sins have reached to heaven, and God has remembered her iniquities." (Revelation 18:4-5)

VII THE RELIGION OF THE GREAT HARLOT

"Come out of her, *my people*." The call is addressed to those who belong to God but have been entangled with Babylon. To believers who have been seduced by her comforts, intoxicated by her pleasures, compromised by her systems.

Come out.

This is not a call to physical isolation—we cannot leave the world entirely, nor does God ask us to. It is a call to spiritual separation. To disentangle our hearts from Babylon's values. To withdraw our worship from her gods. To refuse her mark, whatever the cost.

The call requires discernment. Babylon is not merely "out there"—she is subtle, and her influence seeps into our hearts, our churches, our assumptions, our desires. Coming out of her is a lifelong work of sanctification, a progressive untangling, a daily dying to self and rising to Christ.

But it must begin with recognition. You cannot leave what you do not see. You cannot repent of what you do not acknowledge. You cannot be transformed while you remain conformed.

So let the examination begin.

Is your religion genuine, or counterfeit?

Is your faith rooted in the Spirit, or merely in flesh?

Is your heart pure, or merely your behavior modified?

Are you building on rock, or sand?

Are you following Christ, or the harlot?

The ax is laid to the root. May God grant us grace to bear fruit worthy of repentance.

"Search me, O God, and know my heart; try me, and know my anxieties; and see if there is any wicked way in me, and lead me in the way everlasting."

—Psalm 139:23-24

Endnotes

1. Revelation 17:1-5 (NKJV). The vision of the great harlot is one of the most complex and debated passages in Revelation, with interpreters across church history identifying Babylon variously with Rome, apostate religion, or a future world system.
2. The Greek word *thaumazō* in Revelation 17:6, translated "marveled" or "wondered," carries connotations of astonishment that can include horror or shock, not merely neutral amazement. John's reaction suggests revulsion at the sight of religious corruption drunk on the blood of the saints.
3. The harlot's attire—purple and scarlet, gold and precious stones and pearls—evokes both royalty and wealth. Purple dye, extracted from murex shells, was extraordinarily expensive in the ancient world and associated with imperial power. The golden cup suggests liturgical or sacramental imagery perverted to false worship.
4. Revelation 17:15: "Then he said to me, 'The waters which you saw, where the harlot sits, are peoples, multitudes, nations, and tongues'" (NKJV). The imagery suggests a universal religious system exercising influence over diverse populations.
5. The phrase "mother of harlots" (*mētēr tōn pornōn*) indicates that Babylon spawns spiritual offspring—derivative false religious systems that share her essential character while taking different forms across history and cultures.
6. Irenaeus of Lyon (c. 130-202 AD), *Against Heresies* (Adversus Haereses), Book V. Irenaeus was a disciple of Polycarp, who had known the apostle John, giving his interpretation particular weight as representing early apostolic tradition. His discussion of the Antichrist appears in Book V, chapters 25-30.

VII THE RELIGION OF THE GREAT HARLOT

7. Irenaeus, *Against Heresies* V.25.1. The passage emphasizes that the Antichrist will demand worship as God while actually being a servant of Satan—the ultimate religious counterfeit.
8. Hippolytus of Rome (c. 170-235 AD) wrote both a *Commentary on Daniel* and *On Christ and Antichrist* (*De Christo et Antichristo*), developing the prophetic framework established by Irenaeus. Hippolytus was a student of Irenaeus and preserved early Roman traditions of biblical interpretation.
9. Hippolytus, *Commentary on Daniel*, 4.4-9. His interpretation follows the standard four-kingdom scheme (Babylon, Medo-Persia, Greece, Rome) derived from Daniel 2 and 7.
10. The interrelation of the harlot and the beast in Revelation 17 suggests the alliance between false religion and political power—each supporting and legitimizing the other. This pattern recurs throughout history wherever religious institutions compromise with worldly authority for mutual benefit.
11. Victorinus of Pettau (d. c. 304 AD), *Commentary on the Apocalypse*. Victorinus was the first known Latin commentator on Revelation and was martyred during the Diocletian persecution. His commentary, though later revised by Jerome, preserves important early Latin interpretation.
12. Victorinus, *Commentary on the Apocalypse*, 17.1-3. His identification of Babylon with Rome "sitting upon seven hills" reflects the nearly universal early Christian view, though he also recognized the typological significance that would extend beyond Rome.
13. Augustine of Hippo (354-430 AD), *City of God* (*De Civitate Dei*), XIV.28. Augustine's magnum opus, written in response to the sack of Rome in 410 AD, develops the two-cities framework that has shaped Western political theology.

14. Augustine, *City of God*, I.35. Augustine's recognition that the visible church contains both genuine believers and hypocrites ("wheat and tares") provides important nuance for understanding how false religion can exist within ostensibly Christian institutions.
15. Tertullian of Carthage (c. 155-240 AD), *Apologeticus* (Apology), 24. Tertullian's defense of Christians against Roman accusations clarifies that the conflict was fundamentally religious—about the exclusive worship of the one true God versus the syncretistic pluralism of Roman religion.
16. The Roman requirement of a pinch of incense to the emperor's genius was designed to be minimally intrusive—a small acknowledgment that would demonstrate civic loyalty. Christians died rather than perform this seemingly trivial act because they understood that any acknowledgment of Caesar's divinity compromised their exclusive allegiance to Christ.
17. Cyprian of Carthage (c. 200-258 AD), *On the Lapsed* (*De Lapsis*). The crisis of the *lapsi*—Christians who had apostatized under persecution—raised profound questions about church discipline, the nature of faith, and the possibility of restoration after denial of Christ.
18. Cyprian, *On the Lapsed*, 7-8. His military imagery ("armor of faith") emphasizes that resistance to persecution requires prior spiritual preparation—Christians who had not cultivated deep faith were unable to withstand the pressure.
19. Jerome (c. 347-420 AD), *Commentary on Daniel*, IV.11. Jerome's commentary engaged both the literal-historical meaning of Daniel's visions and their eschatological significance for the church's future.
20. Jerome, *Commentary on Daniel*, IV.21. His warning about the deceptive nature of the Antichrist—using sacred language and

spaces to mislead—emphasizes that the final deception will appear religious, not secular.

21. Mark 8:15: "Then He charged them, saying, 'Take heed, beware of the leaven of the Pharisees and the leaven of Herod'" (NKJV). The disciples' confusion (vv. 16-21) about this warning suggests they too had difficulty distinguishing spiritual from material concerns.
22. Mark 8:17: "Do you not yet perceive nor understand? Is your heart still hardened?" (NKJV). Jesus' rebuke indicates that the disciples' failure to understand was not merely intellectual but spiritual—a hardness of heart that prevented perception.
23. The Herodian dynasty, beginning with Herod the Great (37-4 BC) and continuing through his descendants, represented a political compromise: Jewish identity maintained externally while serving Roman imperial interests. The Herodians in the Gospels (Mark 3:6, 12:13) appear as political pragmatists allied with the Pharisees against Jesus.
24. Luke 4:5-7 (NKJV). Satan's claim to authority over "all the kingdoms of the world" is not disputed by Jesus, suggesting a genuine (though limited and temporary) satanic dominion over worldly political systems. See also John 12:31, 14:30, 16:11 where Satan is called "the ruler of this world."
25. Luke 4:8: "Get behind Me, Satan! For it is written, 'You shall worship the LORD your God, and Him only you shall serve'" (NKJV), quoting Deuteronomy 6:13.
26. John 6:15: "Therefore when Jesus perceived that they were about to come and take Him by force to make Him king, He departed again to the mountain by Himself alone" (NKJV). Jesus consistently refused to be co-opted for political purposes, even when the crowds' intentions seemed positive.

27. Acts 1:6: "Lord, will You at this time restore the kingdom to Israel?" (NKJV). Even after the resurrection and forty days of instruction about the kingdom (Acts 1:3), the disciples still conceived of God's purposes in political terms.
28. 1 Samuel 8:5 (NKJV). Israel's demand for a king "like all the nations" reveals the fundamental compromise: they wanted to be distinctive as God's people while simultaneously conforming to surrounding cultures.
29. 1 Samuel 8:7-8 (NKJV). God's interpretation of the request as rejection of His kingship exposes the theological significance of political choices—seeking human leadership can represent a failure to trust divine sovereignty.
30. 1 Samuel 8:18: "And you will cry out in that day because of your king whom you have chosen for yourselves, and the LORD will not hear you in that day" (NKJV). The warning proved prophetic throughout Israel's monarchy.
31. Psalm 146:3-5 (NKJV). This psalm contrasts the futility of trusting in human princes with the blessedness of trusting in God—a theme that runs throughout Scripture.
32. Isaiah 31:1: "Woe to those who go down to Egypt for help, and rely on horses, who trust in chariots because they are many, and in horsemen because they are very strong, but who do not look to the Holy One of Israel, nor seek the LORD!" (NKJV).
33. Isaiah 31:3: "Now the Egyptians are men, and not God; and their horses are flesh, and not spirit" (NKJV). The contrast between flesh and spirit exposes the fundamental category error in trusting political power for what only God can provide.
34. Jeremiah 17:5-8 (NKJV). The contrast between the cursed man who trusts in flesh and the blessed man who trusts in the Lord uses vivid

VII THE RELIGION OF THE GREAT HARLOT

imagery—a shrub in the desert versus a tree by waters—to illustrate the consequences of misplaced trust.

35. The term "Christian nationalism" describes the conflation of Christian faith with national identity, treating a particular nation as having special covenant status with God. While Christians may legitimately love their countries and participate in civic life, Christian nationalism elevates national loyalty to a religious absolute.

36. Philippians 3:20: "For our citizenship is in heaven, from which we also eagerly wait for the Savior, the Lord Jesus Christ" (NKJV). The Greek *politeuma* (citizenship, commonwealth) indicates that believers' primary political identity is heavenly, not earthly.

37. 2 Timothy 1:7: "For God has not given us a spirit of fear, but of power and of love and of a sound mind" (NKJV). Fear-driven political engagement contradicts the Spirit's gift of confidence in God's sovereignty.

38. John Calvin's description of the human heart as "a perpetual factory of idols" appears in *Institutes of the Christian Religion*, I.11.8. Calvin (1509-1564) emphasized the human propensity to create objects of ultimate devotion that compete with God.

39. Jeremiah 17:9: "The heart is deceitful above all things, and desperately wicked; who can know it?" (NKJV). The heart's capacity for self-deception makes political idolatry particularly dangerous—we can convince ourselves that our will to power is actually zeal for God's kingdom.

40. Revelation 13 describes the beast's political authority and the mark required for economic participation. The explicitly political nature of the end-time deception suggests that those who have practiced political idolatry will be predisposed to accept the beast's claims.

41. Hebrews 13:14: "For here we have no continuing city, but we seek the one to come" (NKJV). The pilgrim identity of believers relativizes all earthly political attachments.
42. Hebrews 11:10: "for he waited for the city which has foundations, whose builder and maker is God" (NKJV). Abraham's example establishes the pattern of looking beyond earthly political arrangements to God's ultimate purposes.
43. Genesis 3:5: "For God knows that in the day you eat of it your eyes will be opened, and you will be like God, knowing good and evil" (NKJV). The serpent's promise of self-deification remains the template for all counterfeit religion.
44. Exodus 32:4: "This is your god, O Israel, that brought you out of the land of Egypt!" (NKJV). Aaron's attribution of YHWH's redemptive act to the golden calf exemplifies how false religion co-opts the language of true faith.
45. Hosea 2:5 (NKJV). Hosea's marriage to Gomer served as prophetic sign-act illustrating Israel's spiritual adultery—pursuing other gods while claiming covenant relationship with YHWH.
46. Isaiah 1:11-14 (NKJV). God's rejection of Israel's sacrifices despite their technical correctness reveals that external religious observance without corresponding heart transformation is abomination.
47. Isaiah 1:15: "When you spread out your hands, I will hide My eyes from you; even though you make many prayers, I will not hear. Your hands are full of blood" (NKJV).
48. Jeremiah 7:4-11 (NKJV). The "temple sermon" confronted the popular belief that the temple's presence guaranteed Jerusalem's safety, regardless of the people's behavior—a form of religious magical thinking.
49. Matthew 21:13: "It is written, 'My house shall be called a house of prayer,' but you have made it a 'den of thieves'" (NKJV), quoting

VII THE RELIGION OF THE GREAT HARLOT

Isaiah 56:7 and Jeremiah 7:11. Jesus' temple cleansing applied Jeremiah's critique to His own generation.

50. Ezekiel 8:9-12 (NKJV). The vision of secret idolatry by Israel's elders within the temple precincts represents the most shocking form of religious corruption—those responsible for maintaining pure worship privately practicing idolatry.

51. The phrase "The LORD does not see us, the LORD has forsaken the land" (Ezekiel 8:12, NKJV) reveals practical atheism—the functional denial of God's omniscience and presence even while maintaining religious positions.

52. Ezekiel 8:14 (NKJV). Tammuz was a Mesopotamian deity associated with fertility and the cycle of seasons. The ritual mourning for Tammuz's annual "death" was incompatible with worship of YHWH but had been imported into the temple precincts.

53. Ezekiel 8:16 (NKJV). The twenty-five men with their backs to the temple worshipping the sun likely represented the twenty-four priestly courses plus the high priest—the religious leadership of Israel engaged in blatant syncretism.

54. Romans 1:25: "who exchanged the truth of God for the lie, and worshiped and served the creature rather than the Creator, who is blessed forever. Amen" (NKJV). Sun worship exemplifies the fundamental exchange at the heart of idolatry—worship of creation instead of Creator.

55. Hebrews 1:1-2: "God, who at various times and in various ways spoke in time past to the fathers by the prophets, has in these last days spoken to us by His Son" (NKJV). The progressive revelation of God culminating in Christ means that genuine knowledge of God is available, refuting both agnosticism and the claim that all religious paths are equally valid.

56. Deuteronomy 29:29: "The secret things belong to the LORD our God, but those things which are revealed belong to us and to our children forever, that we may do all the words of this law" (NKJV). The distinction between secret and revealed things establishes appropriate epistemic humility while affirming real knowledge.
57. Acts 4:12: "Nor is there salvation in any other, for there is no other name under heaven given among men by which we must be saved" (NKJV). Peter's declaration before the Sanhedrin affirms the exclusive sufficiency of Christ for salvation.
58. John 14:6: "Jesus said to him, 'I am the way, the truth, and the life. No one comes to the Father except through Me'" (NKJV). Jesus' self-identification as the exclusive way to the Father cannot be softened into one path among many without emptying the statement of meaning.
59. Matthew 7:13-14: "Enter by the narrow gate; for wide is the gate and broad is the way that leads to destruction, and there are many who go in by it. Because narrow is the gate and difficult is the way which leads to life, and there are few who find it" (NKJV).
60. Luke 15:25-28 (NKJV). The elder brother's anger at his father's welcome of the prodigal reveals a transactional understanding of relationship that had never grasped the father's gracious heart.
61. Luke 15:29-30 (NKJV). The elder brother's accounting language ("these many years I have been serving you," "I never transgressed your commandment") reveals service motivated by expectation of reward rather than love.
62. Luke 18:11: "The Pharisee stood and prayed thus with himself, 'God, I thank You that I am not like other men—extortioners, unjust, adulterers, or even as this tax collector'" (NKJV). The Pharisee's prayer is addressed to himself and uses God as audience for self-congratulation.

VII THE RELIGION OF THE GREAT HARLOT

63. Luke 18:14: "I tell you, this man went down to his house justified rather than the other; for everyone who exalts himself will be humbled, and he who humbles himself will be exalted" (NKJV).
64. 1 Corinthians 3:12-15 (NKJV). Paul's imagery of building materials tested by fire applies to the quality of Christian work and ministry, warning that even genuine believers may suffer loss at the judgment if their works prove to be worthless.
65. Matthew 7:22-23 (NKJV). The terrifying possibility of self-deceived religious workers who expect acceptance and receive rejection emphasizes that supernatural activity is not self-validating.
66. Luke 15:31-32 (NKJV). The father's response to the elder brother is invitation, not condemnation—offering relationship that has always been available but never received.
67. Psalm 73:25-26: "Whom have I in heaven but You? And there is none upon earth that I desire besides You. My flesh and my heart fail; but God is the strength of my heart and my portion forever" (NKJV). Asaph's declaration after wrestling with the prosperity of the wicked concludes that God Himself is the ultimate reward.
68. Hebrews 2:14-15 (NKJV). The writer identifies fear of death as the mechanism of Satan's bondage over humanity, which Christ's death and resurrection have broken.
69. Galatians 5:19-21 (NKJV). Paul's catalogue of "works of the flesh" includes not only obvious bodily sins but also relational and religious sins—dissensions, heresies, selfish ambitions—indicating that fleshly religion can take many forms.
70. 2 Timothy 3:1-5 (NKJV). Paul's description of "perilous times" emphasizes that end-time corruption will maintain religious appearance ("form of godliness") while denying spiritual power.
71. Matthew 23:27-28 (NKJV). Jesus' metaphor of whitewashed tombs—externally attractive, internally corrupt—applies to any

religion that maintains outward conformity while harboring unchanged hearts.

72. Matthew 24:24: "For false christs and false prophets will rise and show great signs and wonders to deceive, if possible, even the elect" (NKJV). The severity of end-time deception requires divine protection for the elect to avoid being swept away.

73. 2 Thessalonians 2:9: "The coming of the lawless one is according to the working of Satan, with all power, signs, and lying wonders" (NKJV). Supernatural activity accompanying the Antichrist will make discernment difficult for those not grounded in truth.

74. Matthew 3:1-2: "In those days John the Baptist came preaching in the wilderness of Judea, and saying, 'Repent, for the kingdom of heaven is at hand!'" (NKJV). John's ministry of preparation emphasized moral transformation, not merely ritual observance.

75. Matthew 3:7-10 (NKJV). John's confrontation of the religious leaders demanded fruit (evidence) of repentance, not merely claims of covenant membership.

76. Ezekiel 34:2-4 (NKJV). God's indictment of Israel's shepherds addresses leaders who exploit rather than serve, who feed themselves rather than the flock—a pattern recurring throughout church history.

77. James 3:1: "My brethren, let not many of you become teachers, knowing that we shall receive a stricter judgment" (NKJV). The warning about stricter judgment for teachers emphasizes the accountability of spiritual leadership.

78. James 1:22-24 (NKJV). James's distinction between hearers and doers addresses the self-deception of those who engage with Scripture intellectually without allowing it to transform behavior.

79. Titus 1:16: "They profess to know God, but in works they deny Him, being abominable, disobedient, and disqualified for every

VII THE RELIGION OF THE GREAT HARLOT

good work" (NKJV). The gap between profession and practice is practical atheism—verbal acknowledgment contradicted by lived denial.

80. Matthew 7:21: "Not everyone who says to Me, 'Lord, Lord,' shall enter the kingdom of heaven, but he who does the will of My Father in heaven" (NKJV). The repetition of "Lord, Lord" indicates emphatic confession that is nevertheless inadequate without corresponding obedience.
81. Luke 6:46: "But why do you call Me 'Lord, Lord,' and not do the things which I say?" (NKJV). Jesus' question exposes the contradiction inherent in claiming His lordship while refusing His authority.
82. James 2:14, 17: "What does it profit, my brethren, if someone says he has faith but does not have works? Can faith save him?... Thus also faith by itself, if it does not have works, is dead" (NKJV). James's emphasis on works as evidence of faith complements Paul's teaching on justification by faith—genuine faith produces visible fruit.
83. 2 Corinthians 13:5: "Examine yourselves as to whether you are in the faith. Test yourselves. Do you not know yourselves, that Jesus Christ is in you?—unless indeed you are disqualified" (NKJV). Paul's call to self-examination presumes that genuine faith can be verified by evidence.
84. Matthew 5:3-10 (NKJV). The Beatitudes describe the character of citizens of God's kingdom, providing criteria for evaluating genuine versus counterfeit spirituality.
85. Galatians 5:22-24 (NKJV). The fruit of the Spirit serves as the primary evidence of genuine transformation—character qualities that cannot be manufactured by religious effort but only produced by the Spirit's work.

86. Romans 12:1-2 (NKJV). Paul's appeal for consecration—presenting bodies as living sacrifices, being transformed by renewed minds—establishes the positive vision of sanctification that contrasts with the harlot's religion.
87. 2 Thessalonians 2:9-12 (NKJV). Paul's teaching about "strong delusion" sent by God upon those who rejected truth indicates that persistent refusal of revelation results in judicial hardening—the loss of capacity to discern.
88. Revelation 18:4-5: "Come out of her, my people, lest you share in her sins, and lest you receive of her plagues. For her sins have reached to heaven, and God has remembered her iniquities" (NKJV). The call to separation is addressed to God's people who have become entangled with Babylon's systems.
89. Psalm 139:23-24: "Search me, O God, and know my heart; try me, and know my anxieties; and see if there is any wicked way in me, and lead me in the way everlasting" (NKJV). David's prayer for divine examination models the appropriate response to warnings about self-deception.

VIII

THE ANTICIPATION OF RELIGION

The Blessed Hope That Propels the Pilgrim

The Fire That Does Not Consume

In the basement on Bergen Street, Newark, eighteen believers huddled against the cold, their bodies wasted by hunger, their faces gaunt from years of persecution. By every earthly measure, they were defeated. The world had moved on without them. The systems of power had excluded them. The pleasures of Babylon were forever closed to those who refused her mark.

And yet.

Yet Sister Magdalena's eyes held a light undiminished by starvation. Brother Thomas, trembling with fear, worshipped undetected by the drones. Young Sarah, frail from violation, sang hymns of anticipation with a voice stronger than her body.

"*Maranatha,*" they whispered. *Our Lord, come.*

What sustained them was not grim determination or endurance. It was anticipation—burning, blazing, unquenchable anticipation in Christ's return. This blessed hope transformed present suffering into what Paul called "light affliction" that was "but for a moment," making tribulation bearable in the light of promised redemption.

This anticipation is the fire that does not consume, the hope that propels rather than paralyzes. This is not escapist eschatology but energizing faith—the future breaking into the present, shaping how we live, suffer, love, and worship.

The call to redeem religion is not finally about the present. It does not only concern piety for piety's sake, morality for morality's sake, spiritual disciplines as ends in themselves. It is about preparation. It is about longing. It is about a love we foretaste now but will fully know then.

Augustine captured this when he wrote: *"You have made us for Yourself, O Lord, and our hearts are restless until they rest in You."* The restlessness is not a defect; it is a design. We were made for something—*Someone*—we have not yet fully received. The ache is evidence of the promise. The longing points to the fulfillment.

The Guarantee of the Spirit

How can we have such confidence? How can we anticipate with certainty what we have not yet seen?

Paul gives the answer in his letter to the Ephesians:

"In Him you also trusted, after you heard the word of truth, the gospel of your salvation; in whom also, having believed, you were sealed with the Holy Spirit of promise, who is the guarantee of our inheritance until the redemption of the purchased possession, to the praise of His glory." (Ephesians 1:13-14)

The Holy Spirit is the *guarantee*—the Greek word is *arrabon*, meaning a down payment, a deposit, or a first installment. When you purchase a house, the earnest money demonstrates your serious intention and legally commits you to complete the transaction. The Spirit is God's earnest money. His presence in us is the down payment of the inheritance to come.

This is why the Spirit's indwelling matters so profoundly. Not as power for service or guidance for decisions, but as *evidence*. Evidence that we belong to God. Evidence that the transaction has begun. Evidence that what has been promised will be completed.

"He who has begun a good work in you will complete it until the day of Jesus Christ."(Philippians 1:6)

The Spirit who regenerated us will glorify us. The Spirit who sealed us will present us. The Spirit who groans within us, interceding with sighs too deep for words, will one day bring us to the place where groaning gives way to glory.

Can you feel Him? In your quietest moments, in your deepest prayers, in the ache that nothing earthly satisfies—that is the Spirit bearing witness with your spirit that you are a child of God, and if a child, then an heir.

"The Spirit Himself bears witness with our spirit that we are children of God, and if children, then heirs—heirs of God and joint heirs with Christ, if indeed we suffer with Him, that we may also be glorified together."(Romans 8:16-17)

Joint heirs with Christ. Whatever He inherits, we inherit with Him. His glory becomes our glory. His kingdom becomes our kingdom. His eternity becomes our eternity.

This is not wishful thinking. This is Spirit-attested reality.

Working Out What God Works In

But does this future hope paralyze present action? Does anticipation of glory make us passive in the present?

Precisely the opposite.

"Therefore, my beloved, as you have always obeyed, not as in my presence only, but now much more in my absence, work out your own salvation with fear and trembling; for it is God who works in you both to will and to do for His good pleasure."(Philippians 2:12-13)

Work out your salvation—not *for* salvation, as if we could earn it, but work it *out*, as a musician works out the implications of a melody, as a mathematician works out the implications of an equation. God has worked salvation *in*; now we work it *out*. God has planted the seed; now it grows and bears fruit.

The "fear and trembling" is not terror of rejection but awe at the privilege. We are co-laborers with God. We are participants in our own transformation. We are not passive recipients but active respondents.

And notice the grounds of our effort: "for it is *God* who works in you." We work *because* He works. Our effort is response to His initiative, cooperation with His operation, participation in His transformation.

This is how the believers in the basement endured—not only waiting, but actively working out what God was working in. Prayers were participation, hymns cooperation, acts of love the Spirit's fruit displayed in them.

Anticipation propels action. The athlete who sees the finish line runs harder, not slower. The bride who sees the wedding day approaching prepares more earnestly, not less. The believer who sees the return of Christ approaching purifies herself, just as He is pure (1 John 3:3).

Kept from Deception by Burning Hope

The greatest of dangers in these last days is deception—the subtle counterfeits that lead even the elect astray, if that were possible. How will believers be kept from deception when the lies are so plausible, the signs so impressive, the social pressure so overwhelming?

By hope.

This may seem counterintuitive. We might expect the answer to be knowledge—careful study of prophecy to recognize the signs. Or discernment—the spiritual gift that enables us to distinguish truth from error. Or community—the support of fellow believers who can test and confirm.

VIII THE ANTICIPATION OF RELIGION

All of these are important. But beneath them all is hope. Burning, blazing, unquenchable hope in the return of Christ.

Those who hope in the wrong thing can be deceived by anything that resembles their hope. If we hope for health and wealth and worldly success, we can be deceived by anyone who promises these things in Jesus' name. If we hope for escape from suffering and difficulty, we can be deceived by anyone who offers a comfortable Christianity.

But if we hope for *Christ Himself*—if our deepest longing is not for what He gives but for who He is—then no counterfeit can satisfy. The lover who longs for the beloved cannot be deceived by a photograph, no matter how flattering. The bride awaiting the bridegroom cannot be fooled by an impersonator, no matter how convincing.

"Beloved, now we are children of God; and it has not yet been revealed what we shall be, but we know that when He is revealed, we shall be like Him, for we shall see Him as He is. And everyone who has this hope in Him purifies himself, just as He is pure." (1 John 3:2-3)

Everyone who has *this hope*—hope in *Him*, in seeing Him, in being made like Him—purifies himself. Hope produces holiness. Anticipation produces action. Longing for Christ produces resistance to counterfeits.

The believers in Newark were not deceived because they sought only Jesus—not the Architect or Babylon's pleasures, but His face and His voice: 'Well done.' They longed for home.

As C.S. Lewis wrote: *"If we find ourselves with a desire that nothing in this world can satisfy, the most probable explanation is that we were made for another world."*

They were made for another world, and no substitute could ever quench that longing. Their hope endured, unbreakable.

The Shortened Days

In His Olivet Discourse, Jesus made a remarkable statement about the great tribulation:

"For then there will be great tribulation, such as has not been since the beginning of the world until this time, no, nor ever shall be. And unless those days were shortened, no flesh would be saved; but for the elect's sake those days will be shortened."(Matthew 24:21-22)

For the elect's sake, the days will be shortened.

There is pastoral comfort here that we must not miss. God knows the limits of His people's endurance. He will not allow the trial to extend beyond what they can bear. He measures the suffering with precision, and He will cut it short.

Picture the basement believers, strength gone and hope stretched thin. Then—the sky splits. The trumpet sounds. The Lord descends.

Just in time.

Not early, because the refining is necessary. Not late, because the limits are real. But precisely on time, at the exact moment when faith has been proved and hope has been tested and love has been purified.

Sister Magdalena had asked, "How much longer?" The Spirit had answered, "Very soon." And when the shout of the archangel finally came, it was not a moment too late. She had been stretched to her limit—and then the stretching stopped, and glory began.

This is the mercy woven into even the hardest providence. God knows our frame. He remembers that we are dust. And He will not break the bruised reed or quench the smoldering wick.

The Rapture of the Remnant

What shall we say of that moment—the moment when the trumpet sounds, when the dead in Christ rise, when the living are caught up together with them in the clouds?

Paul describes it with breathless wonder:

VIII THE ANTICIPATION OF RELIGION

"Behold, I tell you a mystery: We shall not all sleep, but we shall all be changed—in a moment, in the twinkling of an eye, at the last trumpet. For the trumpet will sound, and the dead will be raised incorruptible, and we shall be changed. For this corruptible must put on incorruption, and this mortal must put on immortality." (1 Corinthians 15:51-53)

A mystery. A transformation. In the twinkling of an eye.

The bodies that have been weakened by hunger will be made incorruptible. The bodies that have been violated and abused will be made glorious. The bodies that have aged and diminished will be renewed in eternal youth. Death itself will be swallowed up in victory.

And then—oh, then—face to face with Jesus.

"For now we see in a mirror, dimly, but then face to face. Now I know in part, but then I shall know just as I also am known." (1 Corinthians 13:12)

Face to face. No more veils. No more distance. No more seeing through a glass darkly. The One we have loved without seeing, the One we have trusted without touching, the One whose presence we have known by the Spirit but never by sight—we will see Him. We will know Him. We will be known by Him.

And we will be with Him forever.

"And thus we shall always be with the Lord." (1 Thessalonians 4:17)

Always. Forever. Without interruption. Without ending. Without any threat of separation.

As the ancient church father Cyprian wrote: *"A great thing awaits us, beloved brethren, if we persevere in faith and labor. We shall reign with Christ. We shall see God. We shall be joyful in perpetual salvation. There shall be no more death, no more mourning. There the Lord shall receive us, and shall wipe away every tear from our eyes, and joy shall be as eternity of life."*

The Wounded Bride

The Knock in the Night

In the Song of Solomon, there is a passage that the church has long understood as a portrait of the soul's longing for Christ—and the cost of that longing.

The bride is sleeping, but her heart is awake. Then comes the voice of her beloved:

"I sleep, but my heart is awake; it is the voice of my beloved! He knocks, saying, 'Open for me, my sister, my love, my dove, my perfect one; for my head is covered with dew, my locks with the drops of the night.'" (Song of Solomon 5:2)

He comes in the night. He comes when it is inconvenient. He comes covered with the dew of darkness, having been out in the cold while she lay warm in bed. And he asks her to open.

But she hesitates:

"I have taken off my robe; how can I put it on again? I have washed my feet; how can I defile them?" (Song of Solomon 5:3)

The excuses are small, domestic, reasonable. She has already undressed for the night. Her feet are clean. To rise now would mean discomfort, inconvenience, the disruption of her settled state.

How often does Christ knock, and we offer Him similar excuses? We have made ourselves comfortable. We have arranged our lives. To respond to His call would require disruption, sacrifice, the abandonment of our carefully constructed ease.

But then her heart stirs:

"My beloved put his hand by the latch of the door, and my heart yearned for him. I arose to open for my beloved, and my hands dripped with myrrh, my fingers with liquid myrrh, on the handles of the lock." (Song of Solomon 5:4-5)

She rises. She goes to the door. Her hands drip with myrrh—the fragrance of devotion, the costliness of love poured out.

But when she opens the door:

VIII THE ANTICIPATION OF RELIGION

"I opened for my beloved, but my beloved had turned away and was gone. My heart leaped up when he spoke. I sought him, but I could not find him; I called him, but he gave me no answer." (Song of Solomon 5:6)

He is gone. Her hesitation cost her his presence. Now she must seek him—not in the warmth of her chamber but in the darkness of the city streets.

This is the experience of the soul that has tasted Christ and then, through complacency or delay, lost the sense of His nearness. The beloved does not abandon permanently, but He withdraws that we might seek Him more earnestly. He hides Himself that we might pursue Him more desperately. The absence creates a longing that presence alone could never produce.

The Watchmen's Wounds

What happens next is startling:

"The watchmen who went about the city found me. They struck me, they wounded me; the keepers of the walls took my veil away from me." (Song of Solomon 5:7)

The watchmen—those who should have helped her, those charged with protecting the city, those who represented authority and order—these are the ones who wound her. They do not assist her search; they assault her. They do not honor her devotion; they strip away her veil, her covering, her dignity.

The church fathers saw in this passage a prophecy of what the bride of Christ would suffer at the hands of those who should have been her protectors. Religious authorities. Civil powers. Those entrusted with guardianship who instead became persecutors.

The believers in our story knew this wounding intimately. They were struck by the very institutions that claimed to serve human flourishing. They were wounded by governments that promised protection. Their veils—their dignity, their rights, their standing in society—were stripped away by the keepers of the walls.

But notice: the bride does not stop seeking.

She does not conclude that the beloved is not worth the cost. She does not return to her bed and pull the covers over her head. She does not say, "If seeking him means suffering at the hands of the watchmen, then I will seek him no more."

The wounds do not quench her longing. They intensify it.

This is the nature of true love for Christ. It is not deterred by suffering. It does not calculate cost and conclude the price is too high. The bride who truly loves will seek her beloved through the blows of the watchmen, through the stripping of dignity, through the darkness of the night. She will seek him because she must—because life without him is no life at all.

The Daughters' Suggestion

After her wounding, the bride encounters the daughters of Jerusalem, and they ask her a question that carries the weight of temptation:

"What is your beloved more than another beloved, O fairest among women? What is your beloved more than another beloved, that you so charge us?" (Song of Solomon 5:9)

On the surface, this seems like innocent curiosity. They want to know what makes her beloved so special. But beneath the question lies a subtle suggestion: *Are you sure he is worth all this trouble? What makes him better than any other? Perhaps you should lower your standards. Perhaps you should settle for someone who does not require such costly pursuit.*

The world asks the church this question in every generation.

"What is your Christ more than any other religious figure? Why do you suffer for him when you could have peace by accommodating? Why do you insist on his exclusive claims when tolerance would cost you nothing? Why not blend your devotion with other loyalties? Why not settle for a beloved who makes fewer demands?"

The temptation to self-protect whispers: *Stop seeking. The watchmen will only wound you again. Stay in your bed. Keep your veil. Preserve your dignity. Find a beloved who can be had without cost.*

The temptation to give up murmurs: *He left you. He did not answer when you called. Perhaps he does not want to be found. Perhaps your love is unrequited. Perhaps the whole pursuit has been folly from the start.*

The daughters of Jerusalem represent every voice that counsels compromise, every pressure that urges accommodation, every reasonable argument for abandoning the costly search for Christ alone.

The Bride's Declaration

But the bride does not waver. Instead of doubting her beloved, she declares him:

"My beloved is white and ruddy, chief among ten thousand. His head is like the finest gold; his locks are wavy, and black as a raven. His eyes are like doves by the rivers of waters, washed with milk, and fitly set. His cheeks are like a bed of spices, banks of scented herbs. His lips are lilies, dripping liquid myrrh. His hands are rods of gold set with beryl. His body is carved ivory inlaid with sapphires. His legs are pillars of marble set on bases of fine gold. His countenance is like Lebanon, excellent as the cedars. His mouth is most sweet, yes, he is altogether lovely." (Song of Solomon 5:10-16)

She does not answer their question with argument. She answers with adoration. She does not defend her choice with logic. She describes her beloved until the daughters themselves must see why he is worth any cost.

"Chief among ten thousand." There is no comparison. There is no other beloved who could take his place. Ten thousand alternatives could be offered, and none would suffice.

"Yes, he is altogether lovely." Not partially lovely. Not lovely in some respects while disappointing in others. *Altogether* lovely. Completely. Wholly. Without defect or lack.

This is how the bride cuts through the temptation to settle. Not by gritting her teeth in determination alone, but by *beholding*. She looks at her beloved, she remembers who he is, she recounts his beauties—and in the recounting, every other option fades to nothing. The watchmen's wounds become badges of honor. The stripped veil becomes a small price. The night search becomes adventure rather than affliction.

When we know who Christ is—truly know, not merely intellectually assent—no suffering can make us abandon the pursuit. When we have seen his glory, the glory as of the only begotten of the Father, full of grace and truth, we cannot be content with lesser loves. When we have tasted that the Lord is good, the world's alternatives taste like ashes.

The bride's staunch determination is not stoic willpower. It is the natural response of a heart captivated by beauty. She seeks because she must. She endures because she cannot imagine doing otherwise. She presses on because he is altogether lovely, and nothing less will satisfy.

The Question Turned

The daughters, having heard her description, are themselves moved:

"Where has your beloved gone, O fairest among women? Where has your beloved turned aside, that we may seek him with you?" (Song of Solomon 6:1)

The temptation has been reversed. They no longer suggest she settle for less. They want to join her search. Her declaration of his worth has awakened their own longing.

This is the power of authentic devotion. When the world sees Christians who love Christ so deeply that no suffering can deter them, who speak of Him with such adoration that His beauty becomes visible through their words, who seek Him with such determination that the watchmen's blows

VIII THE ANTICIPATION OF RELIGION

cannot turn them back—the world begins to wonder if perhaps this beloved is worth seeking after all.

Our witness is not primarily in our arguments but in our affections. The world will never be persuaded that Christ is worth having by those who treat Him as barely worth keeping. But when they see a bride who has been wounded and stripped and yet rises again to seek Him, declaring Him altogether lovely—they may begin to ask, "Where has your beloved gone, that we may seek him with you?"

The Bride's Confidence

And the bride's answer reveals that she has found what she sought:

"My beloved has gone to his garden, to the beds of spices, to feed his flock in the gardens, and to gather lilies. I am my beloved's, and my beloved is mine. He feeds his flock among the lilies." (Song of Solomon 6:2-3)

"I am my beloved's, and my beloved is mine."

The seeking has ended in finding. The night has given way to dawn. The wounds have become pathways to deeper intimacy. She knows where he is. She knows she belongs to him. She knows he belongs to her.

This is the confidence that sustained the believers in the basement on Bergen Street. They had sought Christ through the long night of tribulation. They had been wounded by watchmen—by governments, by systems, by those who should have protected them. They had heard the suggestions of the daughters of Jerusalem—the world's counsel to compromise, to accommodate, to settle for a beloved less demanding.

But they had beheld His beauty. They had declared Him altogether lovely. And in the declaring, their determination had become unshakeable.

"I am my beloved's, and my beloved is mine."

No Architect could compete with that. No pleasure the beast offered could compare. No threat of the watchmen could make them abandon the search. They belonged to Christ, and Christ belonged to them, and nothing in all creation could separate them from that love.

This is the anticipation that cuts through every temptation—to self-protect, to give up, to settle for lesser loves. It is not blind stubbornness. It is not mere willpower. It is vision. It is the beholding of One who is altogether lovely, and the recognition that having seen Him, we can never be satisfied with anything less.

The wounds of the watchmen are real. The night is dark. The suggestions to settle are relentless.

But He is altogether lovely.

And that is enough.

"Set me as a seal upon your heart, as a seal upon your arm; for love is as strong as death, jealousy as cruel as the grave; its flames are flames of fire, a most vehement flame. Many waters cannot quench love, nor can the floods drown it. If a man would give for love all the wealth of his house, it would be utterly despised." (Song of Solomon 8:6-7)

Many waters cannot quench this love. The floods of tribulation cannot drown it. All the wealth of Babylon—all her pleasures, all her securities, all her comforts—would be utterly despised by the one who has found the Beloved.

Let the watchmen strike.

Let the daughters question.

Let the night grow darker still.

We will seek Him until we find Him.

For He is altogether lovely.

And He is ours.

Heaven Coming to Earth

We must correct a common misunderstanding that has weakened eschatological hope for generations.

VIII THE ANTICIPATION OF RELIGION

The Christian hope is not "going to heaven when we die." It is heaven *coming to earth*. It is the renewal of all things. It is resurrection and restoration, not escape and abandonment.

N.T. Wright has helpfully recovered this biblical emphasis:

"The whole point of what Jesus was up to was that he was doing close up, in the present, what he was promising long-term, in the future. And what he was promising for that future, and doing in that present, was the coming of heaven to earth, the coming of God's kingdom, God's will being done on earth as it is in heaven."

The Lord's Prayer itself teaches us this: "Your kingdom come, Your will be done, *on earth as it is in heaven.*" Not our escape from earth to heaven, but heaven's invasion of earth. Not the abandonment of creation, but its redemption. Not the salvation of souls away from bodies, but the resurrection of bodies in a renewed creation.

John's vision at the end of Revelation makes this explicit:

"Now I saw a new heaven and a new earth, for the first heaven and the first earth had passed away. Also there was no more sea. Then I, John, saw the holy city, New Jerusalem, coming down out of heaven from God, prepared as a bride adorned for her husband. And I heard a loud voice from heaven saying, 'Behold, the tabernacle of God is with men, and He will dwell with them, and they shall be His people. God Himself will be with them and be their God.'" (Revelation 21:1-3)

The New Jerusalem *comes down out of heaven*. God's dwelling place is *with humanity*. The tabernacle—the place of God's presence—is *among mortals*.

This is the original design reclaimed. In Eden, God walked with humanity in the cool of the day. At Sinai, He dwelt among Israel in the tabernacle. In Christ, the Word became flesh and "tabernacled" among us (John 1:14—the Greek word is the same). In the church, we are being built together as a dwelling place of God by the Spirit.

But all of this is anticipation. All of this is foretaste. The full reality awaits the new creation, when God's presence will pervade every corner of existence, when the division between heaven and earth will be healed, when creation will be liberated from its bondage to decay and brought into the glorious freedom of the children of God (Romans 8:21).

This is what we await. Not harps on clouds. Not disembodied spiritual existence. But resurrection bodies in a renewed cosmos. The physical creation brought to its intended glory. The world as God always meant it to be.

Irenaeus, writing in the second century, understood this:

"For the whole creation waits for and expects the manifestation of the sons of God; and if it waits for and expects them, surely it is not destined for corruption but for incorruption and glory."

The Present Power of Future Hope

What does this anticipation produce in us now? Not passivity but passion. Not withdrawal but engagement. Not resignation but resistance.

The believers in the basement were not escapists. They were not so heavenly minded that they were no earthly good. They cared for one another. They rescued the victims of trafficking. They shared their meager resources. They maintained community in the face of atomization.

Their hope for the future did not diminish their love in the present—it *intensified* it. Precisely because they knew this world was not all there is, they were free to give themselves fully to others. Precisely because they knew their own lives were secure in Christ, they could risk those lives for their neighbors. Precisely because they knew death had been defeated, they could face death without terror.

The apostle Peter draws the connection explicitly:

VIII THE ANTICIPATION OF RELIGION

"Therefore gird up the loins of your mind, be sober, and rest your hope fully upon the grace that is to be brought to you at the revelation of Jesus Christ." (1 Peter 1:13)

"Rest your hope fully"—not partially, not occasionally, not as one factor among many, but *fully*—upon the grace that is coming. And notice what this hope produces: girded minds (mental readiness), sobriety (clear-headed living), and—in the verses that follow—holiness, love, and spiritual growth.

Peter continues:

"Since you have purified your souls in obeying the truth through the Spirit in sincere love of the brethren, love one another fervently with a pure heart." (1 Peter 1:22)

Hope purifies. Hope produces fervent love. Hope enables endurance.

The author of Hebrews celebrates the heroes of faith who lived by this hope:

"These all died in faith, not having received the promises, but having seen them afar off were assured of them, embraced them and confessed that they were strangers and pilgrims on the earth. For those who say such things declare plainly that they seek a homeland... But now they desire a better, that is, a heavenly country. Therefore God is not ashamed to be called their God, for He has prepared a city for them." (Hebrews 11:13-16)

They saw the promises afar off. They embraced them. They confessed their pilgrim status. And God was not ashamed to be called their God.

The Love We Foretaste Now

The call to redeem religion is ultimately a call to love—to love God with all our heart, soul, mind, and strength, and to love our neighbors as ourselves.

But what kind of love is this? Not sentiment. Not emotional fluctuation. Not self-serving affection that evaporates when the cost becomes too high.

It is the love of anticipation—the love that tastes something now and longs for fullness then.

Every genuine experience of God's presence is a foretaste. Every answered prayer is a down payment. Every moment of worship when heaven seems near is an appetizer of the feast to come. Every experience of Christian community—real, honest, sacrificial community—is a preview of the communion of saints in glory.

And because these are foretastes, they create longing. The more we taste, the more we hunger. The more we experience, the more we anticipate. The partial does not satisfy; it intensifies desire for the complete.

"For we know in part and we prophesy in part. But when that which is perfect has come, then that which is in part will be done away." (1 Corinthians 13:9-10)

Now we know in part. Then we will know fully. Now we love imperfectly. Then we will love perfectly. Now we see dimly. Then we will see face to face.

Bernard of Clairvaux, the great medieval mystic, wrote:

"We taste Thee, O Thou living Bread, and long to feast upon Thee still; we drink of Thee, the Fountainhead, and thirst our souls from Thee to fill."

Tasting and longing. Drinking and thirsting. This is the paradox of Christian experience—the more we receive, the more we desire. Not because God is insufficient, but because we are not yet fully capable of receiving all He offers. Our capacities are expanding, and with each expansion comes a deeper awareness of how much more there is.

If We Fall by Sword or Fire

Not all believers will survive to see Christ's return. Many have fallen. Many will fall. The believers in the basement had buried seven of their company. Throughout history, countless saints have passed through death before the trumpet sounded.

VIII THE ANTICIPATION OF RELIGION

Does this diminish hope? Not at all.

For those who die in Christ, the hope is simply realized sooner, not later. They are "absent from the body and present with the Lord" (2 Corinthians 5:8). They are with Christ, which is "far better" (Philippians 1:23). They rest from their labors, and their works follow them (Revelation 14:13).

And they too await the resurrection. They too anticipate the new creation. They too will receive glorified bodies when the trumpet sounds. The dead in Christ rise first—they are not left behind but given priority in the great gathering.

This is why death has lost its sting. Not because death is pleasant—it remains an enemy—but because death is not final. Death is a passage, not an ending. Death is the doorway to the presence of Christ, and beyond that presence lies the resurrection of the body and the renewal of all things.

The martyrs understood this. They could face fire and sword and wild beasts because they knew that death could not separate them from the love of God in Christ Jesus. They could lose their lives because they knew that, in Christ, they would find them again.

As Polycarp said when threatened with fire: *"You threaten me with fire that burns for an hour and is soon extinguished; but you do not know the fire of the coming judgment and eternal punishment, reserved for the ungodly. But why do you delay? Bring what you will."*

He had no fear of the fire that burned for an hour because he had hope for the glory that would never be extinguished.

The Eternal Bond

What awaits us is not individual salvation but *communion*. Not escape from judgment but *relationship*. Not existence in heaven but *intimacy with Christ*.

Jesus' high priestly prayer in John 17 reveals what He desires for us:

"Father, I desire that they also whom You gave Me may be with Me where I am, that they may behold My glory which You have given Me; for You loved Me before the foundation of the world."(John 17:24)

He desires that we be *with Him*. That we behold His glory. That we share in the love that has flowed between Father and Son from before the foundation of the world.

This is the destiny for which we were created. Not autonomous existence. Not independent fulfillment. But union with Christ, participation in the divine communion, eternal belonging.

The early church father Athanasius captured this with his famous statement: *"He became what we are that we might become what He is."* The incarnation, the cross, the resurrection, the ascension—all of it was aimed at our union with God. Christ descended that we might ascend. He became human that we might become partakers of the divine nature (2 Peter 1:4).

And when we finally see Him face to face, we will be "like Him, for we shall see Him as He is" (1 John 3:2). The transformation will be complete. The union will be consummated. The bond will be eternal.

The Voice of the Bridegroom

The book of Revelation closes with an exchange of longing—the Spirit and the Bride calling out, and Christ responding:

"And the Spirit and the bride say, 'Come!' And let him who hears say, 'Come!' And let him who thirsts come. Whoever desires, let him take the water of life freely."

—Revelation 22:17

The Spirit and the Bride say *Come!* This is not an invitation to unbelievers (though it includes that). It is the cry of the church to her Lord. *Come, Lord Jesus. Come quickly. Do not delay.*

And Christ responds:

"He who testifies to these things says, 'Surely I am coming quickly.'"

—Revelation 22:20

"Surely I am coming quickly." The word is *tachu*—swiftly, suddenly, without delay once the time has arrived. He is coming. It is certain. It is imminent. It is sure.

And the church responds with the final prayer of Scripture:

"Amen. Even so, come, Lord Jesus!"

—Revelation 22:20

Amen. So be it. Let it be so. We agree. We consent. We long.

Even so, come, Lord Jesus. Despite the cost. Despite the tribulation. Despite the suffering still ahead. Come anyway. Come quickly. Come now.

This is the heartbeat of anticipating faith. Not "if it be Your will, Lord, someday, perhaps, when convenient." But *Come!* Urgent, desperate, passionate, yearning. The bride calling for the bridegroom. The creation groaning for redemption. The Spirit interceding with groanings too deep for words.

The Work Before Us

Until He comes, we have work to do.

Not frantic work, as if the kingdom depended on our efforts alone. Not anxious work, as if we could miss our destiny by failing to achieve enough. But joyful work. Purposeful work. Work that flows from anticipation rather than anxiety.

We are to "occupy until He comes" (Luke 19:13, KJV). We are to be faithful servants, managing what the Master has entrusted, ready to give an account at His return. We are to make disciples, teaching them to observe all that He commanded. We are to love one another, that the world may know we are His disciples. We are to pursue holiness, purifying ourselves as He is pure. We are to care for the poor, the orphan, the widow, the stranger, loving, even serving our enemies—for in serving them, we serve Him.

But all of this work is infused with hope. It is not the grim determination of those who have only this life to make their mark. It is the eager anticipation of those who know the Master is returning and want to be found faithful when He arrives.

"Therefore, my beloved brethren, be steadfast, immovable, always abounding in the work of the Lord, knowing that your labor is not in vain in the Lord." (1 Corinthians 15:58)

Your labor is not in vain. Nothing done for Christ is wasted. No cup of cold water given in His name is forgotten. No act of love, no word of witness, no deed of mercy will fail to receive its reward when the Lord appears.

The Final Word

In the basement on Bergen Street, Sister Magdalena lifted her eyes toward a sky that was splitting open. The trumpet was sounding. The Lord was descending. Everything she had believed, everything she had hoped, everything she had longed for across sixty-three years of pilgrimage was being vindicated before her eyes.

She had kept her body pure in a world that celebrated impurity. She had refused the mark in a world that rewarded conformity. She had clung to Christ when clinging cost everything.

And now He was coming for her.

She felt her body changing—the hunger vanishing, the frailty dissolving, the weariness transformed into energy beyond anything she had ever known. She felt herself rising, lifted by a power not her own, carried toward the clouds where her Beloved waited.

And then she saw Him.

Not as she had imagined, though imagination had done its best. Not as the paintings depicted, though art had made its attempts. But *Him*—more

VIII THE ANTICIPATION OF RELIGION

real than anything she had ever seen, more beautiful than anything she had ever conceived, more present than anyone had ever been.

His eyes met hers. And in that meeting, every question was answered. Every sorrow was healed. Every longing was fulfilled.

"Well done," He said.

And she knew, in that moment, that everything—every tear, every trial, every temptation resisted, every cross carried—had been worth it. More than worth it. Infinitely, eternally, gloriously worth it.

"For I consider that the sufferings of this present time are not worthy to be compared with the glory which shall be revealed in us." (Romans 8:18)

The glory was being revealed. And it was beyond comparison.

This is the anticipation of religion. Not only doctrine to be believed. Not a duty to be performed. But burning, blazing, unquenchable hope that transforms how we live, how we love, how we suffer, how we serve.

We foretaste now what we will fully know then.

We love imperfectly now what we will love perfectly then.

We see dimly now what we will see clearly then.

But the foretaste is real. The love is genuine. The sight, however dim, is true.

And the One we anticipate is faithful.

He who promised is coming.

Maranatha.

Even so, come, Lord Jesus.

"Now may the God of hope fill you with all joy and peace in believing, that you may abound in hope by the power of the Holy Spirit."

—Romans 15:13

"The grace of our Lord Jesus Christ be with you all. Amen."

—Revelation 22:21

Soli Deo Gloria. Glory to God alone.

Endnotes

1. The Greek word *Maranatha* appears in 1 Corinthians 16:22 and can be parsed as either *marana tha* ("Our Lord, come!") or *maran atha* ("Our Lord has come"). The first parsing expresses eschatological longing; the second, confessional affirmation of Christ's presence. Both meanings resonate with the church's posture of anticipation.

2. 2 Corinthians 4:17: "For our light affliction, which is but for a moment, is working for us a far more exceeding and eternal weight of glory" (NKJV). Paul's characterization of his sufferings—shipwrecks, beatings, imprisonments, stonings—as "light affliction" only makes sense in light of the glory that awaits.

3. Augustine of Hippo, *Confessions*, I.1. This famous opening prayer—"You have made us for Yourself, O Lord, and our hearts are restless until they rest in You" (*fecisti nos ad te et inquietum est cor nostrum, donec requiescat in te*)—expresses the fundamental human condition of longing for God that only finds satisfaction in Him.

4. Ephesians 1:13-14 (NKJV). The Greek *arrabōn* (ἀρραβών), translated "guarantee" or "earnest," was a commercial term for a down payment or deposit that legally committed the buyer to complete the purchase. Its use for the Spirit indicates that God has irrevocably committed Himself to completing our redemption.

5. The concept of the Spirit as "down payment" (*arrabōn*) appears three times in the New Testament: Ephesians 1:14, 2 Corinthians 1:22, and 2 Corinthians 5:5. In each case, the Spirit's present indwelling guarantees future glorification.

6. Philippians 1:6: "being confident of this very thing, that He who has begun a good work in you will complete it until the day of Jesus Christ" (NKJV). Paul's confidence in the Philippians' perseverance

VIII THE ANTICIPATION OF RELIGION

is grounded not in their strength but in God's faithfulness to complete what He has started.

7. Romans 8:16-17 (NKJV). The Spirit's internal testimony (*summarturei*—"bears witness together with") provides assurance of adoption and inheritance. The connection between suffering with Christ and being glorified with Him indicates that participation in His sufferings is the pathway to participation in His glory.

8. Philippians 2:12-13 (NKJV). The apparent tension between "work out your own salvation" and "it is God who works in you" resolves when understood as synergy—human effort responding to and cooperating with divine initiative, not replacing it.

9. The phrase "fear and trembling" (*phobos kai tromos*) appears also in 1 Corinthians 2:3, 2 Corinthians 7:15, and Ephesians 6:5. It suggests not terror but reverent awe and serious engagement with sacred responsibility.

10. 1 John 3:3: "And everyone who has this hope in Him purifies himself, just as He is pure" (NKJV). John establishes a direct connection between eschatological hope and present sanctification—the expectation of seeing Christ produces the desire to be like Him.

11. C.S. Lewis, *Mere Christianity* (London: Geoffrey Bles, 1952), Book III, Chapter 10. Lewis's argument from desire—that the existence of a longing that nothing in this world can satisfy suggests we were made for another world—has become one of the most influential modern statements of the *argumentum e desiderio*.

12. Matthew 24:21-22 (NKJV). Jesus' statement that the tribulation days will be "shortened" (*koloboō*—cut short, amputated) for the elect's sake reveals divine mercy limiting the duration of suffering. The phrase "no flesh would be saved" (*ouk an esōthē pasa sarx*)

suggests that without divine intervention, the tribulation would be humanly unsurvivable.

13. 1 Corinthians 15:51-53 (NKJV). Paul's description of the transformation uses the word *mysterion* (mystery)—a previously hidden truth now revealed. The "twinkling of an eye" (*en rhipē ophthalmou*) emphasizes the instantaneous nature of the change.

14. 1 Corinthians 13:12: "For now we see in a mirror, dimly, but then face to face. Now I know in part, but then I shall know just as I also am known" (NKJV). The Greek *esoptrou* refers to the polished metal mirrors of antiquity, which gave imperfect reflections. The contrast is between present, partial knowledge and future, complete knowledge.

15. 1 Thessalonians 4:17: "And thus we shall always be with the Lord" (NKJV). The Greek *pantote* (always, at all times) emphasizes the permanence and uninterrupted nature of the believer's future communion with Christ.

16. Cyprian of Carthage (c. 200-258 AD), *On Mortality* (*De Mortalitate*), 26. Written during the plague of 252 AD, this treatise encouraged Christians facing death to view it as passage to glory rather than tragedy. Cyprian himself was martyred in 258 AD.

17. Song of Solomon 5:2 (NKJV). The church fathers, following Origen's influential commentary, interpreted the Song of Solomon allegorically as depicting the relationship between Christ and the church (or Christ and the individual soul). This interpretive tradition shaped Christian mysticism for centuries.

18. Song of Solomon 5:3 (NKJV). The bride's excuses—comfort already achieved, reluctance to be inconvenienced—represent the spiritual complacency that can delay response to Christ's invitation. The allegorical reading sees here the soul that has grown comfortable and resists the disruption of deeper encounter.

19. Song of Solomon 5:4-5 (NKJV). Myrrh, associated with burial and sacrifice (see Matthew 2:11, John 19:39), suggests the costliness of love. The bride's hands dripping with myrrh as she reaches for the door represents devotion willing to pay the price of response.
20. Song of Solomon 5:6 (NKJV). The beloved's withdrawal after the bride's initial hesitation has been understood by mystics as the experience of divine absence that follows spiritual complacency—not abandonment but discipline designed to rekindle pursuit.
21. Song of Solomon 5:7 (NKJV). The watchmen who wound the bride rather than helping her have been interpreted as religious authorities who persecute genuine seekers, or as the general hostility of the world toward those who pursue Christ single-mindedly.
22. Song of Solomon 5:9 (NKJV). The daughters of Jerusalem's question—"What is your beloved more than another beloved?"—represents the world's incomprehension of exclusive devotion to Christ. The question carries an implicit suggestion that the cost of such devotion is unreasonable.
23. Song of Solomon 5:10-16 (NKJV). The bride's elaborate description of her beloved (*wasf* in Arabic love poetry) serves as both declaration and witness. By articulating his beauties, she renews her own devotion and potentially awakens longing in her hearers.
24. The phrase "chief among ten thousand" (*dagul merevavah*) in Song of Solomon 5:10 indicates incomparability—the beloved stands out among any possible alternatives. The Hebrew *dagul* suggests being conspicuous, distinguished, or banner-like.
25. Song of Solomon 5:16: "Yes, he is altogether lovely" (*kullo machamaddim*). The Hebrew *machamad* (desirable, precious) appears in the plural of intensity, suggesting supreme desirableness. This comprehensive affirmation—"altogether" or "wholly" lovely—admits no defect or disappointment.

26. Song of Solomon 6:1 (NKJV). The transformation of the daughters from skeptics to seekers illustrates how authentic devotion can awaken desire in observers. Their question—"Where has your beloved gone, that we may seek him with you?"—represents evangelistic fruit.

27. Song of Solomon 6:2-3 (NKJV). The bride's declaration "I am my beloved's, and my beloved is mine" expresses mutual possession and covenant relationship. This formula of belonging appears three times in the Song (2:16, 6:3, 7:10), with subtle shifts in emphasis.

28. Song of Solomon 8:6-7 (NKJV). The imagery of love as strong as death, jealousy as cruel as the grave (*sheol*), and flames that cannot be quenched by many waters presents love as an elemental force that transcends all opposition. The "most vehement flame" (*shalhevethyah*) may contain a reference to the divine name (Yah), suggesting love's divine origin.

29. N.T. Wright, *Surprised by Hope: Rethinking Heaven, the Resurrection, and the Mission of the Church* (San Francisco: HarperOne, 2008), 191. Wright's work has been influential in recovering the biblical emphasis on resurrection and new creation over against popular conceptions of "going to heaven."

30. Matthew 6:10: "Your kingdom come. Your will be done on earth as it is in heaven" (NKJV). The Lord's Prayer establishes the direction of eschatological hope—heaven's reality coming to earth, not souls escaping earth for heaven.

31. Revelation 21:1-3 (NKJV). John's vision of the New Jerusalem "coming down out of heaven from God" confirms that the final state is not human ascent to heaven but divine descent to a renewed earth. The "tabernacle of God" (*skēnē tou theou*) dwelling "with men" fulfills the trajectory of divine presence throughout Scripture.

VIII THE ANTICIPATION OF RELIGION

32. John 1:14: "And the Word became flesh and dwelt among us" (NKJV). The Greek *eskēnōsen* (tabernacled, pitched His tent) uses the same root as *skēnē* (tabernacle), connecting the Incarnation to the tabernacle presence and anticipating the final dwelling of Revelation 21.

33. Romans 8:21: "because the creation itself also will be delivered from the bondage of corruption into the glorious liberty of the children of God" (NKJV). Paul's cosmic eschatology encompasses not just human salvation but the liberation of the entire created order.

34. Irenaeus of Lyon (c. 130-202 AD), *Against Heresies* (*Adversus Haereses*), V.36.1. Irenaeus consistently argued against Gnostic spiritualizing of salvation, insisting on bodily resurrection and cosmic renewal as the proper Christian hope.

35. 1 Peter 1:13: "Therefore gird up the loins of your mind, be sober, and rest your hope fully upon the grace that is to be brought to you at the revelation of Jesus Christ" (NKJV). The imagery of girding the loins comes from tucking up long robes for action—Peter calls for mental readiness grounded in hope.

36. 1 Peter 1:22: "Since you have purified your souls in obeying the truth through the Spirit in sincere love of the brethren, love one another fervently with a pure heart" (NKJV). Peter connects purification, truth-obedience, and fervent love (*ektenos*—stretched out, earnest, intense) as the practical outworking of hope.

37. Hebrews 11:13-16 (NKJV). The "strangers and pilgrims" (*xenoi kai parepidēmoi*) identity characterized Old Testament saints who lived by faith in promises they never received in their lifetimes. Their example establishes the pattern of living toward a future that transforms present existence.

38. 1 Corinthians 13:9-10: "For we know in part and we prophesy in part. But when that which is perfect has come, then that which is in

part will be done away" (NKJV). The partial nature of present knowledge intensifies rather than diminishes longing for the fullness to come.

39. Bernard of Clairvaux (1090-1153), *Jesu, Dulcis Memoria* (Jesus, the Very Thought of Thee), stanza 4. Bernard's hymn, one of the most beloved in Christian tradition, expresses the paradox of spiritual longing—tasting that increases rather than satisfies hunger.

40. 2 Corinthians 5:8: "We are confident, yes, well pleased rather to be absent from the body and to be present with the Lord" (NKJV). Paul's confidence about the intermediate state—presence with Christ between death and resurrection—provides comfort for believers facing death.

41. Philippians 1:23: "For I am hard-pressed between the two, having a desire to depart and be with Christ, which is far better" (NKJV). Paul's description of death as "far better" (*pollō mallon kreisson*—much more better, an emphatic expression) indicates that even the intermediate state exceeds present earthly existence.

42. Revelation 14:13: "Blessed are the dead who die in the Lord from now on. 'Yes,' says the Spirit, 'that they may rest from their labors, and their works follow them'" (NKJV). The beatitude for the faithful dead assures that death in Christ leads to rest, and that earthly works have eternal significance.

43. 1 Thessalonians 4:16: "And the dead in Christ will rise first" (NKJV). The priority given to the resurrection of deceased believers indicates that they are not disadvantaged by dying before Christ's return—indeed, they receive glorification first.

44. Polycarp of Smyrna (c. 69-155 AD), *The Martyrdom of Polycarp*, 11.2. Polycarp's words before execution—contrasting the temporary fire of martyrdom with the eternal fire of judgment—became

paradigmatic for Christian martyrdom. His fearlessness derived from hope in resurrection.

45. John 17:24: "Father, I desire that they also whom You gave Me may be with Me where I am, that they may behold My glory which You have given Me; for You loved Me before the foundation of the world" (NKJV). Jesus' high priestly prayer reveals that the ultimate purpose of salvation is not merely rescue from judgment but participation in the eternal love between Father and Son.

46. Athanasius of Alexandria (c. 296-373 AD), *On the Incarnation* (*De Incarnatione Verbi Dei*), 54. The formula "He became what we are that we might become what He is" (*autos gar enēnthrōpēsen, hina hēmeis theopoiēthōmen*) summarizes the patristic understanding of salvation as theosis (deification)—not becoming God in essence but participating in divine life.

47. 2 Peter 1:4: "by which have been given to us exceedingly great and precious promises, that through these you may be partakers of the divine nature, having escaped the corruption that is in the world through lust" (NKJV). Peter's language of becoming "partakers of the divine nature" (*theias koinōnoi phuseōs*) provides biblical foundation for the doctrine of theosis.

48. 1 John 3:2: "Beloved, now we are children of God; and it has not yet been revealed what we shall be, but we know that when He is revealed, we shall be like Him, for we shall see Him as He is" (NKJV). The transformation into Christ's likeness is connected to the beatific vision—seeing Him produces likeness to Him.

49. Revelation 22:17 (NKJV). The call "Come!" appears four times in this verse—twice as the Spirit and Bride's cry for Christ's return, and twice as invitation to those who thirst. The verse thus expresses both eschatological longing and evangelistic invitation.

50. Revelation 22:20: "He who testifies to these things says, 'Surely I am coming quickly.' Amen. Even so, come, Lord Jesus!" (NKJV). The Greek *tachu* (quickly, swiftly) emphasizes not necessarily temporal imminence but the certainty and suddenness of Christ's coming when it occurs. The response "Even so, come" (*Amen, erchou*) is the church's answering cry to Christ's promise.

51. Luke 19:13: "Do business till I come" (NKJV). The KJV's "occupy till I come" translates *pragmateusasthe*—trade, do business, be engaged in activity. The parable of the minas teaches that expectation of the master's return should produce faithful stewardship, not passive waiting.

52. Matthew 28:19-20: "Go therefore and make disciples of all the nations, baptizing them in the name of the Father and of the Son and of the Holy Spirit, teaching them to observe all things that I have commanded you" (NKJV). The Great Commission establishes the church's mission during the period of anticipation—active disciple-making until Christ returns.

53. 1 John 3:3: "And everyone who has this hope in Him purifies himself, just as He is pure" (NKJV). The connection between hope and holiness appears throughout the New Testament—genuine anticipation of Christ's return produces present sanctification.

54. 1 Corinthians 15:58: "Therefore, my beloved brethren, be steadfast, immovable, always abounding in the work of the Lord, knowing that your labor is not in vain in the Lord" (NKJV). Paul concludes his great resurrection chapter with practical exhortation—the certainty of resurrection guarantees that present labor has eternal significance.

55. Romans 8:18: "For I consider that the sufferings of this present time are not worthy to be compared with the glory which shall be revealed in us" (NKJV). Paul's calculation (*logizomai*—reckon, consider,

calculate) weighs present suffering against future glory and finds the comparison absurd. The glory "revealed in us" (*eis hēmas*) suggests glory not merely shown to us but manifested through us.

56. Romans 15:13: "Now may the God of hope fill you with all joy and peace in believing, that you may abound in hope by the power of the Holy Spirit" (NKJV). Paul's benediction identifies God Himself as "the God of hope" (*ho theos tēs elpidos*)—hope is not merely something God gives but a reflection of who He is.
57. Revelation 22:21: "The grace of our Lord Jesus Christ be with you all. Amen" (NKJV). The final words of Scripture are a benediction of grace, appropriate for a book that has revealed both the severity of judgment and the triumph of redemption.
58. "Soli Deo Gloria" (To God Alone Be the Glory) is one of the five *solas* of the Protestant Reformation, expressing the conviction that all glory belongs to God alone. The phrase traditionally appeared at the conclusion of musical compositions and written works as a dedication acknowledging that any good accomplished belongs entirely to God.

BIBLIOGRAPHY

Primary Sources

Apophthegmata Patrum (Sayings of the Desert Fathers). Translated by Benedicta Ward. Cistercian Studies 59. Kalamazoo, MI: Cistercian Publications, 1984.

Athanasius of Alexandria. *Life of Anthony*. Translated by Robert C. Gregg. Classics of Western Spirituality. New York: Paulist Press, 1980.

---------. *On the Incarnation*. Translated by a Religious of CSMV. Crestwood, NY: St. Vladimir's Seminary Press, 1996.

Augustine of Hippo. *City of God* (*De Civitate Dei*). Translated by Henry Bettenson. London: Penguin, 1984.

---------. *Confessions*. Translated by Henry Chadwick. Oxford: Oxford University Press, 1991.

---------. *On the Good of Marriage* (*De Bono Conjugali*). Nicene and Post-Nicene Fathers, Series 1, Vol. 3. Edited by Philip Schaff. Peabody, MA: Hendrickson, 1994.

Basil of Caesarea. *On Social Justice*. Translated by C. Paul Schroeder. Popular Patristics Series. Crestwood, NY: St. Vladimir's Seminary Press, 2009.

---------. *The Longer Rules* (*Regulae Fusius Tractatae*). In *Ascetical Works*, translated by M. Monica Wagner. Fathers of the Church 9. Washington, DC: Catholic University of America Press, 1950.

Bernard of Clairvaux. *On Loving God* (*De Diligendo Deo*). Translated by G.R. Evans. Cistercian Fathers Series. Kalamazoo, MI: Cistercian Publications, 1987.

Bonhoeffer, Dietrich. *Letters and Papers from Prison*. Edited by Eberhard Bethge. Translated by Reginald Fuller et al. New York: Macmillan, 1971.

Brother Lawrence. *The Practice of the Presence of God*. Various editions. Originally compiled 1692.

Calvin, John. *Institutes of the Christian Religion*. Edited by John T. McNeill. Translated by Ford Lewis Battles. 2 vols. Library of Christian Classics 20-21. Philadelphia: Westminster Press, 1960.

Cassian, John. *Conferences*. Translated by Colm Luibhéid. Classics of Western Spirituality. New York: Paulist Press, 1985.

---------. *Institutes*. Translated by Boniface Ramsey. Ancient Christian Writers 58. New York: Newman Press, 2000.

Clement of Alexandria. *Stromata* (Miscellanies). Ante-Nicene Fathers, Vol. 2. Edited by Alexander Roberts and James Donaldson. Peabody, MA: Hendrickson, 1994.

---------. *The Instructor* (*Paedagogus*). Ante-Nicene Fathers, Vol. 2. Edited by Alexander Roberts and James Donaldson. Peabody, MA: Hendrickson, 1994.

Clement of Rome. *First Epistle to the Corinthians*. In *The Apostolic Fathers*, translated by Bart D. Ehrman, vol. 1. Loeb Classical Library. Cambridge, MA: Harvard University Press, 2003.

The Cloud of Unknowing. Edited by James Walsh. Classics of Western Spirituality. New York: Paulist Press, 1981.

Chrysostom, John. *Homilies on the Gospel of Saint Matthew*. Nicene and Post-Nicene Fathers, Series 1, Vol. 10. Edited by Philip Schaff. Peabody, MA: Hendrickson, 1994.

---------. *Homilies on the Statues*. Nicene and Post-Nicene Fathers, Series 1, Vol. 9. Edited by Philip Schaff. Peabody, MA: Hendrickson, 1994.

Cyprian of Carthage. *On Mortality* (*De Mortalitate*). In *Treatises*, translated by Roy J. Deferrari. Fathers of the Church 36. Washington, DC: Catholic University of America Press, 1958.

———. *On the Lapsed* (*De Lapsis*). In *Treatises*, translated by Roy J. Deferrari. Fathers of the Church 36. Washington, DC: Catholic University of America Press, 1958.

The Didache (Teaching of the Twelve Apostles). In *The Apostolic Fathers*, translated by Bart D. Ehrman, vol. 1. Loeb Classical Library. Cambridge, MA: Harvard University Press, 2003.

Evagrius Ponticus. *The Praktikos* and *Chapters on Prayer*. Translated by John Eudes Bamberger. Cistercian Studies 4. Kalamazoo, MI: Cistercian Publications, 1981.

Gregory of Nazianzus. *Oration 14: On the Love of the Poor*. In *Select Orations*, translated by Martha Vinson. Fathers of the Church 107. Washington, DC: Catholic University of America Press, 2003.

———. *Oration 43: Funeral Oration for Basil the Great*. Nicene and Post-Nicene Fathers, Series 2, Vol. 7. Edited by Philip Schaff. Peabody, MA: Hendrickson, 1994.

Gregory the Great. *Pastoral Rule* (*Regula Pastoralis*). Translated by Henry Davis. Ancient Christian Writers 11. New York: Newman Press, 1950.

Guigo II. *The Ladder of Monks* (*Scala Claustralium*). Translated by Edmund Colledge and James Walsh. Cistercian Studies 48. Kalamazoo, MI: Cistercian Publications, 1981.

Hippolytus of Rome. *On Christ and Antichrist* (*De Christo et Antichristo*). Ante-Nicene Fathers, Vol. 5. Edited by Alexander Roberts and James Donaldson. Peabody, MA: Hendrickson, 1994.

———. *Commentary on Daniel*. Ante-Nicene Fathers, Vol. 5. Edited by Alexander Roberts and James Donaldson. Peabody, MA: Hendrickson, 1994.

Ignatius of Antioch. *Letters*. In *The Apostolic Fathers*, translated by Bart D. Ehrman, vol. 1. Loeb Classical Library. Cambridge, MA: Harvard University Press, 2003.

Irenaeus of Lyon. *Against Heresies* (*Adversus Haereses*). Ante-Nicene Fathers, Vol. 1. Edited by Alexander Roberts and James Donaldson. Peabody, MA: Hendrickson, 1994.

Jerome. *Commentary on Daniel*. Translated by Gleason L. Archer Jr. Grand Rapids: Baker, 1958.

John of the Cross. *The Collected Works of St. John of the Cross*. Translated by Kieran Kavanaugh and Otilio Rodriguez. 3rd ed. Washington, DC: ICS Publications, 2017.

The Martyrdom of Perpetua and Felicity. In *The Acts of the Christian Martyrs*, translated by Herbert Musurillo. Oxford: Clarendon Press, 1972.

The Martyrdom of Polycarp. In *The Apostolic Fathers*, translated by Bart D. Ehrman, vol. 1. Loeb Classical Library. Cambridge, MA: Harvard University Press, 2003.

Origen. *Commentary on the Song of Songs*. Translated by R.P. Lawson. Ancient Christian Writers 26. New York: Newman Press, 1957.

———. *On First Principles* (*De Principiis*). Translated by G.W. Butterworth. New York: Harper & Row, 1966.

Teresa of Ávila. *The Collected Works of St. Teresa of Ávila*. Translated by Kieran Kavanaugh and Otilio Rodriguez. 3 vols. Washington, DC: ICS Publications, 1976–1985.

———. *The Interior Castle*. Translated by Kieran Kavanaugh and Otilio Rodriguez. Classics of Western Spirituality. New York: Paulist Press, 1979.

———. *The Life of Teresa of Jesus: The Autobiography of Teresa of Ávila*. Translated by E. Allison Peers. New York: Image Books, 1991.

Tertullian. *Apologeticus* (Apology). Translated by T.R. Glover. Loeb Classical Library 250. Cambridge, MA: Harvard University Press, 1931.

Victorinus of Pettau. *Commentary on the Apocalypse*. Ante-Nicene Fathers, Vol. 7. Edited by Alexander Roberts and James Donaldson. Peabody, MA: Hendrickson, 1994.

Modern Scholarship

Anderson, Laura. *When Religion Hurts You: Healing from Religious Trauma and the Impact of High-Control Religion*. Grand Rapids: Brazos Press, 2023.

Ash, Christopher. *Job: The Wisdom of the Cross*. Preaching the Word. Wheaton, IL: Crossway, 2014.

Balthasar, Hans Urs von. *Mysterium Paschale: The Mystery of Easter*. Translated by Aidan Nichols. San Francisco: Ignatius Press, 1990.

Barton, Ruth Haley. *Sacred Rhythms: Arranging Our Lives for Spiritual Transformation*. Downers Grove, IL: InterVarsity Press, 2006.

Beale, G.K. *The Book of Revelation*. New International Greek Testament Commentary. Grand Rapids: Eerdmans, 1999.

Bonhoeffer, Dietrich. *The Cost of Discipleship*. Translated by R.H. Fuller. New York: Macmillan, 1959. Originally published as *Nachfolge*, 1937.

Boom, Corrie ten, with John and Elizabeth Sherrill. *The Hiding Place*. Washington Depot, CT: Chosen Books, 1971.

———. *Tramp for the Lord*. Fort Washington, PA: CLC Publications, 1974.

Bosch, David J. *Transforming Mission: Paradigm Shifts in Theology of Mission*. American Society of Missiology Series 16. Maryknoll, NY: Orbis Books, 1991.

Bowlby, John. *Attachment and Loss*. 3 vols. New York: Basic Books, 1969–1980.

Brueggemann, Walter. *Sabbath as Resistance: Saying No to the Culture of Now*. Louisville: Westminster John Knox Press, 2014.

Comer, John Mark. *Practicing the Way: Be with Jesus, Become Like Him, Do as He Did*. New York: WaterBrook, 2024.

---------. *The Ruthless Elimination of Hurry: How to Stay Emotionally Healthy and Spiritually Alive in the Chaos of the Modern World*. New York: WaterBrook, 2019.

Dunn, James D.G. *Jesus and the Spirit: A Study of the Religious and Charismatic Experience of Jesus and the First Christians as Reflected in the New Testament*. London: SCM Press, 1975. Reprint, Grand Rapids: Eerdmans, 1997.

Earley, Justin Whitmel. *Habits of the Household: Practicing the Story of God in Everyday Family Rhythms*. Grand Rapids: Zondervan, 2021.

---------. *The Common Rule: Habits of Purpose for an Age of Distraction*. Downers Grove, IL: InterVarsity Press, 2019.

Eklund, Rebekah. *Practicing Lament: A Practical Theological Exploration*. Eugene, OR: Wipf & Stock, forthcoming.

Foster, Richard J. *Celebration of Discipline: The Path to Spiritual Growth*. San Francisco: Harper & Row, 1978. Revised and expanded editions 1988, 1998.

Gorman, Michael J. *Cruciformity: Paul's Narrative Spirituality of the Cross*. Grand Rapids: Eerdmans, 2001.

Hauerwas, Stanley, and William H. Willimon. *Resident Aliens: Life in the Christian Colony*. Nashville: Abingdon Press, 1989.

Johnson, Sue. *Hold Me Tight: Seven Conversations for a Lifetime of Love*. New York: Little, Brown, 2008.

Johnson, Sue, and Brent Bradley. *The Practice of Emotionally Focused Couple Therapy: Creating Connection*. 3rd ed. New York: Routledge, 2019.

Jones, L. Gregory. *Embodying Forgiveness: A Theological Analysis*. Grand Rapids: Eerdmans, 1995.

Kavanaugh, Kieran. *John of the Cross: Doctor of Light and Love*. New York: Crossroad, 1999.

Ladd, George Eldon. *A Commentary on the Revelation of John*. Grand Rapids: Eerdmans, 1972.

Laird, Martin. *Into the Silent Land: A Guide to the Christian Practice of Contemplation*. Oxford: Oxford University Press, 2006.

Langberg, Diane. *Redeeming Power: Understanding Authority and Abuse in the Church*. Grand Rapids: Brazos Press, 2020.

Lewis, C.S. *The Four Loves*. London: Geoffrey Bles, 1960.

---------. *A Grief Observed*. London: Faber and Faber, 1961.

---------. *The Screwtape Letters*. London: Geoffrey Bles, 1942.

---------. *The Weight of Glory and Other Addresses*. New York: Macmillan, 1949.

Linn, Dennis, Sheila Fabricant Linn, and Matthew Linn. *Sleeping with Bread: Holding What Gives You Life*. Mahwah, NJ: Paulist Press, 1995.

McCarthy, Angela. *The Shape of Marriage: Living the Mystery*. San Francisco: Ignatius Press, 2018.

Merton, Thomas. *Spiritual Direction and Meditation*. Collegeville, MN: Liturgical Press, 1960.

Nee, Watchman. *The Release of the Spirit*. New York: Christian Fellowship Publishers, 1965.

Nouwen, Henri J.M. *The Way of the Heart: The Spirituality of the Desert Fathers and Mothers*. San Francisco: HarperSanFrancisco, 1981.

Ortlund, Ray, Jr. *Marriage and the Mystery of the Gospel*. Short Studies in Biblical Theology. Wheaton, IL: Crossway, 2016.

Ouellet, Marc Cardinal. *Mystery and Sacrament of Love: A Theology of Marriage and the Family for the New Evangelization*. Translated by Michelle K. Borras and Adrian J. Walker. Grand Rapids: Eerdmans, 2015.

Packer, J.I. *Knowing God*. Downers Grove, IL: InterVarsity Press, 1973.

Peterson, Eugene H. *A Long Obedience in the Same Direction: Discipleship in an Instant Society*. 2nd ed. Downers Grove, IL: InterVarsity Press, 2000.

Prince, Derek. *Shaping History Through Prayer and Fasting*. New Kensington, PA: Whitaker House, 1973.

Ravenhill, Leonard. *Why Revival Tarries*. Minneapolis: Bethany House, 1959.

Rohr, Richard. *Falling Upward: A Spirituality for the Two Halves of Life*. San Francisco: Jossey-Bass, 2011.

Stark, Rodney. *The Rise of Christianity: How the Obscure, Marginal Jesus Movement Became the Dominant Religious Force in the Western World in a Few Centuries*. Princeton: Princeton University Press, 1996.

Thompson, Curt. *The Soul of Shame: Retelling the Stories We Believe About Ourselves*. Downers Grove, IL: InterVarsity Press, 2015.

Tripp, Paul David. *Suffering: Gospel Hope When Life Doesn't Make Sense*. Wheaton, IL: Crossway, 2018.

Welwood, John. *Toward a Psychology of Awakening: Buddhism, Psychotherapy, and the Path of Personal and Spiritual Transformation*. Boston: Shambhala, 2000.

Wilder, Jim. *Renovated: God, Dallas Willard, and the Church That Transforms*. Colorado Springs: NavPress, 2020.

Wilder, Jim, and Michel Hendricks. *The Other Half of Church: Christian Community, Brain Science, and Overcoming Spiritual Stagnation*. Chicago: Moody Publishers, 2020.

Willard, Dallas. *The Divine Conspiracy: Rediscovering Our Hidden Life in God*. San Francisco: HarperSanFrancisco, 1998.

---------. *The Spirit of the Disciplines: Understanding How God Changes Lives*. San Francisco: HarperSanFrancisco, 1988.

Wright, N.T. *Evil and the Justice of God*. Downers Grove, IL: IVP Books, 2006.

---------. *Surprised by Hope: Rethinking Heaven, the Resurrection, and the Mission of the Church*. San Francisco: HarperOne, 2008.

www.ingramcontent.com/pod-product-compliance
Lightning Source LLC
LaVergne TN
LVHW091657070526
838199LV00050B/2187